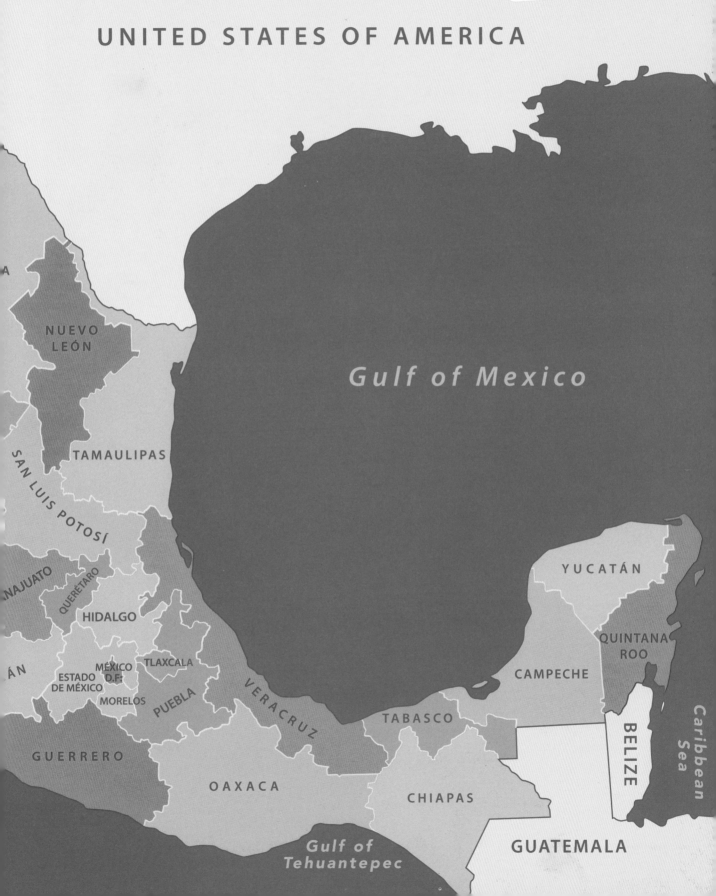

UNITED STATES OF AMERICA

Gulf of Mexico

A

NUEVO
LEÓN

TAMAULIPAS

SAN LUIS POTOSÍ

YUCATÁN

NAJUATO

QUERÉTARO

HIDALGO

QUINTANA
ROO

ÁN

MÉXICO
D.F.

TLAXCALA

CAMPECHE

ESTADO
DE MÉXICO

MORELOS

PUEBLA

VERACRUZ

BELIZE

GUERRERO

TABASCO

*Caribbean
Sea*

OAXACA

CHIAPAS

*Gulf of
Tehuantepec*

GUATEMALA

PATI JINICH

TREASURES
OF THE
MEXICAN
TABLE

PATI JINICH

TREASURES
OF THE
MEXICAN
TABLE

classic recipes, local secrets

Photographs by Angie Mosier

HOUGHTON MIFFLIN HARCOURT
BOSTON · NEW YORK · 2021

For information about permission to reproduce selections from this book, write to trade.permissions@hmhco.com or to Permissions, Houghton Mifflin Harcourt Publishing Company, 3 Park Avenue, 19th Floor, New York, New York 10016.

hmhbooks.com

Library of Congress Cataloging-in-Publication Data
Names: Jinich, Pati, author. | Mosier, Angie, photographer.
Title: Pati Jinich treasures of the Mexican table : classic recipes, local
    secrets / Pati Jinich ; photographs by Angie Mosier.
Description: Boston : Houghton Mifflin Harcourt, [2021] | Includes index.
Identifiers: LCCN 2021018574 (print) | LCCN 2021018575 (ebook) | ISBN
    9780358086765 (hbk) | ISBN 9780358085782 (ebk)
Subjects: LCSH: Cooking, Mexican. | LCGFT: Cookbooks.
Classification: LCC TX716.M4 J5598 2021 (print) | LCC TX716.M4 (ebook) |
    DDC 641.5972—dc23
LC record available at https://lccn.loc.gov/2021018574
LC ebook record available at https://lccn.loc.gov/2021018575

Book design by Ashley Lima
Cover and endpaper design by Tai Blanche
Food styling by Tamie Cook
Prop styling by Thom Driver

Chapter opener texture by freshdesignelements.com
Cover photograph of Pati Jinich © Jen Chase
Map of Mexico © Rainer Lesniewski/Shutterstock

Printed in the United States of America
2 2021
4500836327

Para Dany,
mi más grande refugio.
Para Alan, Sami, y Juju,
mis más grandes regalos
—espero que nuestra comida les de fuertes
alas para conocer, probar, y aprender de mundos nuevos.

ACKNOWLEDGMENTS

I always tell my three boys that Mexican-Americans are doubly blessed. We have two countries, two cultures, two rich and diverse cuisines to draw from, and two languages (sometimes more!), as well as so many beautiful legends, customs, and traditions. Along with that double blessing, though, comes a double responsibility: to represent the place where we come from with our heads held high and to be worthy of the place where we now belong. Shining a light on the food we make and sharing the recipes we have brought to the world is the best way for me to do that.

I could have no better partner in my search for Mexico's food treasures and my endeavors to bring them to an American audience than the team at WETA and Frank Content, coproducers of my National Public Television series, *Pati's Mexican Table,* now in its tenth season. Along with my fellow executive producer, Enrique Perret, we have traveled from the city of Oaxaca to the border wall in Tijuana to Los Mochis in Sinaloa and beyond. Special thanks to the many people who have worked on the series, one season at a time. I am truly indebted to my TV and online audiences, who invite us into their homes and make the recipes in their own kitchens for the people they love: That is what makes our work worthwhile.

I am so proud of my team and coworkers at Mexican Table, the company I started in 2010. What began as a one-person project has turned into a five-person, women-owned company. Kristy Noel and Sofia Viskin work tirelessly with me day in and day out to create and share the content that we have a passion for—thank you for your immense drive and commitment. Pilar Orozco, thank you for your ever-optimistic attitude and team spirit, and thanks to Debbie German, for helping to keep us in check.

Our work would not be possible without the trust and support of our sponsors, partners, and friends who have believed in the mission of *Pati's Mexican Table,* year after year. Special thanks to Matt Saver, my legal advisor, for his always available advice.

I am deeply grateful to everyone at the Mexican Cultural Institute, where I have been resident chef, taught culinary classes, and held special events for the past twelve years, and where I started my journey.

For this book, no one has been more valuable in helping me craft the story of Mexico's culinary riches than the author and journalist Martha Rose Shulman, who helped me polish my sentences and tested so many of my recipes. Her keen intelligence and love of Mexican food inform these pages in countless ways.

My literary agent, David Black, realized from the beginning that my country's classic dishes deserved a major book, and he has had my back at every turn in the history of its making, providing crucial insights and constant support.

To my dear friend Rux Martin, my former editor at Houghton Mifflin Harcourt, who helped me shape the book from its initial idea to its fruition with wise and thorough guidance, how I appreciate your loyalty and help.

At Houghton Mifflin Harcourt, my editor, Sarah Kwak, who pays impeccable attention to every detail, has been a steadfast ally, an enthusiastic companion, and an incredible delight to work with. Thanks to editorial director Karen Murgolo, publisher Deb Brody, Tai Blanche, and Rebecca Springer for their dedicated work on the production of this book. Profound thanks to copy-editor Judith Sutton, who brought her laser eye and infinite knowledge of food to the project.

Angie Mosier, along with food stylist Tamie Cook and prop stylist Thom Driver, always went the extra mile to deliver the delicious immediacy of my favorite dishes with gorgeous photos. Ashley Lima captured the timeless beauty of Mexico in her design for the book. Tai Blanche created the cover.

Thanks to Jen Chase for the cover photo, which was taken spontaneously, right when the sun was hitting the window of my favorite room at the Mexican Cultural Institute.

I am forever indebted to and in awe of the boundless generosity and warmth that we received from the chefs, cooks, artisans, bakers, market vendors, fishermen, artists, historians, and food aficionados in Mexico who shared their space, their food, their recipes, and their stories.

Deep gratitude to my family—my father, Miki Drijanski, and my mother, Susana Roth, and my sisters, Karen, Alisa, and Sharon, who share an irrational passion for food and the stories behind it—you have always been such an inspiration. To my in-laws, Carlos and Perla Jinich, who have always been there to celebrate any triumph, no matter how small or large, and to offer needed words of wisdom when times are tough.

My work and who I am today would not be possible without the unconditional love, patience, encouragment, and kindness of my husband, Dany, and our three sons, Alan, Sami, and Juju—los adoro beyond words. From the very beginning, they have been deeply involved in exploring the food of our home country and how it expresses itself in kitchens abroad. And our new dog, Mila, has also joined the ongoing adventure. I am so grateful to you for jumping into this book!

Un fuerte abrazo,

CONTENTS

INTRODUCTION

At lunchtime on a September day in the Sonoran capital of Hermosillo, a line had formed outside a long, low building with a flame-colored awning. It was at least 115 degrees inside the taqueria, but the owner, Doña Guille, didn't break a sweat. Surrounded by several blazing mesquite grills, she draped a sheet of dough over one arm and stretched it fluidly with her fist until it reached her armpit and was almost transparent. Then she slapped it onto an inverted iron disk—actually a repurposed harrow, seasoned by decades of use—where the tortilla blistered instantly. She deftly snatched it off with her fingers and plopped a ladleful of *carne con chile*, fork-tender shredded beef bathed in a sumptuous rust-red chile sauce, onto it. She squirted on some guacamole salsa, rolled the whole thing up, and handed it to me. I could hardly get my jaw around it. The tortilla was made with the sweet flour from wheat grown nearby, flecked with beef cracklings, and infused with rustic smoke. The filling soaking its way through the tortilla had a mellow beefy intensity. It was a cowboy-sized burrito meant for the ranch-sized appetite of a *vaquero*. I'd never tasted anything like it.

For more than a dozen years, I've been on a quest to discover the best of Mexico's culinary treasures that have held families together and kept communities connected. Like that carne con chile, they are heirloom recipes passed down from one generation to the next. My search has taken me deep into my home country, from a small Mayan hut in the Yucatán jungle to the bustling, labyrinthine Centro de Abastos market in the city of Oaxaca, to the food stands of Nogales. Some dishes are local masterpieces, the pride of a single town. Others have gained a following beyond their region, their fame traveling outward in seismic waves to the rest of the country and sometimes rippling over the border.

Every state in Mexico—there are thirty-two of them—has a trove of such beloved dishes. *Chilorio*, shredded pork cooked in its own fat until caramelized, then cooked some more in a fruity chile and tomato sauce, began as a neighborhood favorite, the specialty of home kitchens in the tiny town of Mocorito in

Sinaloa. To satisfy the demand, people opened little factories right in their homes. It didn't take long for the dish's fame to spread beyond Sinaloa, and now it is a national sensation. For every celebrated classic like chilorio, carne asada, mole poblano, and tres leches cake, there are dozens of equally irresistible finds that you might not know even if you're Mexican, unless you're from the area the specific dish comes from.

Although people often speak of "Mexican food" as if it were just one thing, in reality, the cuisine of my native country is as complex and varied as its terrain. Mexico encompasses the tropics of the Yucatán Peninsula and the wheat farms and cattle ranches of Chihuahua and Sonora. It stretches from the flat, steamy Gulf Coast to the Sierra highlands of central Mexico to deserts that extend their sand dunes straight into the Sea of Cortez. There are regions, subregions, and micro regions, each with its own unique and rich culinary profile. You can find local treasures everywhere, sometimes in places as small as a remote village or a rancho or even within just one family.

The wealth of our foodscape is the product not only of the land but also of thousands of years of history. Native ingredients like chiles, beans, squash, tomatoes, tomatillos, corn, avocados, peanuts, pineapples, chocolate, and vanilla had been cultivated for millennia but had never been seen by a European until the Spanish arrived in the sixteenth century. They brought new staples that grew into fundamentals in our cooking: pork, beef, wheat, rice, spices like cinnamon, and olive oil, to name just a few.

As a result of this complex layering of ingredients, you will find recipes in this collection that date back hundreds or even thousands of years, like an unforgettable Yucatecan dish of seared white beans, herbs, and pumpkin seeds, with the Maya name of *tok seel*; or *chulibul,* green beans in a fresh corn puree, which has been eaten in the state of Campeche since pre-Hispanic times. But you'll also want to try such relatively recent arrivals as tacos Árabes, an exquisite melding of Mexico and the Middle East, the gift of Lebanese immigrants in Puebla. And when we borrow a dish from the Spanish, like flan, we make it our own—I give you the version all Mexicans hanker for here.

The recipes speak of rainy afternoons deep in mountain forests, enjoying a bowl of mushroom soup laced with epazote; of lingering sunny days at a beach on the Sea of Cortéz, devouring messy seafood tostadas dressed with three salsas. They recall fiestas on the southern coast of Oaxaca, savoring a luscious whipped-potato cazuela with confettied vegetables as colorful as the traditional dresses of the women who make it. They evoke quick lunches standing at a street food stand in the city of Guadalajara, dipping a crusty sandwich stuffed with carnitas first into tomato broth, then into a spicy chile de árbol sauce, as the juices run down your arms. These dishes embody the ingenuity, warmth, and humor of the Mexican people, often expressed in evocative names like "dance with your wife" migas or "come back to life" seafood cocktail. And if there is a story to go with a recipe, like the local legend that accompanies the miners' fish soup from Chihuahua called bear soup, it gets passed along too, always with a smile.

For each of the recipes in this book, the journey ended in my Maryland home kitchen, where I repeatedly cooked each one of these classics for my husband and boys to be sure it was the best expression of itself and that you could make it with ease. When somebody has a knack for getting the flavor of a dish just right, so that you want to come back for more, we say that he or she has *buen sazón*. These recipes are written to help guide you to that buen sazón. They are *de batalla,* from the battle, meaning they are versatile workhorses that may become essential to your own repertoire. Make carne con chile one day and enjoy it with rice and beans; the next day, wrap it in a burrito. Take the time to cook chilorio on Sunday, then transform it into a quesadilla on Monday.

I hope you will learn from and enjoy these treasures that we have inherited from the generations before us over the centuries, and that you, in turn, will pass them on.

All of the ingredients called for in this book are easily findable online if you can't get them at your own market. Stock your pantry with the essentials—dried chiles, canned tomatoes (for when good ripe tomatoes are not available), and white onions—and you'll be good to go.

Dried Chiles: The Big Five

These five chiles will get you to the finish line in most of my recipes:

1. Anchos (page 324)
2. Chipotles, preferably moritas, which are smaller (page 133)
3. Guajillos (page 16)
4. Pasillas (page 127)
5. Chiles de árbol (page 124)

And sometimes:

6. Colorados (page 103)

SUBSTITUTIONS

If you're caught short, try these switch-outs:

▶ Guajillos can be substituted for colorados.

▶ Chiles de árbol or even red pepper flakes can stand in for the heat of chiltepín chiles.

Two Indispensable Canned Chiles

1. Chipotle chiles in adobo (page 133)
2. Pickled jalapeños in brine

Fresh Chiles

Most supermarkets have the fresh chiles you will need for these recipes: jalapeños and their hotter cousin, serranos (these can be substituted for one another); poblanos; and, sometimes, Anaheim chiles, aka New Mexico chiles; as well as habaneros for some feisty fresh heat.

Tomatoes: Straight Talk

Roma (aka plum) tomatoes are what Mexicans use most often. (These are the same tomatoes preferred for Italian recipes.) Dense and fleshy, they have a low moisture content. For that reason, they're great for sauces and salsas, especially salsas that call for roasted tomatoes, since they don't release too much juice.

More important than the variety, however, is the ripeness of the tomatoes. Ripe local tomatoes are always preferable to Romas that are hard and green. In the colder months, some hydroponic brands of tomatoes can deliver a fullness of flavor approaching that of ripe local tomatoes, but they are expensive.

However, most of us aren't lucky enough to live in a place where we can get ripe tomatoes year-round. When local tomatoes aren't in season, canned tomatoes are the best stand-in. Their flavor is superior to that of out-of-season fresh tomatoes. For sauces, I choose whole canned tomatoes. For recipes that call for roasted tomatoes, canned fire-roasted tomatoes are an excellent substitute. (They don't need to be roasted again.) In recipes that call for diced or chopped tomatoes, canned crushed tomatoes are fine.

White Onions

White onions are the choice in most of Mexico. They are clean and fresh-tasting. Since they are lower in sulfur than yellow onions, they don't dominate when raw, and their higher water content makes them crunchier, perfect for salsas and other raw dishes. If you have only yellow onions in your pantry, you can use them, but the taste will be a bit sweeter, the texture mushier.

SOUPS

GARLIC SOUP / **SOPA DE AJO** 9

SPRING ONION AND TOMATO SOUP WITH MELTY CHEESE / **SOPA DE CEBOLLITAS CON QUESO** 10

CORN SOUP WITH QUESO FRESCO / **SOPA DE ESQUITES CON QUESO** 12

GUAJILLO MUSHROOM SOUP / **SOPA DE HONGOS CON GUAJILLO** 14

PINTO BEAN SOUP WITH MASA DUMPLINGS / **SOPA DE OMBLIGO** 17

CHIPOTLE OYSTER SOUP / **SOPA DE OSTIÓN AL CHIPOTLE** 20

MINE WORKERS' FISH SOUP / **CALDO DE OSO** 23

SMOKY CRAB AND SHRIMP SOUP / **CHILPACHOLE DE JAIBA Y CAMARÓN** 27

SWEET LIME AND CHICKEN SOUP / **SOPA DE LIMA** 29

DRESSED-UP CHICKEN SOUP / **CALDO TLALPEÑO** 32

BEEF AND VEGETABLE SOUP / **MOLE DE OLLA** 36

CREAMY TOMATO AND CHICHARRÓN SOUP / **SOPA DE CHICHARRÓN** 38

RED MENUDO / **MENUDO ROJO** 40

Just about every recipe in this chapter has a story. Or maybe I should say *is* a story. It could be about the tiny, completely off-the-grid, magical Sinaloan mountain town called Jinetes de Machado, where I learned to make a creamy bean soup with masa dumplings that has the memorable name "belly button soup." Or it could be about the village of Tlaxiaco, high in the Oaxacan Sierras, where I met an inspiring woman chef named Ixchel Ornelas, who revived me after my long journey with the warming, comforting corn soup with queso fresco that she is known for.

Most of my soups are stories of places like these, since a soup is a warm way of getting to know a culture and its people. In the Yucatán, you would be hard-pressed to find a menu that does not offer the delicately citrusy chicken soup called *sopa de lima*. And everywhere along the Gulf Coast in the state of Veracruz, you will feast on fresh crab and chipotle soup—*chilpachole de jaiba*. In landlocked Chihuahua, I found *sopa de ajo*—garlic soup—not often on menus but a part of the daily meal in most homes. Every family has its favorite versions of these, because soups are more than local; they are also personal.

Of course, there are certain soups that you find all over Mexico. Yet as you move through the country's diverse territories, you will always come upon local variations. The *caldo de res*—beef soup with vegetables—that simmers on stoves in Sonora is different from the one that simmers in Oaxacan pots.

Some soups remind me of home. A smoky mushroom and guajillo soup makes me think of the summer rainy season in central Mexico, when mushroom gatherers take to the hills to hunt for wild mushrooms and then bring their bounty to local markets. The chipotle chicken soup, *sopa Tlalpeña*, from a neighborhood in my hometown, Mexico City, is one of my standbys, and I hope it becomes one of yours.

GARLIC SOUP / **SOPA DE AJO**

Serves 6

If you are in the state of Chihuahua and are invited to a meal in somebody's home, you are likely to be served sopa de ajo. The soup, which has Spanish origins, took root mostly in the central and northern areas of Mexico. Fresh epazote sprigs are typical, as are dried chiles of one type or another, although I don't include chiles here. Sometimes the chiles are cooked in oil along with the garlic and pureed, and sometimes they are toasted or fried and used as a topping.

The soup calls for a lot of garlic cloves, but their flavor is sweet, almost caramelized. I puree the garlic after it has simmered in the seasoned broth, giving the soup a silky texture and intensifying its mushroomy taste.

2 tablespoons plus 1 teaspoon olive oil, plus more for the baking sheet

6 (½-inch-thick) slices baguette, diced

1½ teaspoons kosher salt, or more to taste

Freshly ground black pepper

15 garlic cloves, sliced

8 cups chicken broth

3 sprigs fresh epazote (see note)

2 large eggs

1 cup grated Chihuahua or Monterey Jack cheese (4 ounces)

Preheat the oven to 350 degrees F, with a rack in the upper third. Generously brush a baking sheet with olive oil. Place the baguette pieces on the baking sheet. Sprinkle with ½ teaspoon of the salt and pepper to taste, toss well with your hands, and spread out into an even layer. Bake until crisp and golden brown, 20 to 25 minutes. Remove the croutons from the oven, transfer to a bowl, and set aside.

Heat 2 tablespoons of the olive oil in a large saucepan over low heat. Add the sliced garlic and cook, stirring occasionally, until it has completely softened and is barely beginning to brown along its edges, 7 to 8 minutes; do not burn. Add the chicken broth, epazote sprigs, and the remaining 1 teaspoon salt. Raise the heat to medium, bring to a simmer, and cook for 10 to 12 minutes. Turn off the heat and allow the soup to cool slightly.

Remove the epazote sprigs and pour the broth and garlic into a blender, in batches if necessary. Puree until smooth. Return to the saucepan.

When you're ready to serve, bring the soup back to a simmer over medium heat.

Beat the eggs with the remaining 1 teaspoon olive oil in a small bowl. Stirring the simmering broth with a dinner fork, drizzle in the eggs in the thinnest stream possible. Continue to simmer until the eggs are cooked, about 2 minutes, and remove from the heat.

Ladle into soup bowls, add about 3 tablespoons grated cheese to each serving, and top with the croutons. Serve immediately.

Cook's Note

▶ You can substitute a tablespoon of dried epazote for the fresh. You can also substitute other fresh herbs of your choice, such as cilantro or thyme.

SPRING ONION AND TOMATO SOUP WITH MELTY CHEESE / SOPA DE CEBOLLITAS CON QUESO

Serves 6 to 8

Think of this soup as a cross between a rich, creamy tomato soup and an onion soup with lots of melted cheese. The soup stood out when I was researching the cuisine of Durango, a landlocked state in north-central Mexico with deep culinary traditions, which include a love for butter, cream, and cheese.

Don't let the large number of spring onions (or scallions, which can be substituted) fool you into thinking that this will have an overpowering onion flavor. Cooking the alliums slowly in a generous amount of butter tames their pungency and gives them a mellow sweetness. The final enrichment of copious amounts of grated cheese transforms this into an irresistible queso soup. Serve with toasted crusty bread.

5 tablespoons unsalted butter

1 tablespoon olive oil

30 spring onions or 60 scallions (about 8 bunches), white and light green parts only, thinly sliced (about 8 cups; reserve 1 cup of the light green parts for garnish)

3 garlic cloves, finely chopped

1¼ teaspoons kosher salt, or more to taste

½ teaspoon freshly ground black pepper

2 pounds ripe tomatoes, coarsely pureed in a blender or food processor, or 1 (28-ounce) can crushed tomatoes

3½ cups chicken broth

½ cup crema or heavy cream

2 cups grated melting cheese, such as asadero, Oaxaca, Monterey Jack, or mozzarella (8 ounces)

Heat the butter and olive oil in a large pot over medium heat until the butter is bubbling. Add the spring onions or scallions and cook for about 10 minutes, stirring occasionally, until completely softened. Clear a space in the middle of the pot, add the garlic, and cook for a minute or two, until fragrant. Add 1 teaspoon of the salt and the pepper and stir well.

Stir in the tomatoes and cook for 9 to 10 minutes, stirring occasionally, until they have cooked down and darkened in color.

Add the chicken broth, stir well, and bring to a boil. Reduce the heat to medium-low and simmer for 3 to 4 minutes. Stir in the cream and cook at a gentle simmer for another 5 minutes. Add the remaining ¼ teaspoon salt, or more to taste, then add the cheese and stir so that it melts into the soup. Ladle the soup into bowls, garnish with the reserved spring onions or scallions, and serve.

CREMA

Mexican crema has everything you like about cream, sour cream, and crème fraîche in one delicious bite. Tangy and a little salty, it's thicker than heavy cream but still pourable, thinner than sour cream or crème fraîche. This is why we reach for it so readily to enrich soups, vegetable dishes, and desserts.

Crema is found in Mexican markets and in larger supermarkets. It has a conveniently long shelf life, usually a couple of weeks at least. Once you have it on hand, you'll find all sorts of ways to use it—including eating it by the spoonful.

CORN SOUP WITH QUESO FRESCO / **SOPA DE ESQUITES CON QUESO**

Serves 6

This soup showed me the simpler side of Oaxacan cooking. I had come to Tlaxiaco, high in the Sierra Madre Mountains, to work with Ixchel Ornelas, a leading Oaxacan chef who is spearheading efforts to promote the cooking of her area. She created the soup for her family restaurant El Patio, and it has become so famous in the region that she can't take it off the menu. At 2,100 meters above sea level, this forested region, known as Mixteca Alta, can be cold and rainy, very different from the rest of Oaxaca, and the soup was warming and satisfying after my five-hour trip from Oaxaca City.

Ixchel taught me how to make the most complicated mole I have ever tasted, with more than forty ingredients, but it was her corn soup that stayed in my head for weeks after I got back home. Although it calls for just a handful of ingredients and comes together in about 15 minutes, there is a lot going on when you taste it: the sweetness and crunchiness of the corn; the tanginess of the queso fresco, which is firm when you begin eating the soup, then begins to share itself with the broth; the clean, earthy taste of the epazote; and the heat of the serranos.

2 tablespoons unsalted butter

1 tablespoon vegetable oil

½ cup finely chopped white onion

1 to 2 serrano or jalapeño chiles (to taste), finely chopped

4 cups fresh corn kernels (from 5 to 6 ears) or thawed frozen corn

½ teaspoon kosher salt, or more to taste

¼ cup chopped fresh epazote or cilantro leaves

8 cups chicken broth

1 cup diced queso fresco (4 ounces)

Melt the butter with the oil in a large pot over medium-high heat. Once the butter begins to sizzle, add the onion and chiles and cook for 3 to 4 minutes, until wilted and beginning to color. Add the corn and salt, stir, and cook for 3 minutes, until the kernels begin to soften. Add the epazote or cilantro, stir, and add the chicken broth. Bring to a boil, cover, reduce the heat to low, and simmer for 7 to 8 minutes, until the soup is fragrant and the corn is tender. Adjust the seasonings and remove from the heat.

Ladle the soup into bowls, top with the queso fresco, and serve.

GUAJILLO MUSHROOM SOUP / **SOPA DE HONGOS CON GUAJILLO**

Serves 6 to 8

You find mushroom soup in Mexico year-round, but especially during the summer rainy season in the central part of the country, when foragers go out to the hills before dawn to gather all sorts of exotic varieties and bring them, still glistening with the morning dew, to local markets. With different textures, shapes, and colors, these mushrooms, rarely available in the cities, have whimsical names like birds' feet, little cloves, and blue clouds.

For this soup, you can use wild mushrooms such as chanterelles, trumpets, shiitakes, or oysters (a mix is nice) or cultivated ones such as white buttons, cremini, or baby bellas. Whether made with wild or cultivated varieties, Mexican mushroom soup has a rustic mountain quality. Dried chiles are usually part of the equation; the most common are guajillos, as here, or anchos or chiles de árbol, which can be substituted. All will give the broth a red hue and a smoky taste, but anchos will yield a more bittersweet, chocolaty flavor and chiles de árbol will make it smokier and the heat a bit feistier.

3 dried guajillo chiles, stemmed and seeded

2 tablespoons vegetable oil

1 tablespoon unsalted butter

½ cup finely chopped white onion

3 garlic cloves, finely chopped

2 pounds fresh wild or cultivated mushrooms, or a combination, cut into bite-size pieces

1½ teaspoons kosher salt, or more to taste

½ teaspoon freshly ground black pepper, or more to taste

8 cups vegetable or chicken broth

5 sprigs fresh epazote or cilantro

Lime wedges for serving

Heat a comal or skillet over medium-low heat. Add the guajillo chiles and toast, turning them, until their skin goes from soft and deep red to toasted and mostly browned but not blackened.

Transfer the chiles to a saucepan, cover with hot water, and bring to a boil. Reduce the heat to medium and simmer for about 10 minutes, until the chiles are softened. Transfer to a blender, add 1 cup of their cooking liquid, and cover tightly. Puree until smooth.

Heat the oil and butter in a large pot over medium heat until the butter melts. Add the onion and cook for about 3 minutes, stirring occasionally, until it is softened and the edges are just beginning to brown. Add the garlic, stir, and cook until fragrant, less than a minute. Raise the heat to high, stir in the mushrooms, 1 teaspoon of the salt, and the pepper, and let the mushrooms cook, stirring often. They will release their juices and then, as the juices evaporate, begin to brown, which is what you want; it should take 10 to 12 minutes.

continued

Once all of the mushroom liquid has evaporated, reduce the heat to medium, stir in the pureed chiles, and cook until the puree thickens and most of it has been absorbed by the mushrooms, about 10 minutes. Add the broth, stir, add the epazote or cilantro sprigs, and bring to a simmer. Simmer for 10 minutes, until all the flavors come together. Remove the epazote or cilantro, add the remaining ½ teaspoon salt, taste, and adjust the seasonings.

Serve with lime wedges.

Cook's Notes

► If you want a layer of tomato flavor and a thicker broth, add a tomato to the guajillo chiles as they simmer. Simmer until the chiles are softened and the tomato is mushy, about 10 minutes, then puree with the 1 cup cooking liquid. You can do this with any soup that calls for pureed rehydrated chiles.

► When toasting dried chiles, turn on your stove's exhaust fan to help disperse the fumes from the chiles.

► For soups or stews made with sprigs of fresh herbs that will be removed after cooking, it's useful to tie them together with a short piece of cooking twine so you can fish them out easily.

THE EVER-POPULAR GUAJILLO CHILE

Why do we love guajillos? Because these dried chiles have an elegant taste to match their long, tapered shape and beautiful dark maroon color, and because they contribute an earthy depth of flavor without overwhelming heat, they are one of the most common chiles in Mexican cooking. You find them in salsas and stews, soups and moles, meat dishes, adobos, and rubs.

As a first step, guajillos are almost always stemmed and seeded, and then often toasted on a comal. Be sure to toast them until they turn opaque and a bit brownish, but not until they blacken, which would make them bitter. They can then be ground into a powder, but more often they are rehydrated in hot or simmering water and pureed with other ingredients, including some of the soaking water.

PINTO BEAN SOUP WITH MASA DUMPLINGS / **SOPA DE OMBLIGO**

Serves 6 to 8

I was captivated by the name of this traditional pinto bean soup from the tiny Sinaloan mountain town of Jinetes de Machado: *Ombligo* means belly button! The rich, creamy pureed soup has masa dumplings in it that are shaped into little balls with dimples in them, hence the name. The belly buttons trap the hearty flavors of the soup they cook in, and they also share themselves with the soup, thickening it and permeating it with the flavors of queso fresco and fresh cilantro and mint.

The finished soup seems to beg for a little heat, and because it is Sinaloan, I usually add the region's iconic dried chiltepín chiles. But you can use another dried ground chile of your liking, such as chiles de árbol, to garnish it.

I learned the soup from Maria Elena Machado, the aunt of Gerardo Machado, who invited me to visit the town.

2 tablespoons vegetable oil

½ cup chopped white onion

1 garlic clove, chopped

½ pound ripe tomatoes, chopped, or half a 15-ounce can crushed tomatoes

½ teaspoon kosher salt, or more to taste

½ recipe Basic Simmered Beans (page 156), made with pinto beans, drained, reserving 1 cup of the broth, or 2 (15-ounce) cans pinto beans, drained, plus 1 cup chicken or vegetable broth

8 cups chicken or vegetable broth

FOR THE DUMPLINGS

1 cup masa harina (see note)

1 cup lukewarm water

¼ teaspoon kosher salt, or more to taste

3 tablespoons vegetable oil

3 tablespoons crumbled queso fresco

1 tablespoon chopped fresh cilantro leaves

1 tablespoon chopped fresh mint leaves

Crema or sour cream for garnish (optional)

Sliced scallions, chopped fresh mint and cilantro leaves, and/or crushed dried chiltepín chiles or chiles de árbol for garnish (optional)

Heat the oil in a large heavy pot over medium-high heat. Add the onion and cook for 5 to 6 minutes, until it has softened and the edges are beginning to brown. Add the garlic and cook for another minute, until fragrant and beginning to color. Stir in the tomatoes and salt and cook until the tomatoes have reduced to a thick paste, 5 to 6 minutes.

Add the beans, with the 1 cup of their broth (or the additional 1 cup chicken or vegetable broth), along with 4 cups of the broth. Bring to a boil, reduce the heat to medium, cover partially, and simmer for 10 minutes. The beans should be completely soft and the broth thick and soupy. Remove from the heat.

continued

Meanwhile, make the dumplings: In a medium bowl, combine the masa harina with the water and salt and knead together. The dough will be very coarse and seem dry. Add the oil, queso fresco, cilantro, and mint and mix together until the dough is very soft and homogenous, about 1 minute. Set aside.

Working in batches, puree the soup in a blender until smooth. Pour back into the pot and whisk or stir in the remaining 4 cups broth. Bring to a simmer over medium heat, then reduce the heat to low.

To form the dumplings: Fill a bowl with warm water for moistening your hands. Wet your hands and form the dumplings one at a time: Scoop up enough masa to make a 1-inch ball, roll between your hands into a ball, and make a dimple in the middle with your thumb, then gently drop into the soup. Once all the dumplings have been shaped and added to the soup, gently stir with a wooden spoon to make sure none are sticking to the bottom of the pot. Cover partially and let the soup simmer gently for 15 to 20 more minutes, until the dumplings are cooked through.

Taste the soup for salt and add more to taste if necessary. Serve hot, garnishing each bowl with a spoonful of cream, and sprinkling on scallions, herbs, and/or crushed chiles if you like.

Cook's Notes

► If you have a choice between masa harina for tamales (the package will say "for tamales") or for tortillas, go for the tamal version. Masa harina for tortillas is finer, but it will work.

► You can substitute mild feta or farmers' cheese for the queso.

JINETES DE MACHADO: A TOWN THAT'S ALL IN THE FAMILY

Jinetes de Machado has only been around for about 150 years, and its population has been made up of four generations of a single extended family, the Machados. The cattle-raising family used to be semi-nomadic until they arrived here and made it their home. The village is so remote that during most of the year, the only way to get to it is by mule. There is no electricity or running water, and the people like it that way.

Today there are no more than sixty people living in Jinetes. My host was Gerardo Machado, one of the men of the younger generation. He is devoted to protecting the flora and fauna and is trying to bring in a new kind of ecotourism. He also works to stop illegal logging and the hunting of animals on the verge of extinction, like the mountain jaguar.

The Machados survive on what they grow—they prepare their own masa for tortillas, bake their own bread, make fresh cheeses, and farm all their fruits and vegetables. The only items from the outside world are a few basics like oil, sugar, and flour.

CHIPOTLE OYSTER SOUP / **SOPA DE OSTIÓN AL CHIPOTLE**

Serves 6

I was inspired to make this soup, which is one of my favorites of all time, after I visited the port city of Altata in Sinaloa, on the northeast coast of the Baja Peninsula. A truly hidden gem, Altata is home to a number of thriving oyster farms. The waters of the Pacific Ocean are mineral-rich here, and the oysters are the meatiest, most delicious I've ever tasted.

Decades earlier, I'd eaten a similar soup in a Mexico City cantina on a night out with my future husband and my older sister and her husband. Daniel and I had just started dating, and right after the food came to the table, my sister asked him what his intentions were with her little sister. I was mortified and focused on my fabulous soup, which I never forgot, so I was delighted to be able to re-create it.

I use finely chopped celery, carrots, and leeks in two ways here. For the flavorful, smoky-spicy pureed base, I cook a portion of the vegetables with the chiles and simmer them with roasted tomatoes and the oyster juices. Then the rest are added with the oysters and cooked just until al dente, so they add a delightful tiny crunch. The oysters should be cooked gently and not too long, so they taste and feel like a seafood version of foie gras.

1½ pounds ripe tomatoes (see note)

3 tablespoons vegetable oil

1½ cups finely chopped white onion

1½ cups finely chopped celery

1½ cups finely chopped carrots

1½ cups finely chopped well-rinsed leeks

5 garlic cloves, finely chopped

3 chipotle chiles in adobo sauce, finely chopped, plus 1 tablespoon of the sauce

1 dried chile de árbol, stemmed and chopped, seeds included

1 pound shucked oysters (12 to 15 large), with their juices

1 teaspoon kosher salt, or more to taste

1 teaspoon dried oregano

5 cups Shrimp Broth (page 27) or chicken or vegetable broth

Chopped fresh cilantro leaves for garnish

Quartered limes for serving

Preheat the broiler, with the rack 2 to 3 inches from the heat source. Place the tomatoes on a baking sheet lined with foil and broil for 10 to 12 minutes, turning them over halfway through, until charred and mushy. Remove from the heat. Alternatively, you can roast the tomatoes on a comal or in a large skillet over medium heat, turning them every 4 to 5 minutes. Remove from the heat.

continued

When the tomatoes are cool enough to handle, finely chop them and transfer to a bowl. Make sure to tip in any juices from the baking sheet. Set aside.

Heat the oil in a large pot over medium heat. Add the onion and cook, stirring often, for 5 to 6 minutes, until softened. Stir in 1 cup each of the celery, carrots, and leeks and cook for 3 to 4 minutes, until wilted.

Clear a space in the middle of the pot and add the garlic, chipotles in adobo, adobo sauce, and chile de árbol. Cook, stirring, for a minute, then mix with the vegetables and cook for another minute.

Add the tomatoes, the oyster juices, salt, and oregano, bring to a simmer, and cook until the mixture thickens a bit, 6 to 7 minutes. Add the broth, bring to a simmer, and simmer for 10 minutes, until the color darkens and the soup thickens slightly. Turn off the heat and allow to cool slightly.

Transfer the soup, in batches, to a blender and puree until smooth. Wash and dry the pot.

If you want a very silky texture, place a sieve over the pot and pour the soup through it; otherwise, just return the soup to the pot. Bring to a simmer over medium heat and add the remaining ½ cup each celery, carrots, and leeks. Simmer for 4 to

5 minutes, until the vegetables are cooked to al dente and the soup is a little thicker. Stir in the shucked oysters and any juices and cook for 1 minute, until barely cooked through. Turn off the heat.

Ladle into soup bowls, garnish with cilantro, and offer your guests quartered limes so they can squeeze in some fresh juice before they eat.

Cook's Notes

► You can substitute 1 (28-ounce) can fire-roasted tomatoes for the fresh tomatoes; skip the broiling step.

► When you puree a hot soup, the built-up steam can cause the top of the blender to fly off. To prevent this from happening, always work in batches, filling the blender only halfway. For extra protection, cover the top with a towel before you turn on the blender. Start on low speed, then gradually increase the speed.

MINE WORKERS' FISH SOUP / **CALDO DE OSO**

Serves 6 to 8

I first learned about this soup from a Denver TV producer whom I knew only as Pepe. I was intrigued, because I'd never seen it on a menu, even though I've been to Chihuahua many times. That's because it's not a restaurant dish, but a beloved home-cooked meal.

Pepe described in detail how his mom makes the soup, and after making it, I understood why it's worthy of his nostalgia. How could he ever forget the intense flavor of the tomato-based broth, spiced with both anchos and pickled jalapeños? A small amount of flour is added to the base to give the broth body, a common trick in the northern states of Mexico, where wheat has a stronger presence than corn. The soup is full of vegetables and you can easily make a meal of it. The copper-mine workers who are said to have originated caldo de oso traditionally made it with catfish, a freshwater fish that is abundant in Chihuahua, but the recipe also works well with other white fish. (For the story of how it came to be called bear soup, see the sidebar.)

2 dried ancho chiles, stemmed and seeded

2 tablespoons unsalted butter

2 tablespoons vegetable oil

⅔ cup finely chopped white onion

3 garlic cloves, finely chopped

2 pounds ripe tomatoes, chopped, or 1 (28-ounce) can crushed tomatoes

½ teaspoon dried thyme

½ teaspoon dried marjoram

½ teaspoon dried oregano

¼ teaspoon ground cumin

Kosher salt to taste

1 tablespoon all-purpose flour

8 cups fish or seafood broth, Shrimp Broth (page 27), or water

1 bay leaf

½ teaspoon freshly ground black pepper

1 pickled jalapeño, diced, plus 2 tablespoons of its brine

2 cups peeled and diced carrots

2 cups peeled and diced potatoes

2 pounds catfish, tilapia, cod, or snapper fillets, cut into 2-inch pieces

Lime wedges and plenty of chopped fresh cilantro leaves for serving

Place the ancho chiles in a bowl, cover with about 2 cups boiling water, and let sit for 10 minutes, or until they are plumped. Transfer the chiles and 1 cup of their soaking water to a blender and puree until smooth. Set aside.

Heat the butter and oil in a large pot over medium heat until the butter is bubbling. Add the onion and cook for 4 to 5 minutes, until it is softened and the edges begin to color. Add the garlic, stir, and cook for a minute, until fragrant. Increase the heat to medium-high and stir in the tomatoes. Add the thyme, marjoram, oregano, cumin, and a generous pinch of salt and cook, stirring occasionally, until the tomatoes have softened and cooked down a bit, 6 to 8 minutes. Sprinkle the flour over the tomatoes and onions, stir well, and cook, stirring, until the mixture begins to brown and smell toasty. Add the broth or water and bring to a simmer, stirring.

continued

Stir the pureed anchos into the soup. Add the bay leaf, 1 teaspoon salt, the pepper, pickled jalapeño, and its brine and mix well. Bring back to a simmer, stirring, then reduce the heat to medium, cover partially, and simmer for 15 minutes, stirring occasionally.

Add the carrots and potatoes and continue to simmer for 15 to 20 minutes, until the vegetables are cooked through. Taste and adjust the salt.

Season the fish with salt and pepper, stir into the soup, and simmer for 5 to 8 minutes, or until just cooked through.

Ladle the soup into bowls and pass lime wedges and chopped cilantro at the table.

"BEAR SOUP" WITH NO BEAR

The traditional name for this dish, *caldo de oso*, translates as bear soup. Nope, there is no bear in it. The story goes like this: Almost a century ago, copper-mine workers building the La Boquilla Dam on the Conchos River in Camargo, a mining region in Chihuahua, fed themselves from the bounty of catfish they found in the river. Every day they made catfish soup. After a while, though, they grew so tired of eating it that they began to call it *caldo odioso*, which translates as detestable soup. Eventually, *odioso* got shortened to *oso*. It's a common Mexican practice to make words smaller and use the diminutive, so the name stuck. And while the mine workers at the dam a hundred years ago might have wearied of the soup, the people of Chihuahua adore it, and I know you will too.

SMOKY CRAB AND SHRIMP SOUP / CHILPACHOLE DE JAIBA Y CAMARÓN

Serves 6

Chilpachole, from the Nahuatl words *chilli* (chile) and *patzolli*, meaning something that is mixed, is fun to say and even more fun to eat. Reminiscent of bouillabaisse, it's rich, spicy, and soothing, all at the same time. In the state of Veracruz, where the dish originated, the soup is made with the blue crabs that abound along the state's long, smiling gulf coastline. Sometimes other seafood is added, usually shrimp.

Traditionally the whole crabs are cooked in a rich, velvety chipotle broth thickened with masa. When I began making chilpachole, I used my local Maryland crabs. But because their season is short, I now use crabmeat and shrimp, cooked in a broth made with shrimp shells and, if I can get them, heads, which has the same richness and depth of flavor as one from whole crabs.

Sometimes cooks put jalapeños in the broth instead of chipotles, but I like both. Jalapeño is the fresh version of the chipotle and has a completely different taste. I roast it to coax out its flavors and blend it with the soup base, along with the chipotles and some of their adobo sauce.

Masa yields a thicker, silkier soup, but you can also thicken the soup with crumbled toasted tortillas, which add a rustic flavor that I love.

FOR THE SHRIMP BROTH

1 pound medium shrimp in the shell, preferably head-on

10 cups water

½ white onion

5 garlic cloves, peeled

4 bay leaves

2 teaspoons kosher salt, or more to taste

1 teaspoon black peppercorns

FOR THE SOUP

1½ pounds tomatoes (see note)

3 garlic cloves, not peeled

½ white onion, quartered

1 jalapeño chile

2 chipotle chiles in adobo sauce, plus 2 tablespoons of the sauce

1 teaspoon kosher salt

2 tablespoons olive oil

6 sprigs fresh epazote or 1 tablespoon crumbled dried epazote

¼ cup masa harina, blended with ¼ cup water, or 3 corn tortillas, toasted and crumbled

2 pounds jumbo lump crabmeat, picked over for shells and cartilage

FOR SERVING

Diced avocado (optional)

Sliced crunchy bread (optional)

2 limes, quartered

continued

To make the shrimp broth: Peel and devein the shrimp, removing and reserving the heads, if you have them; refrigerate the shrimp until ready to use them. Place the heads and shells in a medium saucepan. Add the water, onion, garlic, bay leaves, salt, and peppercorns and bring to a boil over medium-high heat, then reduce the heat to medium and simmer for 30 minutes. Strain the broth. You will have about 9 cups; you can freeze what you don't use for the soup. Set aside.

To make the soup: Preheat the broiler, with the rack 2 to 3 inches from the heat source. Place the tomatoes, garlic cloves, onion, and jalapeño on a baking sheet lined with foil and broil for 10 to 12 minutes, turning the vegetables halfway through, until they are charred and the tomatoes are mushy. The garlic will probably be done by the time you turn the vegetables; remove it when it's charred and softened. When it is cool enough to handle, peel it. Alternatively, you can char the vegetables on a comal or large skillet over medium heat, turning them every 4 to 5 minutes. Remove from the heat.

Transfer the charred vegetables to a blender. Add 1 cup of the shrimp broth and the chipotles, adobo sauce, and salt and puree until smooth.

Heat the oil in a large pot over medium heat. Add the vegetable puree and epazote, using the pot lid to shield yourself from splatters, and cook, stirring often, for 10 to 12 minutes, until the mixture thickens and darkens and the flavors intensify.

Combine the masa harina mixture or crumbled tortillas and 1 cup of the reserved shrimp broth in a blender and blend until smooth. Stir into the simmering sauce, along with another 3 cups shrimp broth, bring to a simmer, and simmer for 20 minutes, stirring occasionally and scraping the bottom of the pot.

Add the crab and shrimp and cook for 3 to 4 minutes, until the shrimp is just cooked through.

Garnish the soup with diced avocado and serve with crunchy bread, if you wish, passing the lime quarters for squeezing in.

Cook's Note

▸ You can substitute 1 (28-ounce) can fire-roasted tomatoes for the fresh tomatoes; skip the broiling step for the tomatoes and puree them with the roasted garlic, onion, and jalapeño.

SWEET LIME AND CHICKEN SOUP / **SOPA DE LIMA**

Serves 6

To say this chicken soup is a signature dish of the Yucatán is an understatement. You'll find it on just about every restaurant menu on the peninsula. What makes it uniquely Yucatecan is not just the sweet lime, known as *lima*, the variety of lime that is used there and gives the soup its name as well as its unmistakable flavor, but also the harmonious combination of bell pepper (called *chile dulce* in the region) in the sofrito base, roasted garlic in the broth, and fragrant dried oregano. Even the tortilla chips that garnish the soup are cut differently from those in traditional tortilla soups: They are long strips rather than short strips or wedges.

You can find lima citrus in specialty stores and online, or substitute regular limes or lemons.

5 garlic cloves, not peeled

2 boneless, skinless chicken breasts (about 1½ pounds)

10 cups water

1 teaspoon dried oregano

½ teaspoon dried thyme

3 bay leaves

3 cloves

2½ teaspoons kosher salt, or more to taste

¼ teaspoon freshly ground black pepper

2 tablespoons vegetable oil, plus more for frying the tortilla strips

1 cup chopped red onion

½ pound ripe tomatoes, chopped, with their juices, or half a 15-ounce can crushed tomatoes

1 green or yellow bell pepper, cored, seeded, and chopped

6 to 8 corn tortillas, cut into 2-x-½-inch strips and fried or baked until crisp (page 54)

½ cup chopped fresh cilantro leaves and upper stems for garnish

1 sweet lime (or regular lime or lemon), thinly sliced, for garnish, plus 2 to 3 sweet limes (or regular limes or lemons) for squeezing

1 fresh habanero chile, thinly sliced, for garnish (optional)

Preheat the broiler, with the rack 2 to 3 inches from the heat source. Place the unpeeled garlic cloves on a small baking sheet under the broiler and broil for 5 to 10 minutes, turning from time to time, until the skin is completely charred and blackened and the garlic is soft and mushy. Remove from the heat and set aside to cool slightly; peel when cool enough to handle. Alternatively, you can char the garlic on a preheated comal or skillet, turning it occasionally. Remove from the heat.

Place the chicken breasts in a large pot and cover with the water. Add the charred garlic cloves, oregano, thyme, bay leaves, cloves, 2 teaspoons of the salt, and the pepper and bring to a simmer over medium heat. Skim off the foam, cover partially, reduce the heat to medium-low, and simmer for 30 to 35 minutes, until the chicken is cooked through but still moist. Remove from the heat.

continued

Remove the chicken breasts from the broth and set aside until cool enough to handle, then shred along the grain into thin pieces. Strain the broth into a large bowl and add the shredded chicken.

Rinse and dry the pot. Add the oil and heat over medium-high heat until hot. Add the onion, tomatoes, bell pepper, and the remaining ½ teaspoon salt and cook, stirring often, until the vegetables are very soft, almost a mash, about 10 minutes.

Stir in the chicken broth and chicken and bring to a simmer. Reduce the heat to low, partially cover, and simmer for 8 to 10 minutes, until all the flavors have come together.

Ladle the soup into bowls. Top each serving with a handful of tortilla strips and garnish with some of the cilantro, lime or lemon slices, a squeeze of juice, and, if desired, some sliced habanero for added flavor and heat.

SWEET LIMES

The sweet lime, *Citrus limettioides,* is of Asian origin. It was brought to Mexico by the Spanish and it took hold in the Yucatán Peninsula, where it is now ubiquitous. It goes by various names, such as *lima,* sweet lemon, and limetta. The fruit is plump and round, about 2½ inches in diameter, with smooth, deep green skin that becomes yellow and freckled as the fruit matures. The pulp is a beautiful light green, with a perfumed aroma and an intriguing flavor that is much milder, sweeter—almost floral, but with a hint of bitterness—and less acidic than that of regular limes.

DRESSED-UP CHICKEN SOUP / **CALDO TLALPEÑO**

Serves 6

I love all Mexican chicken soups, but this is one of my favorites, maybe because it comes from my hometown of Mexico City. The soup is named for its place of origin, Tlalpan, which is now a neighborhood in Mexico City but was once a small town on the outskirts.

What identifies a caldo Tlalpeño is the chipotle-seasoned broth and the chickpeas, carrots, and green beans. I give the soup a complex double-strength chipotle base by using both dried chipotles and chipotles in adobo. I cut the carrots into matchsticks and add them and the green beans toward the end of cooking so they have a crisp texture and a nice fresh taste. The garnishes are cilantro, onion, quartered limes, and chopped serranos or jalapeños—and, yes, I insist on all of them, please!

Either epazote or cilantro can be used in the soup, but go for epazote if you can get it. Pureeing the herb with the seasoning base results in a darker, more brick-colored soup; if you add it later and simmer it with the vegetables, the soup will have a brighter red color. The choice is yours.

1 pound ripe tomatoes or 1 (15-ounce) can whole tomatoes

2 garlic cloves, peeled

2 dried chipotle chiles, preferably moritas (page 133), stemmed

3 sprigs fresh epazote or cilantro

1 chipotle chile in adobo sauce

¼ cup coarsely chopped white onion

1½ teaspoons kosher salt, or more to taste

2 tablespoons vegetable oil

6 cups chicken broth

½ pound carrots, peeled and cut into 1-inch-long matchsticks

½ pound green beans, trimmed and cut diagonally into 1-inch pieces

1 (15.5-ounce) can chickpeas, drained and rinsed, or ⅔ cup dried chickpeas, cooked and drained (see note)

4 cups shredded cooked chicken (page 251) or rotisserie chicken

FOR THE GARNISH

1 cup finely chopped white onion

2 to 3 serrano or jalapeño chiles, finely chopped

1 ripe avocado, halved, pitted, and sliced or diced

2 limes, quartered

Place the fresh tomatoes, if using, garlic, and dried chipotles in a medium saucepan. If you want to puree the epazote or cilantro sprigs with the seasoning sauce (see headnote), add them now. Cover generously with water and bring to a boil over medium-high heat. Reduce the heat to medium and simmer for 10 to 12 minutes, until the tomatoes are soft and mushy and their skins are starting to come off, the chipotles are plump, the garlic is soft, and the herbs have wilted.

Using a slotted spoon, transfer the simmered tomatoes, garlic, and epazote or cilantro to a blender. If using canned tomatoes, add them to the blender. Add ¼ cup of the cooking liquid, the chipotle in adobo, onion, and salt and puree until smooth.

continued

Heat the oil in a large pot over medium heat. Add the tomato puree, cover partially, and cook, stirring and scraping the bottom of the pot occasionally, for 8 to 10 minutes, until the sauce thickens and intensifies.

Add the chicken broth and bring to a simmer, then add the carrots, green beans, and chickpeas, along with the epazote or cilantro if you didn't add it earlier, and bring to a simmer. Simmer for 5 to 6 minutes, then stir in the shredded chicken and simmer for another 3 to 4 minutes to heat through.

Ladle the soup into soup bowls and pass the onion, serrano, avocado, and limes so everyone can garnish their caldo Tlalpeño to taste.

Cook's Note

► Dried chickpeas cook more evenly if you soak them first, for at least 6 hours, and up to 24 hours. Drain the chickpeas and place in a large saucepan. Cover with water by 2 inches and bring to a boil over high heat, then reduce the heat to medium-low and cook, partially covered, for 1 hour. Add salt to taste and simmer for another 30 minutes, or until the chickpeas are soft but not breaking apart.

BEEF AND VEGETABLE SOUP / MOLE DE OLLA (PAGE 36)

BEEF AND VEGETABLE SOUP / **MOLE DE OLLA**

Serves 8 to 10

Mole de olla is a deeply comforting brothy beef and vegetable soup. Mexicans enjoy it year-round, even in the summer. You will see vendors ladling sizzling-hot mole de olla from large pots (*olla* means cooking pot) in markets in the central part of the country at the peak of the midday heat, because paradoxically, it fills you up as it cools you down.

Despite its name, this soup has nothing in common with the rich, complex moles of Oaxaca and Puebla. Here the word just means a mix of ingredients, in this case a puree of reconstituted dried chiles and roasted tomatoes, tomatillos, and sesame seeds that flavors the beef broth. It's a *caldo de res*, a practical and economical one-pot dish that varies from one part of the country to another. The broth of this one is a deep burnt orange—tangier and a little spicier than the typical version.

In Mexico, mole de olla gets its tangy flavor from xonocostles, a sour cactus fruit. Tomatillos, which I substitute here, have a similarly tart flavor. Lime wedges are served alongside for everybody to squeeze into their bowls to further brighten the taste.

Eating the soup is a ritual that becomes personalized. Some people have a bowl of the broth, then go back for the meat and vegetables and chase the bites with warm corn tortillas. Others like to eat the corn on the cob before moving on to the rest of the soup, while others—like me—prefer to eat everything at the same time. *The photo is on page 35.*

3 pounds beef stew meat, such as chuck or shank, cut into 1½- to 2-inch chunks

1 white onion, cut in half

3 garlic cloves, peeled

4 to 5 sprigs fresh mint

3 bay leaves

1 tablespoon kosher salt, or more to taste

10 cups water

3 dried ancho chiles, stemmed and seeded

3 dried pasilla chiles, stemmed and seeded

1 pound tomatoes (see note)

¼ pound tomatillos (2 to 4, depending on size), husked and rinsed

2 tablespoons sesame seeds, lightly toasted

2 chayote squash, peeled and cubed (about 3 cups)

1 large zucchini, trimmed and cubed (about 3 cups)

¾ pound green beans, trimmed and cut into 1-inch pieces (about 2 cups)

3 or 4 ears fresh corn, husked and cut into thirds

FOR GARNISH

1 cup finely chopped white onion

½ cup coarsely chopped fresh cilantro leaves and upper parts of stems

3 or 4 limes, quartered

Put the meat, onion, garlic cloves, mint, bay leaves, and salt in a large heavy pot, add the water, and bring to a boil over medium-high heat. Skim off any foam that has risen to the surface and reduce the heat to low. Continue to skim until there is no more visible foam, then cover and simmer for 1 hour.

Meanwhile, place both kinds of chiles in a medium bowl, cover with boiling water, and soak for 10 to 15 minutes, until plumped.

Preheat the broiler, with the rack 2 to 3 inches from the heat source. Place the tomatoes and tomatillos on a baking sheet lined with foil and broil for 10 minutes, or until they are completely charred and mushy, turning them halfway through. Transfer to a blender. Add the sesame seeds and chiles, along with ¼ cup of their soaking liquid, and blend until smooth.

After the meat has simmered for an hour, uncover the pot and remove the onion, garlic, and mint (don't worry if some of these remain). Pour in the chile mixture and stir to blend. Cover and simmer for another 30 minutes, or until the broth and meat are nicely enriched with the chile puree.

Remove the lid, taste, and adjust the salt. Add the chayote, raise the heat to medium, cover partially, and simmer for 15 minutes. Add the zucchini, beans, and corn, cover partially, and simmer for another 10 minutes, or until the zucchini and beans are tender but not mushy.

Serve the soup in wide bowls, making sure that each bowl includes meat, corn, chayote, green beans, and zucchini. Pass the garnishes at the table.

Cook's Note

► You can substitute 1 (15-ounce) can fire-roasted tomatoes for the fresh tomatoes. Skip the broiling step for the tomatoes, and puree them with the roasted tomatillos and other ingredients.

TOMATILLOS: THE LITTLE TOMATOES THAT AREN'T

Tomatillos look like small light green tomatoes wrapped in papery husks. But although they are related to tomatoes, green regular tomatoes can't stand in for them. They have their own distinctive flavor profile, tangy and tart rather than sweet. They go by different names in different regions, among them *tomate, tomate verde,* and *tomate de cascara* (husk tomato).

Many large supermarkets stock tomatillos in the produce section. When you shop for them, don't be shy about peeking under the husks to make sure that they are firm and bright green, with no hidden bruises or wrinkles. The skin of the fruit is often sticky, which is normal, and it will wash away when you rinse the tomatillos after husking them.

Tomatillos are traditionally simmered or roasted, with the exception of salsa verde cruda, where they're used raw. But more and more, cooks are taking advantage of their sprightly sourness and adding them raw to sauces and soups as well as to salads.

CREAMY TOMATO AND CHICHARRÓN SOUP / **SOPA DE CHICHARRÓN**

Serves 6 to 8

The deep-fried pork rinds called *chicharrones* are one of the most beloved snacks of Mexico and increasingly, in the United States. But until recently I'd never heard of chicharrón soup, which has become wildly popular in my hometown of Mexico City and surrounding areas. A couple of fancy restaurants initiated the trend, and people loved it so much that they started making it at home. The soup is almost like a tomato bisque, with some wonderful spice from the guajillo chiles and the addictive background flavor of the chicharrones, which give the pureed soup a creamy texture. My friend Mara Yañez, a Mexico City native, shared her recipe with me as I was finishing my second bowl.

2 pounds ripe tomatoes or 1 (28-ounce) can whole tomatoes

½ white onion, quartered

2 garlic cloves, peeled

5 dried guajillo chiles, stemmed and seeded

8 cups chicken broth

½ pound chicharrones, broken into bite-size pieces

2 tablespoons vegetable oil

½ teaspoon kosher salt, or more to taste

FOR GARNISH

Crumbled chicharrones

1 avocado, halved, pitted, and diced

Chopped fresh cilantro leaves and upper parts of stems (optional)

Lime wedges (optional)

Combine the tomatoes, onion, garlic, and chiles in a large pot. Add the chicken broth and bring to a boil over medium-high heat. Reduce the heat to medium and add the chicharrones. Cover partially and return to a simmer, then use the back of a cooking spoon to push the chicharrón pieces into the broth to submerge them. Cover partially again and simmer for 15 minutes, or until the chicharrones are softened. Turn off the heat and let the soup cool for about 10 minutes.

Puree the soup in batches in a blender until creamy and smooth.

Rinse and dry the pot and set over medium heat. Add the oil, and when it is hot, pour in the pureed soup. Season with salt, stir well, bring to a simmer, and simmer for 5 minutes, or until the soup darkens a bit in color and the flavors intensify. Remove from the heat and taste for salt.

Ladle into bowls and garnish with crumbled chicharrones, the diced avocado, and, if you wish, some chopped cilantro leaves. Serve, passing lime wedges at the table.

MEXICO'S FAVORITE MUNCHIES

Salty and crunchy, with a bumpy, crispy, porous surface that is perfect for absorbing all sorts of flavors and sauces, chicharrones can stand in for tortilla chips as dippers for salsas and guacamole. They are great to munch on with a cold beer or a Michelada, the spicy beer and tomato juice cocktail. Look for them in the chips aisle, often labeled as pork rinds or cracklings.

RED MENUDO / **MENUDO ROJO**

Serves 8 generously

In Mexico, menudo—tripe soup—is a special-occasion or certain-day-of-the-week dish, or even a certain-time-of-day dish, and that day or time or occasion varies from region to region. It may be a Sunday specialty in one place, a Friday specialty in another. It's also considered one of the most effective hangover foods, a survival stew, a nourishing pick-me-up, an overall what-you-need-to-get-going one-pot-meal. Oh, and it is delicious! I find the texture of the tripe irresistible—soft and tender, yet with a slightly resistant, delicately spongy chew.

Although I like all types of menudo—red, green, and white—I am a devotee of the red version, enriched with a blend of chiles that give it its deep color, maybe because that's what I grew up eating in Mexico City. This recipe is a classic take. You can leave out the calves' feet if you can't get them, but if you have a Mexican meat market nearby, you'll find them there, and they add a lot of flavor and body. And you can substitute canned hominy for the dried (see note). But whatever you do, don't leave out the fresh mint that both seasons the broth and garnishes the finished soup.

FOR THE SOUP

½ pound dried hominy (also called giant white corn; maíz mote pelado)

1 head garlic, cut horizontally in half, loose papery outer layer removed

1 white onion, halved

3¾ teaspoons kosher salt, or more to taste

3 pounds beef tripe, preferably equal parts honeycomb tripe and book (bible) tripe (see note)

2 pounds calves' feet, cut into 2 to 4 pieces (optional; see note)

½ cup white vinegar

1 teaspoon dried oregano

15 sprigs fresh mint, tied with kitchen twine

FOR THE CHILE PUREE

4 dried colorado or guajillo chiles, or a mix, stemmed and seeded

2 garlic cloves, peeled

½ teaspoon cumin seeds, lightly toasted

½ teaspoon coriander seeds, lightly toasted

FOR THE GARNISHES

2 cups coarsely chopped fresh mint leaves

2 cups coarsely chopped fresh cilantro leaves and upper stems

1 cup finely chopped white onion

5 or 6 limes, halved

Ground or crushed dried chiltepín chile (page 141) or dried chile piquín or chile de árbol

Dried oregano

Warm corn tortillas, corn tostadas, or crunchy bread for serving (optional)

To make the soup: If using dried hominy, soak it in water to cover for 12 to 24 hours; drain in a colander and rinse well. Place the hominy in a large pot, add 4 quarts water, one half of the garlic head, and an onion half. Bring to a boil over high heat, reduce the heat to medium, skim off the foam, cover partially, and simmer for 2½ to 3 hours, until the hominy "blooms," or opens like a flower. Add ¾ teaspoon of the salt, stir, and remove from the heat. Remove the onion and garlic and discard; set the hominy aside.

Meanwhile, rinse the tripe and calves' feet, if using, in several changes of cold water. In a container large enough to hold the tripe and calves' feet, combine the vinegar, 4 cups water, and 2 teaspoons of the salt and stir to dissolve the salt. Add the tripe, calves' feet, and enough additional water to cover and soak for 30 minutes. Drain in a colander and rinse well. Cut the tripe into bite-size pieces, 1 to 1½ inches.

Combine 5 quarts water and the remaining onion and garlic half in a very large soup pot or a stockpot. If using the calves' feet, add them to the pot and bring the water to a boil over high heat. Reduce the heat to medium and simmer, partially covered, for 20 minutes. Skim off any foam. Add the tripe to the pot, along with the remaining 1 teaspoon salt, the oregano, and mint-sprig bundle, and bring to a boil. Reduce the heat to low and simmer, partially covered, for 4 hours, or until the tripe is soft and tender but still has some texture. Remove the garlic and onion and discard.

Meanwhile, make the chile puree: Place the dried chiles and garlic in a small saucepan, cover with water, and bring to a boil. Reduce the heat to medium-low and simmer for 10 to 15 minutes, until the chiles are softened. Remove from the heat and transfer the chiles and garlic to a blender, along with ½ cup of the cooking water. Add the cumin and coriander seeds and puree until smooth. Set aside.

To finish the soup: If you used the calves' feet, remove them from the pot with a slotted spoon and set aside to cool until you can handle them. Then remove the meaty and gelatinous pieces and discard the bones. Cut the meat and gelatinous bits into smaller pieces and stir back into the pot.

Add 4 cups hot water to the tripe and bring back to a simmer. Add the chile puree and the cooked hominy and its broth and stir well to combine. Bring to a simmer and simmer for another 20 to 30 minutes to blend the flavors. Taste and adjust the salt.

Arrange the garnishes in small bowls on the table, and set out the tortillas, tostadas, or bread. Serve and let your guests customize their menudo.

continued

Cook's Notes

- You can substitute 4 cups canned hominy (from two 15-ounce cans), rinsed and drained for the dried. Add it at the end of cooking, with the chile puree, along with an additional cup of water. In that case, you'll need just half an onion and half a garlic head.

- There are three types of beef tripe, which is the edible lining of a cow's stomach, each from a different stomach compartment (there are four stomach compartments, sometimes referred to simply as stomachs, but only three of them have linings that are suitable for tripe). The two called for in this recipe are honeycomb, from the second compartment, which has a diamond-shaped raised pattern across its surface and is considered the most coveted type, and book, or bible, tripe, from the third compartment, which has stacked folds that look like pages of a book. The third type is blanket tripe, from the first compartment, which looks like a solid, shaggy sheet.

- You can substitute beef tendon for the calves' feet.

- The flavors in menudo just get better if it's made ahead. You can make it 3 to 4 days in advance, cover, and refrigerate, then reheat when ready to serve. You will need to add more water when you reheat it, as the tripe will continue to soak up broth as it sits.

MENUDO: A REGION IN A BOWL

Mexico, being a nose-to-tail country, adores offal meats and noses, ears, and tails too. We love to taco these meats, but we also turn them into hearty soups and stews. Probably the most well-known and widely appreciated of these is menudo. In Yucatán, it's called *mondongo*. Other places know it as *pancita*.

Like the colors in the country's flag, menudo can be red, green, or white. When enriched with a dried chile sauce, and sometimes with tomatoes, it can go deep red for menudo rojo. It can go green in menudo verde with a fresh green chile sauce and sometimes tomatillos. And we also flavor menudo with aromatics only, for the white version, menudo blanco.

But however the dish is prepared, it starts off as a caldo—a brothy soup like caldo de pollo or caldo de res, but made with tripe (*pancita*) and sometimes with other organs and meats as well, such as calves' feet or cheeks.

Then menudo is taken down one path or another, depending on regional traditions, to take it to a more complex level. Sometimes you can identify the region by your bowl of menudo. Sonora adds its chile colorado; central Mexico and Michoacán might use pasillas; the Yucatán adds achiote paste.

Menudo isn't just a dish created in the spirit of not wasting anything from the animal; it's also one that brings out the maximum flavor from every bit used.

TACOS, QUESADILLAS, BURRITOS, AND TAMALES

MELTED CHEESE WITH GUAJILLO AND GARLIC MUSHROOMS / **QUESO FUNDIDO CON HONGOS AL AJILLO CON GUAJILLO** 46

SINCRONIZADAS WITH POBLANO, CHEESE, AND CHORIZO / **SINCRONIZADAS CON RAJAS Y CHORIZO** 49

SONORAN SHRIMP AND SCALLOP TOSTADAS / **CACHOREADAS DE CALLO Y CAMARÓN** 52

GOVERNOR'S SHRIMP TACOS / **TACOS GOBERNADOR DE CAMARÓN** 55

DOUBLE-STACKED SHRIMP AND CHEESE TACOS / **TACOS BRAVOS DE TOÑO** 58

SHRIMP AND POTATO BURRITOS / **BURRITOS DE MACHACA DE CAMARÓN CON PAPA** 61

THREE-CHEESE CHICKEN ENCHILADAS / **ENCHILADAS DE POLLO CON TRES QUESOS** 64

CHICKEN CODZITOS / **CODZITOS DE POLLO** 66

DROWNED CRISPY BEEF AND POTATO TAQUITOS / **TAQUITOS DORADOS AHOGADOS** 69

SONORAN CARNE ASADA TACOS / **TACOS DE CARNE ASADA ESTILO SONORA** 72

CRUNCHY CARNE ASADA TOSTADAS / **LORENZAS DE CARNE ASADA** 74

BEEF AND POTATO CHIMIS / **CHIMICHANGAS DE GUISADO DE RES CON PAPA** 76

TONGUE TACOS / **TACOS DE LENGUA** 79

PUEBLA-STYLE PORK TACOS / **TACOS ÁRABES** 81

MIXED MEAT TACOS / **TACOS CAMPECHANOS** 83

CHILE-MASA QUESADILLAS / **ENCHILADAS POTOSINAS** 86

POTATO AND POBLANO SOPES / **SOPES CON PAPAS Y RAJAS** 90

PLANTAIN MOLOTES WITH PICADILLO FILLING / **MOLOTES RELLENOS DE PICADILLO** 93

SWEET POTATO AND BLACK BEAN TAMALES / **TAMALES DE CAMOTE CON FRIJOL** 96

TAMALES WITH FRESH CORN, CHEESE, AND GREEN CHILE / **TAMALES DE ELOTE CON RAJAS DE CHILE VERDE Y QUESO** 101

ACHIOTE CHICKEN TAMALES / **MINI PIBIS DE POLLO** 105

TRADITIONAL FLOUR TORTILLAS / **TORTILLAS DE HARINA** 108

CHUBBY FLOUR TORTILLAS / **TORTILLAS DE HARINA GORDITAS** 110

HOMEMADE CORN TORTILLAS / **TORTILLAS DE MAÍZ** 114

How did indigenous people more than a thousand years ago figure out that they could liberate the nutrition packed inside kernels of dried corn by soaking them in an alkaline solution, then grinding those kernels into a mash that could eventually be transformed into so many foods—or even an edible plate? And how did they discover that those tortillas could be crisped to serve as spoons, snacks, or toppings that make an already delicious dish even more unforgettable? It took no time at all for the Spanish settlers to accept this way of eating and adapt it to flour tortillas in the northern part of Mexico, where the wheat that they brought with them thrived. It's not surprising that the foods that gained the earliest foothold north of the border were tacos, burritos, quesadillas, and enchiladas—food wrapped in or piled on tortillas.

The dishes in this chapter, all based on *masa* (dough)—corn, flour, even plantains—are often referred to collectively as *antojos*. *Antojo* is the word for craving, but it also means whim. We Mexicans crave certain foods at certain times, and many of our antojos tend to be street foods like tacos, tostadas, quesadillas, or chimichangas. Because we love these dishes, we often use the diminuitive endearment *antojito* when talking about them.

Whether you use store-bought or make your own corn and flour tortillas, they empower you to make so many types of dishes, from simple quesadillas with poblanos, cheese, and chorizo to saucy shrimp and cheese tacos. In this chapter, you'll also find new kinds of tacos that you probably won't get at your neighborhood taco truck, like the fried taquitos from Yucatán called *codzitos*, and other crispy tacos filled with beef, pinto beans, and potatoes that you "drown" in a tasty broth, then garnish with crunchy cabbage and pickled onion. And if you haven't tried tongue tacos yet, you really must: Tongue may very well be the most tender meat you'll ever taste and the very essence of beef.

In some ways, almost every chapter in this book could have been folded into this one, because we love to "taco" our food, and there are so many things that are just begging to be taco'd. Certain eating rituals in Mexico, like the carne asada cookouts that are practically a weekly event for families in Sonora, are all about tacos. Yes, carne asada is also about the meat, but you would never have it without flour tortillas. In fact, I sometimes had trouble deciding which chapter certain recipes belonged in, because our preferred way to eat so many of our favorite foods is to *taquear* them—tuck them inside of or pile them on top of a tortilla or a tostada. If a dish is terrific, it will probaby work as a filling or a topping. Chicken tinga? Perfect for a taco. The meat stew known as birria? It shines the brightest inside a taco. So I am hoping that you will come to believe, as Mexicans do, that "taco" is also a verb.

MELTED CHEESE WITH GUAJILLO AND GARLIC MUSHROOMS / QUESO FUNDIDO CON HONGOS AL AJILLO CON GUAJILLO

Serves 4 to 6

I don't know a single Mexican who doesn't drool over the thought of queso fundido. The dish is exactly what the name says: melted cheese—tons of it. It's not a dip, not a sauce. You throw one or more delicious melting cheeses into a traditional earthenware cazuela or a baking dish and heat it in the oven until the cheese not only melts, but becomes bubbly on top and crusty all around the edges.

Then there are the toppings. Restaurants in Mexico City offer toppings separately on their menus, such as strips of roasted poblanos (*rajas*) with caramelized onions, different kinds of chorizo, cultivated or wild mushrooms cooked with epazote, or dried chiles. Here I've opted for thinly sliced mushrooms cooked with slivered guajillo chiles in garlic-infused olive oil.

Most people I know like their queso fundido on flour tortillas, but you can opt for corn tortillas if you prefer. If you have some salsas and guacamole or avocados on hand, put them on the table for optional add-ons.

¼ cup olive oil

6 garlic cloves, peeled, plus 2 tablespoons finely chopped garlic

¾ cup finely chopped white onion

2 dried guajillo chiles, stemmed, seeded, and finely chopped or snipped with scissors

1 pound mixed mushrooms, such as white button, baby bella, and wild mushrooms, thinly sliced

¾ teaspoon kosher salt, or more to taste

¼ teaspoon freshly ground black pepper, or to taste

4 cups grated mixed melting cheeses, such as asadero, Oaxaca, Monterey Jack, or mozzarella (1 pound)

8 to 10 flour and/or corn tortillas

Guacamole or 1 ripe avocado, halved, pitted, and sliced (optional)

Salsa(s) of your choice for serving (optional)

Preheat the oven to 450 degrees F, with a rack in the upper third. Lightly oil a large shallow baking dish.

Heat the oil in a medium saucepan over medium heat. Add the whole garlic cloves and cook, stirring occasionally, until they soften and brown, 7 to 8 minutes. Remove with a slotted spoon and discard, leaving the flavored oil behind.

Add the onion and guajillo chiles and cook, stirring, for 1 to 2 minutes, just until the onion begins to soften. Add the chopped garlic, stir, and cook for a minute, until fragrant. Stir in the mushrooms, salt, and black pepper and cook, stirring occasionally, until all the mushroom juices have been released and begun to evaporate and the mushrooms have begun to color, 8 to 10 minutes. Remove from the heat, taste, and adjust the salt.

continued

Combine the cheeses thoroughly and arrange in the baking dish. Bake for 12 to 15 minutes, or until the cheese is completely melted. Top with the mushrooms, return to the oven, and bake for another 7 to 8 minutes, until the cheese is bubbling, the edges are crusty, and the top is lightly browned.

Meanwhile, heat a comal or large skillet over medium-low heat for at least 5 minutes. One or two at a time, depending on the size of your comal or pan, heat the tortillas, making sure they are not overlapping, until warm, puffed, and browned in spots, about a minute per side. Place in a tortilla warmer or wrap in a clean cloth or kitchen towel.

Serve the queso bubbling hot from the oven, with the warm tortillas and guacamole or avocado slices and salsa, if desired. Let everyone assemble their own tacos at the table.

SINCRONIZADAS WITH POBLANO, CHEESE, AND CHORIZO / **SINCRONIZADAS CON RAJAS Y CHORIZO**

Makes 3 sincronizadas; serves 5 or 6 as an appetizer, 3 as a main course

Sincronizadas are two-tortilla quesadillas, typically made with flour tortillas. The filling is sandwiched between the tortillas, and the quesadillas are heated on both sides until the cheese melts and the tortillas crisp a little. One of the things I love about sincronizadas is that you can get more filling into them than you can get into a regular quesadilla—and I always want to overstuff my quesadillas!

When I was growing up, we often had sincronizadas for dinner. Our main meal was the *comida* at midday, and dinner was lighter. Sincronizadas fit the bill perfectly, and there was always something delicious on hand to fill them with.

These quesadillas are very popular in the northern state of Coahuila. The tortillas are lavished with melted cheese and spicy chorizo, and the finished sincronizadas are topped with roasted poblano chiles and caramelized onions. They can be cut into triangles and served as an appetizer, or you can enjoy them whole, as a full meal, morning, noon, or night.

1 pound Mexican chorizo, casings removed and coarsely chopped

2 tablespoons vegetable oil

1 medium white onion, halved and thinly sliced

4 fresh poblano chiles, roasted, sweated, peeled, seeded, and cut into 2-inch-long strips (page 176)

½ teaspoon kosher salt

6 large (8- to 10-inch) flour tortillas

1½ cups grated melting cheese, such as asadero, Oaxaca, Monterey Jack, or mozzarella (6 ounces), or more to taste

Heat a large skillet over medium heat. Add the chorizo and cook for 5 to 6 minutes, until crisp and browned, breaking the meat apart into smaller pieces with a couple of wooden spoons or spatulas. Scrape into a bowl.

Return the pan to the heat, add the oil, and stir in the onion. Cook, stirring occasionally and scraping the bottom of the pan to release any tasty residue from the chorizo, until the onions have completely wilted and are light brown around the edges, 12 to 15 minutes. Stir in the poblano strips and salt and cook for another 3 to 4 minutes. Transfer to a bowl.

Heat a comal or large skillet over medium-low heat for at least 5 minutes. One or two at a time, place the tortillas on the comal or skillet, without overlapping. Top each one with ½ cup of the grated cheese and spread it evenly over the tortilla. Do the same with one-third of the chorizo. Top with another tortilla and press down gently. Once the first tortilla has browned lightly on the bottom, turn the quesadilla over and cook for a couple of minutes, until all of the cheese has melted and both tortillas are lightly colored. Transfer to a platter and keep warm. Repeat with the remaining tortillas and filling.

continued

When all of the quesadillas are done, place on a cutting board and cut into 4 triangles each. Transfer to a platter, spoon the poblano and onion mixture on top, and serve.

Cook's Notes

▸ You can also use the poblano and onion mixture to fill the quesadillas, spooning it on top of the chorizo.

▸ Large flour tortillas, 8 to 10 inches in diameter, are used for sincronizadas. Regular 5- to 6-inch flour tortillas are used for tacos.

MEXICAN CHORIZO

Mexican chorizo is unlike most other fresh pork sausages. It's seasoned with a mix of spices as well as dried chiles, which give it a distinctive burnt-red color and flavor. There's also a splash of vinegar in the mix, imparting a unique acidity and allowing the meat to crisp beautifully as it fries.

Different from Spanish chorizo, which is smoked and cured and doesn't require cooking, Mexican chorizo is raw and needs to be cooked. If you can't find Mexican chorizo, you can try other Latin raw chorizos such as Salvadorean, or use spicy Italian sausage instead.

The chorizo sold in the U.S. tends to be less fatty than that in Mexico, so I heat 1 or 2 tablespoons of oil in the pan before adding the meat. I remove the casing and coarsely chop the meat, then add it to the hot pan and break it up into smaller pieces with two wooden spoons or spatulas as it browns. Chicken, turkey, and vegetarian chorizos are leaner than regular chorizo, and you will likely need to add more oil when browning any of them.

SONORAN SHRIMP AND SCALLOP TOSTADAS / CACHOREADAS DE CALLO Y CAMARÓN

Makes 6 to 8 large tostadas; serves 6 to 8 as an appetizer, 3 to 4 as a main course

This is one messy tostada, as most tostadas are—but this one is even messier! Sonorans are so passionate for them that they gave them a sexy name that comes from the regional slang term for making out—*cachorear*. When you eat them, you will see why; they are crave-worthy from bottom to top. The crunchy tostadas are slathered with a layer of mayo before being piled high with the seafood and at least three salsas, then crowned with ripe avocado slices.

Cachoreada is usually made with raw shrimp and scallops or with a combination of raw and cooked seafood. In this take, the shrimp and scallops are seared but left rare and juicy in the center.

FOR THE MAYONNAISE

½ cup mayonnaise

Grated zest of 1 lime

Kosher salt and freshly ground black pepper

FOR THE TOSTADAS

1 pound medium shrimp, peeled and deveined

1 pound sea scallops, tough side muscles removed

1 teaspoon kosher salt

½ teaspoon freshly ground black pepper

2 tablespoons unsalted butter

2 tablespoons vegetable oil

6 to 8 corn tostadas (page 54)

Salsa Bandera with Jicama and Pineapple (page 138)

1 ripe avocado, halved, pitted, and sliced

All-Purpose Seasoning Sauce (page 142)

Hot sauce for serving

To make the mayonnaise: Combine the mayonnaise with the lime zest in a small bowl. Season with salt and pepper to taste, mix well, and set aside.

To make the tostada filling: Season the shrimp and scallops with the salt and pepper. Heat 1 tablespoon of the butter with 1 tablespoon of the oil in a large skillet over high heat. Once the butter has begun to foam, add the shrimp. Cook for 1 or 2 minutes per side, just until nicely seared and browned on the outside and just cooked through. Scrape into a bowl. Return the skillet to the heat, add the remaining 1 tablespoon each butter and oil, and heat until the butter foams. Add the scallops and cook for a minute per side, or until the tops and bottoms are browned and the centers are no longer translucent; they should be medium-rare. Remove from the heat. As soon as you can handle them, slice the scallops thin and set aside.

To build the tostadas: Spread about a tablespoon of mayo on each tostada, top with a layer of scallops, a couple of tablespoons of the salsa, and a layer of shrimp. Finish with some avocado slices, top them with a couple of tablespoons of seasoning sauce, and add hot sauce to taste. Serve immediately, passing the remaining seasoning sauce at the table.

Of course you can buy tostadas and tortilla chips (*totopos*), but you'll love the irresistible toasty aroma and fresh snap that you get from making your own. You have a choice of methods: You can fry the tortillas, bake them, or toast them on a comal or in a skillet. Frying adds another flavor dimension because of the oil; baked tortillas can be a bit more resilient; and those toasted on a comal or in a skillet have a slightly charred taste, which I love. I use that method often for tostadas, but not for chips, as it takes too long because of all the flipping that is required.

Tostadas

TO FRY: Fill a large skillet with ½ inch of vegetable oil and heat over medium heat for 4 to 6 minutes, or until hot but not smoking. The edge of a tortilla should bubble enthusiastically when you dip it into the oil. If the oil is sufficiently hot, the tostadas will not be greasy. One at a time, fry the tortillas for about 45 seconds to a minute per side, using rubber-tipped tongs or a skimmer to flip them over, until tan and crisp. Do not let them become dark brown, or they will taste bitter. Remove from the oil and drain on paper towels or stand on their edges in a deep metal strainer set over a bowl.

TO BAKE: Preheat the oven to 350 degrees F, with the racks in the middle and lower third. Oil a couple of baking sheets. Place the tortillas in a single layer on the sheets. Bake for 15 minutes. Turn the tortillas and bake for another 5 to 10 minutes, until tan and crisp.

TO TOAST: Heat a comal or large skillet over medium-low heat for at least 5 minutes. One by one, toast the tortillas, turning occasionally, until crisp, 6 to 10 minutes. Be careful not to burn them.

Tortilla Chips (*Totopos*) or Strips

Tortilla chips usually get a nice sprinkling of kosher salt just after they come out of the oil or oven or off the comal. Instead of cutting the tortillas into wedges for chips, you can cut them into strips, as wide and long as you want; just adjust the cooking time as necessary.

TO FRY: Cut the tortillas into wedges or strips and follow the directions for frying tostadas above, cooking in batches and being careful not to crowd the pan. Drain on paper towels and sprinkle with salt while still hot.

TO BAKE: Preheat the oven to 350 degrees F, with the racks in the middle and lower third. Oil a couple of baking sheets. Lightly brush or spray the tortilla wedges or strips with oil. Place in a single layer on the baking sheets. Bake for 15 minutes. Turn over and return to the oven for another 5 to 10 minutes, until tan and crisp; do not allow them to get too dark. Remove from the oven, sprinkle with salt, and let cool before serving.

GOVERNOR'S SHRIMP TACOS / **TACOS GOBERNADOR DE CAMARÓN**

Makes 10 to 12 tacos; serves 4 or 5

A Mazatlán restaurant called Los Arcos claims to have invented these tacos in the early 1990s to surprise Francisco Labastida Ochoa, then governor of the state of Sinaloa. It was well known among the governor's friends that he adored his wife's shrimp tacos, so the chef at the restaurant set out to match them. The governor liked the Los Arcos tacos so much that the chef named them in his honor. Since then, tacos gobernador have spread all over the state as well as outside of Sinaloa, up and down the Baja Peninsula and beyond. I have even eaten them in Los Angeles and Miami.

It's obvious why they are so popular. They have a ton of cheese (essential), along with the shrimp, so they are really a cross between a taco and a quesadilla. The filling for this version includes slivered onions, poblanos, and just a bit of tomato. I go for a very thick sauce, made with tomato paste, some sauce from chipotles in adobo, and Worcestershire sauce, which we call *salsa Inglesa*. The tacos are typically made with corn tortillas, but when I was in Sinaloa, I noticed that many locals asked for them in flour tortillas.

3 tablespoons unsalted butter

1 medium white onion, cut into thin slivers

1 fresh poblano chile, seeded and cut into thin slivers

3 garlic cloves, finely chopped

1 tomato, cut into thin slivers

2 tablespoons sauce from chipotles in adobo

1 tablespoon tomato paste

1 teaspoon Worcestershire sauce

½ teaspoon kosher salt

¼ teaspoon freshly ground black pepper, or to taste

1½ pounds medium to large shrimp, peeled, deveined, and cut into large chunks

10 to 12 corn or flour tortillas

2 cups grated melting cheese, such as asadero, Oaxaca, Monterey Jack, or mozzarella (8 ounces), or more to taste

Salsa of your choice for serving (optional)

Guacamole for serving (optional)

Heat the butter in a large skillet over medium-high heat. Once it melts and begins to foam, add the onion and poblano and cook until wilted, 3 to 4 minutes. Stir in the garlic and cook until fragrant, about 1 minute. Stir in the tomato and cook until it begins to soften, about 1 minute. Add the adobo sauce, tomato paste, Worcestershire sauce, salt, and pepper, stir well, and cook for another minute.

Add the shrimp and cook until they are just cooked through and change color, 1 to 2 minutes. Scrape the filling into a bowl, so that the shrimp do not continue to cook.

continued

GOVERNOR'S SHRIMP TACOS / **TACOS GOBERNADOR DE CAMARÓN** continued

Heat a comal or large skillet over medium-low heat for at least 5 minutes. One or two at a time, heat the tortillas for about a minute on each side. Place 2 heaping tablespoons of the shredded cheese on each warm tortilla and once it begins to melt, add a generous spoonful of the shrimp mixture, fold in half, and continue heating, turning from time to time, until the cheese has melted and the tortillas have begun to lightly brown and become a little crispy.

Serve the tacos as soon as you cook them, with salsa and guacamole, if desired, or cover the first batches and keep warm while you make the remaining tacos.

DOUBLE-STACKED SHRIMP AND CHEESE TACOS /
TACOS BRAVOS DE TOÑO

Makes 8 double tacos; serves 4 or 5

Tacos bravos is very much in the Sonoran tradition of super-dressed, super-sauced, and super-cheesy shellfish dishes. It's one of the specialties of Toño Contreras, the owner of Mariscos El Rey in Hermosillo. Toño began his career selling seafood on the beach, then he opened a little stand, and now he has a few restaurants under his belt. His tacos are irresistible through and through. The tortillas are dipped in a spicy tomato sauce, set on a griddle until they begin to crisp, covered with cheese, and then, just as the cheese begins to melt, they're stacked by twos and topped with buttery seared shrimp. The combined sauce and oozing cheese form a crust on the tortilla stacks as they heat on the comal.

2 pounds ripe tomatoes or 1 (28-ounce) can whole tomatoes

4 garlic cloves, peeled

2 to 3 dried chiles de árbol, stemmed

2 teaspoons dried oregano

2 tablespoons tomato paste

1 teaspoon kosher salt, plus more for seasoning the shrimp

2 tablespoons vegetable oil, plus more for cooking the tacos

2 pounds medium shrimp, peeled and deveined

Freshly ground black pepper

2 tablespoons unsalted butter

16 corn tortillas

3 cups grated melting cheese, such as asadero, Oaxaca, Monterey Jack, or mozzarella (12 ounces)

1 large ripe avocado, halved, pitted, and thinly sliced

Combine the fresh tomatoes, if using, garlic, and chiles de árbol in a medium saucepan, cover with water, and bring to a boil over medium-high heat. Reduce the heat and simmer for about 10 minutes, until the tomatoes, garlic, and chiles are soft. Drain and transfer to a blender.

Add the oregano, tomato paste, and salt to the blender, add the canned tomatoes, if using, and puree until smooth.

Heat 1 tablespoon of the oil in a medium saucepan over medium heat. Pour in the tomato puree, using the lid to to shield yourself from splatters, cover partially, and cook, stirring occasionally, for 5 to 6 minutes, until the mixture has thickened and darkened. Remove from the heat.

Season the shrimp with salt and pepper. Heat 1 tablespoon of the butter with 1 tablespoon of the oil in a large skillet over high heat. Once the butter melts and begins to foam, add half the shrimp and sear for a minute or so per side. They should be browned on the outside but just cooked through. Be careful not to overcook, or they will be rubbery. Scrape into a bowl and repeat with the remaining butter, oil, and shrimp.

Heat a comal or large skillet over medium heat for at least 5 minutes. Add a tablespoon or two of oil to the surface.

continued

Briefly dip a tortilla into the sauce, making sure the entire tortilla is coated (I use a pair of rubber-tipped tongs, but you can just use your hands), and lay on the pan. Dip a second tortilla into the sauce and lay in the pan next to the first one, making sure the tortillas are not overlapping (see note). Top each tortilla with about 2 tablespoons shredded cheese and cook for a couple of minutes, until the cheese begins to melt and the bottoms of the sauced tortillas begin to dry and brown a little. Then, using a spatula, scrape up one tortilla and stack on top of the other one, cheese side up. Don't worry if the tortilla you scraped up sticks and tears a little bit or if it does not sit evenly on top of the other one. Spoon some seared shrimp on top of the stack, gently fold the stack in half, and cook for a couple of minutes longer, turning the stack over occasionally, until the cheese has begun to ooze out and create a crust.

Top with slices of ripe avocado and serve (these are best straight out of the comal), or transfer to a plate or platter and cover with foil to keep warm while you cook the remaining stacks.

Cook's Note

► If your pan isn't large enough to hold two tortillas without overlapping, for each stack, dip and cook one tortilla, topping it with cheese, remove it from the pan, and dip and cook a second tortilla, then stack them together, top with some shrimp, and finish cooking as above.

SHRIMP AND POTATO BURRITOS / **BURRITOS DE MACHACA DE CAMARÓN CON PAPA**

Makes 8 to 10 burritos; serves 8 to 10

Machacar means to crush, mash, or pound. Traditional machaca, which is used in many ways, is made with thin slices of beef that are pounded, salted, and sun-dried, like jerky, then rehydrated and mashed until very finely shredded. Today the term has expanded to include versions with fresh seafood, usually different kinds of fish and shrimp. This one, from the coast of Sinaloa, is phenomenal. The shrimp are barely cooked, so that they stay sweet and moist, then they're pounded until mashed. Tomatoes are cooked with feisty serrano chile, smoky dried chipotles, onion, garlic, and crunchy sesame seeds until almost caramelized, then the shrimp and cooked diced potatoes are folded in and cooked until heated through. My favorite way to serve this machaca is the most traditional—as a filling for burritos, with a tangy raw salsa verde on the side.

2 dried chipotle chiles, preferably moritas (page 133)

Kosher salt

1 pound medium shrimp, peeled and deveined

¾ pound red potatoes, peeled and cut into very small dice (¼ inch or smaller)

3 tablespoons vegetable oil

½ cup finely chopped white onion

1 serrano chile, stemmed and finely chopped

2 garlic cloves, finely chopped

3 tablespoons sesame seeds

1½ pounds ripe tomatoes, finely chopped, or 1 (28-ounce) can crushed tomatoes

8 to 10 flour tortillas

Raw Salsa Verde (page 120) or other salsa of choice

Place the dried chipotle chiles in a bowl, cover with boiling water, and let soak for 10 to 12 minutes, until plumped and softened. Drain, stem, seed, and finely chop.

Fill a medium saucepan with water, salt generously, and bring to a boil over high heat. Add the shrimp and cook for 1 minute, until pink and barely cooked through. Remove with a slotted spoon and set aside. Add the potatoes to the boiling water, reduce the heat to medium-high, and cook for 5 to 7 minutes, until soft. Drain and set aside.

When the shrimp have cooled enough to handle, working in batches, place them in a sturdy plastic bag and pound with a meat pounder or the bottom of a small heavy skillet until broken apart and mashed.

continued

SHRIMP AND POTATO BURRITOS /
BURRITOS DE MACHACA DE CAMARÓN CON PAPA
continued

Heat the oil in a large skillet over medium-high heat. Add the onion and cook for 3 to 4 minutes, until softened and beginning to brown. Add the serrano and chipotle chiles, stir, and cook for a minute. Add the garlic and sesame seeds, stir, and cook for another minute, until the garlic is fragrant and the sesame seeds are toasted. Add the tomatoes and ½ teaspoon salt and cook until the tomatoes are soft and pasty, 5 to 8 minutes. Add the shrimp and potatoes, stir well, and mash everything together for another minute. Taste and adjust the salt. Remove from the heat.

Heat a comal or large skillet over medium-low heat for at least 5 minutes. One or two at a time, add the tortillas to the pan, without overlapping, and heat for about a minute per side, until they become pliable and softer and begin to puff and color in spots. Add 3 heaping tablespoons of the machaca to each tortilla. Fold one side of each tortilla over to enclose the filling, then fold in the sides and roll up into a burrito. Once they are assembled, you can heat the burritos for another minute if you want them a bit toasted, or eat them still soft, as soon as they are assembled.

Serve with the salsa.

THREE-CHEESE CHICKEN ENCHILADAS / ENCHILADAS DE POLLO CON TRES QUESOS

Serves 6

These luscious enchiladas are emblematic of the cooking of northern Mexico, where people are crazy about cream, cheese, and colorado chiles. In true northern style, not only are the enchiladas generously sauced with the region's favorite red salsa, but they also have three kinds of cheese as well as Mexican crema. Some enchiladas, like these, are nestled into baking dishes, covered with sauce and cheese, and baked; others are just filled, sauced, and served.

16 corn tortillas

Double recipe Colorado Chile Red Salsa (page 128)

4 cups shredded cooked chicken (page 251) or rotisserie chicken

1 cup crema or sour cream

2 cups grated Oaxaca cheese or mozzarella (8 ounces)

2 cups grated asadero, Muenster, or Monterey Jack cheese (8 ounces)

1 cup crumbled Cotija cheese or grated Pecorino Romano or Parmigiano-Reggiano (4 ounces)

1 ripe avocado, halved, pitted, and sliced, for garnish (optional)

Preheat the oven to 400 degrees F, with a rack in the middle. Heat a comal or large skillet over medium-low heat for at least 5 minutes.

One or two at a time, heat the tortillas on the comal or skillet, without overlapping, for about a minute per side, until malleable and warm. Cover or wrap in a kitchen towel to keep warm.

Pour about 1 cup of the salsa into a 9-x-13-inch baking dish and spread it evenly over the bottom. One by one, place each tortilla on a cutting board and sprinkle about ¼ cup of the chicken evenly down the middle. Roll up into a chubby soft taco and place seam down in the baking dish. Pour the remaining salsa over the enchiladas and top with the cream. Cover with the grated cheeses and sprinkle the Cotija, Romano, or Parmesan over the top.

Bake for 15 to 20 minutes, or until the cheese has completely melted and begun to lightly brown around the edges. Serve hot, with sliced avocado (if desired).

CHICKEN CODZITOS / **CODZITOS DE POLLO**

Makes 18 codzitos; serves 6

Codzitos (from the Mayan word *kots,* meaning little rolled-up taco), a favorite in the Yucatán, are tightly rolled tacos that are deep-fried until irresistibly crunchy, then dressed with a red salsa and garnished with a generous amount of crumbly, salty aged cheese. (In Mexico City and other parts of the country, deep-fried rolled tacos are called *flautas* or taquitos dorados.) The kind I like the most are stuffed with shredded chicken and sauced with a satisfyingly spicy thick Yucatecan sauce with tomatoes, onion, and banana peppers (or güero chiles, or their Yucatecan cousins, *xcatic*). I love biting into the layers of crunch around the moist chicken, with the sauce and cheese over the top.

The traditional cheese for codzitos is a Yucatecan cheese called queso sopero. It's similar to Cotija, which you can find more easily. You can also use añejo, or, if you prefer a less salty, moister cheese, sprinkle the codzitos with queso fresco.

> 1½ **pounds ripe tomatoes, coarsely chopped, or 1 (28-ounce) can crushed tomatoes**
>
> ¼ **medium white onion, coarsely chopped**
>
> 2 **fresh banana chiles, güero chiles, or xcatic chiles (page 184), coarsely chopped**
>
> 1 **teaspoon kosher salt, or more to taste**
>
> **Leaves from 5 sprigs fresh epazote or cilantro, coarsely chopped**
>
> 1 **cup chicken broth**
>
> 2 **tablespoons vegetable oil, plus more for deep-frying**
>
> 4 **cups shredded cooked chicken (page 251) or rotisserie chicken**

> **Freshly ground black pepper**
>
> 18 **corn tortillas**
>
> 1 **cup grated Cotija or añejo cheese or queso fresco (4 ounces), or more to taste**

Combine the tomatoes, onion, chiles, salt, epazote or cilantro, and chicken broth in a blender and puree until smooth.

Heat the 2 tablespoons oil in a medium saucepan over medium heat. Add the tomato puree and cook, stirring often, until it has thickened and darkened a little and the flavors have intensified, 15 to 18 minutes. Turn off the heat.

Season the shredded chicken with salt and pepper to taste.

Heat a comal or large skillet over medium-low heat for at least 5 minutes. Before rolling the tortillas into codzitos, heat them one by one for about a minute per side, until warm and pliable (this step is important, because it will prevent the tortillas from breaking when you roll them). Then place a couple of tablespoons of shredded cooked chicken down the center of each tortilla and roll up as tightly as you can. As you go, spear 2 or 3 codzitos at a time together with a wooden toothpick, sticking the toothpick through the middle and making sure to insert it through the seams, so they will hold their shape.

Fill a large skillet with about 1 inch of oil and heat over medium heat for 5 to 6 minutes. Place a cooling rack on a baking sheet lined with paper towels.

continued

Test the oil by dipping a tortilla into it: The oil should immediately and exuberantly bubble around it. When the oil is hot, carefully add the codzitos in batches, being careful not to over-crowd the pan, and fry them for 2 to 3 minutes per side, until golden and evenly crisped. (The oil lets you know when the codzitos are done, because the bubbling will get a bit slower.) Remove the cozitos from the oil and drain on the rack. Make sure to allow the oil to heat back up before adding the next batch. Remove the toothpicks.

To serve, place the codzitos on a platter or divide among plates, dress with the sauce, and top generously with the grated cheese.

Cook's Note

► As an alternative to frying, you can cook the codzitos on a comal or in a large skillet over medium-low heat, turning them a few times as they brown and crisp on all sides. This will take a little bit longer, about 15 minutes or so.

MAKING SOMETHING FROM (ALMOST) NOTHING

The codzitos that are most widely eaten in the Yucatán are not filled at all. They're like a deep-fried version of a *taquito de nada*, or taco with nothing, an unfilled rolled-up warm tortilla sprinkled with salt. You can add a schmear of butter after you heat up the tortilla, then sprinkle on the salt.

The crisp sauced little codzitos are some-what like the simplest chilaquiles (tortilla chips bathed in sauce), which I always find irresistible, but the tortillas are rolled up instead of cut into triangles, the way they are in chilaquiles. With the layers of rolled tortilla, the fried cylinders seem to crunch more than flat tortilla chips, and those layers of crunch are delicious to bite into, with the sauce and cheese.

Codzitos are sold ready-made in markets and stores, to be brought home, sauced, and garnished with cheese at a moment's notice. They make an easy quick lunch, dinner, or even breakfast.

DROWNED CRISPY BEEF AND POTATO TAQUITOS / **TAQUITOS DORADOS AHOGADOS**

Makes 40 taquitos; serves 12

I've been eating taquitos—rolled stuffed corn tortillas that are typically fried and addictively crunchy—my whole life, but I'd never had "drowned" crispy taquitos in broth until Miguel Taniyama, one of Sinaloa's most popular chefs and a proud ambassador of all that the state has to offer, introduced me to them at a stand in the central market in Culiacán.

The tortillas are filled with a hearty mix of beef, potatoes, and refried beans, rolled up tightly, and fried until crisp and brown. Then they are topped with shredded cabbage, pickled onions, crema, and queso fresco and doused with a rich spiced-up beef broth that smells and tastes so good that you feel it has healing powers. As you eat, the tacos go from crunchy to softer in the broth, and you'll find yourself wanting more.

2 pounds boneless beef chuck, rump roast, or other stewing meat, cut into 2-inch pieces

1 white onion, halved

10 garlic cloves, peeled

1 bay leaf

2 dried guajillo chiles, stemmed and seeded

1 tablespoon black peppercorns

1 ripe tomato or 1 canned tomato

2 large carrots, cut into thick slices

1 tablespoon kosher salt, plus more to taste

Freshly ground black pepper

3 large Yukon gold potatoes, peeled and halved

1 cup Basic Refried Beans (page 158), made with pinto beans, or canned beans

40 corn tortillas

Vegetable oil for deep-frying

FOR SERVING

1 head cabbage, cored and shredded

1 cup crema or sour cream, or to taste

1 cup crumbled queso fresco, or to taste

Pickled red onions (see note)

Put the meat, onion, garlic cloves, bay leaf, chiles, peppercorns, tomato, carrots, salt, and pepper to taste in a Dutch oven or a large heavy pot. Add enough water to cover by at least 1 inch. Bring to a boil over high heat, then reduce the heat to medium-low, skim off any foam, cover, and simmer for 1½ hours, or until the meat is cooked through but not falling apart.

Add the potatoes and simmer for another 1 hour, or until the meat and potatoes are fork-tender and you can easily shred the meat.

With a slotted spoon, transfer the meat and potatoes to a large bowl. Strain the broth into a saucepan and bring to a boil. Reduce the heat to medium and simmer, uncovered, for 30 minutes, until slightly reduced. Taste and adjust the salt.

Meanwhile, transfer the meat to a cutting board and finely chop. Mash the potatoes in the bowl. Add the refried beans and chopped meat to the potatoes and mash and mix together until well combined. Season with salt and pepper.

continued

Heat a comal or large skillet over medium-low heat for at least 5 minutes. One or two at a time, heat the tortillas for about 1 minute per side, until warm and pliable. (This step is important, because it will prevent the tortillas from breaking when you roll them into taquitos.) Place 2 tablespoons of the beef and potato mixture on one half of the warm tortilla (I like them really chubby) and roll up tightly. As you go, insert a wooden toothpick through 2 or 3 taquitos, making sure to spear them through the seams so they will hold their shape.

Heat 1 inch of oil in a large skillet over medium heat for about 5 minutes, or until it is hot enough to bubble exuberantly when you dip the end of a taquito into it. Place a cooling rack on a baking sheet lined with paper towels.

Carefully add the taquitos to the oil in batches, being careful not to overcrowd the pan. Fry on the first side until crisp and golden, 1½ to 3 minutes, then turn and repeat on the other side. (The oil lets you know when the taquitos are done because the bubbling will get a little slower.) Remove from the oil and transfer to the cooling rack. Make sure to allow the oil to heat back up before adding the next batch. Remove the toothpicks.

To serve, place 3 or 4 taquitos in each wide soup bowl or deep rimmed plate. Top with the shredded cabbage, crema, queso fresco, and pickled red onions. Ladle about a cup of hot broth over the taquitos to drown them. Alternatively, you can serve the broth on the side for dunking, so guests can drown their taquitos as they please.

Cook's Note

▶ To make pickled onions, toss 1 cup thinly sliced red onions with 2 tablespoons freshly squeezed lime juice, 1 tablespoon white vinegar, 3 tablespoons vegetable oil, and salt and pepper to taste. Let sit for at least 15 minutes before serving, or cover and refrigerate for up to 5 days. *The photo is on page 125.*

CHANGING THE CONVERSATION IN SINALOA

If you could create the perfect setting for rich farmland, it would look like Sinaloa, with the ocean to the west and a mountain range to the east, where rains feed into vast rivers that run through the lush valley in between. Almost 40 percent of Mexico's produce comes from Sinaloa.

In that same fertile farmland, unfortunately, another crop flourishes that is the root of one of Mexico's biggest problems: opium. Sinaloa and particularly its capital, Culiacán, have lived through some hard times. But the proud people of Sinaloa, like the chef Miguel Taniyama, my guide to the food in the city, are changing the conversation. Tani, as his friends call him, believes that opening the world's eyes to the culinary riches of his state is the first step on a new path for Sinaloans. "We grow so many of Mexico's vegetables. We are the biggest producers of tomatoes, we raise much of the beef, and we have wild blue Pacific shrimp, which are unlike any other. Until now we've guarded our recipes, but it's time to show the world what we do in the kitchen."

SONORAN CARNE ASADA TACOS / TACOS DE CARNE ASADA ESTILO SONORA

Makes 12 to 16 tacos; serves 6 to 8

Carne asada—grilled sliced beef, usually skirt or flank steak—is popular throughout Mexico, but in Sonora, with its wide-open country and fields blanketed with wheat, its hot dry weather, and its roaming cattle, carne asada is a way of life. The term applies not only to the dish itself, but also to the event where it's served, which is a weekly ritual. The people here are proud of their beef, and of their knowledge of the carne asada experience that they have cultivated over the centuries. Their expertise begins with how they raise and care for their cattle, and extends to how they cut the meat and grill it, always over an open wood and charcoal fire, using the most basic tools, with nothing more than coarse salt for seasoning.

There are plenty of professional *parrilleros*—grill masters—throughout Sonora and the rest of Mexico. But in Sonora, there is a parrillero in every home. With the tips on the opposte page, you too can become one. Families love to host carne asadas, and it is an honor to be invited to one, since this means they are really letting you in.

FOR THE CARNE ASADA

¼ large white onion for cleaning the grill

Beef fat cut from the meat if it is fatty, beef tallow (available online), or vegetable oil for greasing the grill

2 pounds boneless top sirloin, sliced into ½-inch-thick steaks

1 (2-pound) boneless chuck roast, sliced into ½-inch-thick steaks

4 teaspoons kosher salt, or to taste (about 1 teaspoon per pound of meat)

FOR THE TACOS

12 to 16 large (8- to 10-inch) flour tortillas

Fiesta Refried Beans (page 159)

Fire-Roasted Sonoran Chunky Salsa (page 123)

Guacamole with Chile Verde (page 152)

To make the carne asada: Prepare a hot fire in a charcoal or gas grill. If using a charcoal grill, the fire is ready when the coals are glowing red but entirely covered with gray ash and you can hold your hand 5 to 6 inches above them for only 4 or 5 seconds.

Using a pair of tongs, rub the onion quarter over the grill to clean. Using the tongs, rub the beef fat or vegetable oil over the grill to further season it.

Working in batches if necessary, grill the meat: Season the top of the steaks generously with salt just before you put them on the grill, salted side up. Grill for 4 to 5 minutes, until deep seared grill marks have developed on the bottoms of the steaks and the meat juices have started rising and bubbling over the tops. Turn and grill for another 3 to 4 minutes for medium-rare. As the meat is cooked, remove it from the grill and place in a covered dish or container. Allow the meat to rest for 5 minutes before cutting.

One by one, cut the steaks into ½-inch dice or thinly slice them, cutting against the grain (if cutting the meat into dice, start by cutting it against the grain). Return the sliced meat to the covered dish to keep warm as you work.

To heat the tortillas: Reduce the grill heat to medium if using gas. Or, if using charcoal, set the tortillas on a cooler part of the grill. Heat the tortillas for about 1 minute per side, until puffed, lightly browned, and heated through. Wrap in a clean kitchen towel or put them in a tortilla warmer to keep warm, then bring to the table, along with the meat, beans, salsa, and guacamole.

To assemble the tacos, spread some refried beans on the middle of a warm tortilla, add a generous amount of meat, and top the meat with salsa and guacamole to taste. Your taco should be so full that it's difficult to close it.

PELÍN'S CARNE ASADA TIPS

While we were on location in Ciudad Obregón, our self-appointed local guide, Joséí Luis Lambarri (nicknamed Pelín), spontaneously invited me and my crew to his home for a carne asada. It was a truly humbling experience. In no time and with no advance notice, his mother-in-law prepared guacamole, Pelín shopped for the right kinds of meat, and his wife made the salsa and then ran to the corner for tortillas. Within an hour of his invitation, we were enjoying the full, incredible Sonoran carne asada experience.

Pelín gave me lots of tips on what really matters for a successful carne asada.

► The cut of meat matters, a lot. It should be a combination of top sirloin (*palomilla* or *aguayón*), for its mild taste and tender texture, and chuck (*diezmillo*) with all of its fat, for its deep beefy flavor and sturdy chew.

► Clean and season the grill with raw onion and beef tallow or fat cut from a fatty piece of beef (by the butcher or by you at home), so the grill is ready to welcome the meat. (You can use vegetable oil for this if necessary.)

► Preparing the grill for medium-high to high heat is crucial, as is knowing when the fire is ready—in the case of a charcoal grill, never when the flames are still running wild, but when they have calmed down and the charcoal has turned red and is covered in gray ash.

► Salt the meat generously. Many, including Pelín, insist on seasoning it on one side only, right before you throw it on the grill. Salting this way creates an instant dry brine that seasons the meat from the top down as it cooks, giving the bottom surface a clean char.

► Watch the meat carefully so you know when to turn it—when you see drops of moisture on the surface. Forget about a timer. Turn the meat only once, and cook it on the second side for a shorter amount of time.

► Let the meat rest before you cut it and then, most important, you have to cut it fast, and always against the grain, into thin slices or cubes, as everybody will be more than ready to start making their tacos. A parrillero can hardly keep up.

CRUNCHY CARNE ASADA TOSTADAS / **LORENZAS DE CARNE ASADA**

Makes 12 tostados; serves 6

Everybody loves the combination of beans and melted cheese on a crisp corn tortilla. In Sonora, cooks have taken this concept to the highest level with the *Lorenza*. Corn tortillas are sprinkled or brushed with water and sprinkled with salt, then tossed onto the grill where the meat was cooked. Then the crunchy tostadas are slathered with seasoned refried beans mixed with cheese, topped with more cheese, and returned to the grill so that the cheese melts and the tortillas crisp a bit more. They are crowned with the juicy cubed carne asada and dressed with guacamole and salsa.

Although in northern Mexico carne asada is usually eaten with the region's phenomenal flour tortillas, the Lorenza is the exception. Corn tortillas are used because they are more resilient: They can be heated until crunchy without burning.

Meat from Sonoran Carne Asada Tacos (page 72), just cooked and still warm

12 corn tortillas

Kosher salt

Fiesta Refried Beans (page 159) or other refried beans

3 cups grated melting cheese, such as asadero, Oaxaca, Monterey Jack, or mozzarella (12 ounces)

Fire-Roasted Sonoran Chunky Salsa (page 123)

Guacamole with Chile Verde (page 152)

After grilling the meat, reduce the heat to medium if using a gas grill. If using a charcoal grill, use a cooler part of the grill for toasting the tortillas.

Cut the meat into ½-inch dice and keep warm.

Brush the tortillas with water and sprinkle with salt on both sides. Toast on the grill for 2 to 3 minutes per side, or until lightly colored on both sides and crispy.

Slather about 2 heaping tablespoons of refried beans on each crisp tortilla and top with ¼ cup grated cheese. Return to the grill and heat until the cheese melts and the tortillas turn a darker brown.

Transfer the tostadas to a platter, top with the meat, and bring to the table, along with the salsa and guacamole. Let your guests add salsa and guacamole to their own taste.

BEEF AND POTATO CHIMIS / CHIMICHANGAS DE GUISADO DE RES CON PAPA

Makes 8 to 12 chimichangas; serves 4 to 6 generously

Chimichanga or chivichanga? Are these Mexican or Mexamerican? These crispy pan-seared burritos from the state of Sonora answer yes to all of the above. The chimi (or chivi) is a craved favorite on both sides of the border. Sonora and Arizona were one geopolitical entity for a long time, and the two states are still strongly interconnected. This dish is also popular in the northern Mexican states of Chihuahua and Sinaloa, and north of the border, it's beginning to feel the love in other states besides Arizona.

Chimichangas are made with large flour tortillas. The filling of this one is pure Sonoran comfort, a savory mix of tender stewed beef, sautéed onions, potatoes, tomatoes, and lots of diced roasted Anaheim chiles, the ingredient that most identifies this as a dish from northern Mexico. Everything is moistened with the delicious broth from the simmered meat and cooked until the flavors come together and intensify. The filling is equally delicious tucked into flour tortillas for tacos, or rolled up for burritos. But my family votes for the chimi as the best vehicle for it.

FOR THE MEAT

2 pounds boneless beef chuck, cut into 1- to 2-inch pieces

1 cup chopped white onion, plus ½ onion

6 garlic cloves, peeled

3 bay leaves

1 tablespoon kosher salt

1 teaspoon black peppercorns

1 teaspoon dried oregano

½ teaspoon coriander seeds

½ teaspoon cumin seeds

2 tablespoons vegetable oil

¾ pound potatoes, such as Yukon gold (3 medium), peeled and diced (about 2 cups)

½ pound ripe tomatoes, chopped, or half a 15-ounce can crushed tomatoes

4 fresh Anaheim chiles, roasted, peeled, seeded, and diced (page 176)

FOR THE CHIMICHANGAS

8 to 12 large (8- to 10-inch) flour tortillas

2 tablespoons vegetable oil

2 cups shredded romaine or iceberg lettuce

1 cup crumbled queso fresco

Crema or sour cream (optional)

Diced tomatoes (optional)

Diced ripe avocado (optional)

Fire-Roasted Sonoran Chunky Salsa (page 123) or other salsa of your choice

To cook the meat: Place the meat in a Dutch oven or other large heavy pot, cover generously with water, and bring to a boil over high heat. Skim off the foam, reduce the heat to medium-low, and add the onion half, garlic, bay leaves, 2 teaspoons of the salt, the peppercorns, oregano, coriander, and cumin seeds and stir well. Cover and cook for 1½ hours, or until the meat is fork-tender and shreds easily.

continued

Remove the meat from the broth and set aside; strain the broth. Reserve 1½ cups of the broth for this recipe and refrigerate or freeze the rest for another use. Once the meat has cooled enough to handle, shred it or chop into small pieces.

Heat the oil in the Dutch oven or a large deep skillet over medium heat. Add the chopped onions and the potatoes, season with ½ teaspoon of the salt, and cook for about 10 minutes, stirring occasionally, until the onions have softened and the potatoes have begun to brown. Stir in the tomatoes and cook for 3 to 5 minutes, or until they are soft and mushy. Add the chiles and the remaining ½ teaspoon salt and cook for another 3 to 4 minutes, stirring often, until the ingredients are well blended. Stir in the meat and the reserved 1½ cups broth and cook until the broth is mostly absorbed and the potatoes have completely softened. Remove from the heat.

To make the chimichangas: Heat a large skillet over medium-low heat for at least 5 minutes. One at a time, heat the tortillas for about a minute per side, until warmed through. Remove from the heat and top with a couple of generous spoonfuls of the beef mixture. Fold one side of the tortilla over to enclose the filling, then fold in the sides and roll up into a burrito.

Heat the oil in the skillet over medium heat. When the oil is hot, working in batches so you don't crowd the pan, add the chimichangas seam side down and fry for a minute on each side, or until lightly colored.

Garnish with the lettuce, queso, and, if desired, the cream, tomato, and avocado. Serve with the salsa on the side.

Cook's Note

► There are a few keys to success with chimis. Always heat the flour tortillas before you fill and roll them. Make sure the oil is hot before you put the chimis in the pan, but not too hot, as flour tortillas are delicate and can easily burn. Place the chimis seam side down so that the seam seals as they cook. You can serve them garnished with the lettuce and cheese, but let people add their own crema and salsa so that the chimis don't get soggy.

CHIMI, BURRITO, OR TACO?

The differences between a chimi, a burrito, and a flour tortilla taco are subtle. To make soft tacos, warm flour tortillas and fill with the beef or other mixture, adding the garnishes along with the beef, if you wish, and fold over. For burritos, warm the tortillas, add the filling, and roll up, or make into a package by folding in both sides. The garnishes can go inside with the filling or outside. For chimis, warm the flour tortillas, add the filling, and roll up, tucking in the sides. Seal and lightly crisp either by deep-frying or shallow-frying, as in this recipe. The garnishes go on top.

TONGUE TACOS / **TACOS DE LENGUA**

Makes 10 to 12 tacos; serves 3 or 4

Don't turn the page! You may think you don't like tongue, but you probably haven't ever had it the way we prepare it in Mexico. Cooked in the Mexican way, it has a soft, luxuriant texture and a majestically subtle flavor. We simmer tongue gently, with lots of garlic and onion and herbs, until it is silky-tender. Then we chop it or slice it thin, brown it with onions in a little oil, pile it onto warm corn tortillas, add crunchy raw chopped onion and some cilantro, and spoon on the salsa of your choice (I always go for salsa verde). These tacos will make a tongue-to-tail convert of you if you aren't one already.

FOR THE TONGUE

1 whole beef tongue (3 to 4 pounds), cut into 2 or 3 pieces

1 head garlic, papery outer layer removed, cut horizontally in half

1 white onion, cut in half

5 bay leaves

1 tablespoon kosher salt

15 black peppercorns

1 teaspoon dried marjoram

1 teaspoon dried thyme

1 teaspoon dried oregano

FOR THE TACOS

2 teaspoons vegetable oil

½ cup finely chopped onion

Kosher salt and freshly ground black pepper

10 to 12 corn tortillas, warmed

Salsa verde of your choice (pages 118 to 121)

¼ cup coarsely chopped fresh cilantro leaves and upper stems

2 or 3 limes, cut into wedges

To cook the tongue: Place the tongue, garlic, onion, bay leaves, salt, peppercorns, marjoram, thyme, and oregano in a large pot. Add enough water to cover by 2 to 3 inches and bring to a boil over high heat. Reduce the heat to medium-low, cover tightly, and simmer for 3 hours, or until the tongue is very tender. Check the water halfway through and top up with hot water if necessary; the tongue should remain submerged. Turn off the heat and allow the tongue to cool slightly in the broth. Don't let it cool completely, as it is easier to peel when warm or hot.

Remove the tongue from the broth and place on a cutting board. Using a small sharp knife and your hands, peel away the outer layer of skin as well as the bottom layer of the tongue, with the membranes, and discard. Cut the tongue into ¼-inch dice.

To make the tacos: Heat the oil in a large skillet over medium heat. Add half the chopped onion and cook, stirring, until softened. Stir in the diced tongue, season with salt and pepper to taste, and cook for 4 to 5 minutes, stirring occasionally, until the tongue is lightly browned and the onion has completely softened. Transfer to a bowl.

Fill the warm tortillas with a generous amount of the tongue. Arrange on a platter or plates, spoon some salsa verde on top of each one, sprinkle with the rest of the onion and the cilantro, and serve, passing lime wedges for squeezing.

PUEBLA-STYLE PORK TACOS / **TACOS ÁRABES**

Makes 6 to 8 large tacos; serves 3 or 4 generously

Tacos Árabes are a specialty of Puebla, home to one of Mexico's most significant Lebanese communities. They are so popular that the city boasts more than three dozen taco Árabes restaurants and stands, each with its own fiercely devoted fan base.

Thinly sliced pork is marinated in a lemony, oniony herbal marinade. At most stands, the meat is cooked on a spit, then shaved off, but sometimes it's seared on a griddle. Then the meat and onions are placed on pitas and topped with salsa. The final embellishment is a Mexicanized tahini drizzle, which is tart, creamy, and rich.

You don't need a rotisserie spit for this recipe. I have tested the dish using a grill, griddle, and skillet, with equally delicious results. As long as the pork is cut thin, into what we call *bistec*, marinated, and then cooked over high heat so that it crisps a little on the outside to get the semblance of fire-cooked shawarma, you are set to go. Use a cut of pork that has some fat in it, which will season and baste the meat as it cooks.

Note that the pork must be marinated for at least 2 hours, and up to 24 hours.

FOR THE MARINADE

½ teaspoon cumin seeds

½ teaspoon coriander seeds

2 teaspoons dried oregano

1 teaspoon dried thyme

⅓ cup freshly squeezed lime juice

¼ cup olive oil

1 tablespoon white vinegar

4 garlic cloves, peeled

¼ cup slivered white onion

4 teaspoons kosher salt

½ teaspoon freshly ground black pepper

2 cups coarsely chopped fresh parsley leaves

2 cups coarsely chopped fresh mint leaves

FOR THE PORK AND TACOS

4 pounds boneless pork butt (see note), very thinly sliced (¼ inch or thinner)

2¾ cups slivered white onions

Vegetable oil for cooking the pork

6 to 12 large thin pita breads or 6 to 8 large (8- to 10-inch) flour tortillas

Chipotle Peanut Salsa (page 132) or Street-Style Salsa (page 124)

Puebla Tahini Sauce (page 143)

To make the marinade: Heat a small skillet over medium-low heat. Add the cumin and coriander seeds and toast, shaking the pan or stirring, for 20 to 30 seconds. Add the oregano and thyme and cook, stirring, for another 10 to 15 seconds, until fragrant. Transfer to a blender.

Add the lime juice, olive oil, vinegar, garlic, onion, salt, and pepper to the blender and puree until smooth. Add the parsley and mint and pulse a few times, just until the herbs are coarsely pureed. You want a textured marinade.

continued

To marinate the pork: Place a layer of the meat in a large bowl. Cover with some of the marinade and then a layer of onions. Cover with more of the marinade. Continue with the layers, making sure that both the meat and the onions are covered with marinade. Cover, refrigerate, and marinate for at least 4 hours, and up to 24 hours.

To make the tacos: Prepare a hot fire in a charcoal or gas grill. Or heat a large nonstick skillet over high heat. Brush the cooking surface with oil. Cook the meat in batches (leave the onions in the bowl, or most of them—it's fine if some of the onions stick to the meat), taking care not to overcrowd the grill or pan, turning the meat once, for 3 to 5 minutes per side, until it is cooked through and has a nice char all over the surface. As you cook, transfer the cooked meat to a lidded container, or transfer to a platter and cover tightly with foil.

If using a grill, use a vegetable grill pan to cook the onions. Grill the onions, turning with tongs, until tender and lightly browned, about 5 minutes. Or cook the onions in the skillet. Scrape the cooked onions over the meat.

Slice the meat into approximately 1-x-¼-inch strips. As you cut it, return it to the covered container so it stays warm.

Heat a comal or large skillet over medium-low heat. Working in batches, heat the pita bread or tortillas, turning once, until warmed through and lightly browned on both sides. Wrap the first batches in a clean kitchen towel to keep warm, or use a tortilla warmer.

To assemble the tacos, arrange a generous amount of meat and onions on the middle of or inside each pita bread or tortilla (the traditional way is to top the pitas as if they were tortillas). Top with the salsa, drizzle on the tahini sauce, and serve.

Cook's Note

► Some *carnicerias* sell pork butt already thinly sliced (*bistec de cerdo*), or you can ask your butcher to slice it for you.

HOW RELIGIOUS FREEDOM LED TO A NEW TACO

The ancestors of Mexico's modern Lebanese community, mostly Christian but some Jewish, began to come to Mexico in the 1800s, seeking religious freedom. They settled in Veracruz, the Yucatán, and the southern port city of Tampico. Later waves of Lebanese immigrants settled in Puebla and Mexico City. One of Mexico's most iconic dishes, tacos al pastor, evolved from shawarma, the thinly sliced spit-roasted Lebanese meat dish that was originally made with lamb. Lamb eventually gave way to pork, and the spices were also tweaked. Although Puebla is not home to the largest Lebanese community in Mexico (that honor goes to Mérida), it is the city where Lebanese culinary culture has had an immense impact, with tacos Árabes being one of the city's most sought-after specialties.

MIXED MEAT TACOS / **TACOS CAMPECHANOS**

Makes 8 tacos; serves 4

When you put together an assortment of meats with different flavors and textures in a taco, you get tacos campechanos (*campechanear* is a slang word that means to combine). It's hard to find a recipe for them in a cookbook, probably because they are such a taco-stand specialty that nobody ever thinks of making them at home. Yet they're so good and filling (*campechano* can also mean hearty) and so easy to make that they will amp up your taco repertoire.

This classic version combines flank steak (*suadero*); longaniza, a type of Mexican chorizo that is heavy on the achiote seasoning; and chicharrones. The flank steak is simmered until it is very tender and falling apart, then crisped in the pan in longaniza fat and mixed with bites of the highly seasoned sausage and crunchy, airy, salty crumbs of pork cracklings. The result is such a delicious combination that you will immediately understand the meaning of *campechano*.

2 pounds flank steak, cut into 1-inch pieces

2 garlic cloves, peeled

½ white onion

3 bay leaves

1 teaspoon kosher salt

1 teaspoon black peppercorns

1 tablespoon vegetable oil

½ pound longaniza or Mexican chorizo, casings removed and chopped

½ pound chicharrones, crumbled or finely chopped

FOR SERVING

8 corn tortillas

1 cup finely chopped white onion

1 cup chopped fresh cilantro leaves and upper stems

Street-Style Salsa (page 124) or other salsa of your choice

Put the flank steak, garlic, onion, bay leaves, salt, and peppercorns in a large saucepan. Cover generously with water and bring to a boil over high heat. Reduce the heat to medium-low, skim off any foam, cover, and cook for 1½ hours, or until the meat is completely tender and falling apart. Remove from the heat and set aside until the meat is cool enough to handle.

Remove the meat with a slotted spoon and chop into small pieces. Set aside.

Heat a large skillet over medium-high heat and add the oil. Add the longaniza or chorizo and brown for about 5 minutes, breaking it into smaller pieces with a couple of wooden spoons or spatulas until crumbled and crispy. Add the chopped flank steak, stir, and cook for a few more minutes, until the flank steak starts to brown as well. Stir in the chicharrones, mix everything together, and turn off the heat.

continued

Heat a comal or large skillet over medium-low heat for at least 5 minutes. One or two at a time, heat the tortillas for about a minute per side, until warmed through, with brown specks on both sides. Wrap the first batches in a clean kitchen towel to keep warm or use a tortilla warmer.

Assemble the tacos and serve, or let people assemble their own, adding some of the meat mix to each tortilla and topping it with some chopped onion, cilantro, and salsa.

LONGANIZA

Longaniza is a unique type of Mexican chorizo that is thinner and longer than regular chorizo. It isn't twisted into separate sausages in the casings, like chorizo, but left as one long link. The most famous longaniza in Mexico comes from the town of Valladolid, in the Yucatán. It's flavored with achiote paste and bitter orange and smoked over a wood fire. As with any Mexican chorizo, longaniza must be cooked before eating. If you don't find it, you can substitute Mexican chorizo or even spicy Italian sausage.

CHILE-MASA QUESADILLAS / ENCHILADAS POTOSINAS

Makes about 20 quesadillas; serves 10

Enchiladas potosinas are quesadillas made with masa that has been seasoned with a dried chile paste. In this version, I use a combination of ancho chiles and chiles de árbol, giving the dough a beautiful reddish-orange color and a beguiling flavor with a touch of heat. The tortillas are folded over a filling of queso fresco mixed with cooked tomatoes, tomatillos, and onion seasoned with garlic and chile, and the edges are sealed so that the filling is completely enclosed. The enchiladas are cooked on a lightly oiled griddle. These are called enchiladas not because they are anything like what we typically think of when we hear the word, but because *enchilada* can also mean something that has chile added to it.

Enchiladas potosinas are one of the most iconic dishes of the state of San Luis Potosí, in the north-central part of the country. They are so popular there and in the surrounding central states that you can even find them in gas stations. When my sisters and I were growing up, my dad traveled often to Querétaro, a state that shares a border with San Luis Potosí, and he always picked up a couple of boxes of them on his way home. My mom shallow-fried them, and we'd eat them right out of the frying pan.

FOR THE CHILE PUREE

2 to 3 dried ancho chiles, stemmed and seeded

1 to 2 dried chiles de árbol, stemmed

1 garlic clove, peeled

½ teaspoon kosher salt

FOR THE FILLING

2 tablespoons vegetable oil, plus more for cooking the enchiladas

½ cup chopped white onion

1 serrano or jalapeño chile, finely chopped

1 garlic clove, minced

2 ripe tomatoes or 2 canned tomatoes, finely chopped

2 tomatillos, husked, rinsed, and finely chopped

¼ teaspoon salt, or more to taste

1½ cups crumbled queso fresco (about 6 ounces)

FOR THE TORTILLAS

2 to 2½ cups masa harina, as needed

1¼ cups water

To make the chile puree: Place the ancho chiles, chiles de árbol, and the whole garlic clove in a small saucepan, cover with water, and bring to a boil over medium-high heat. Reduce the heat to medium and simmer for about 10 minutes, until the chiles and garlic are soft.

continued

Transfer the chiles and garlic to a blender, along with ¾ cup of the cooking liquid. Add the salt and puree until smooth. Scrape into a small bowl and set aside.

To make the filling: Heat the 2 tablespoons oil in a large skillet over medium-high heat. Add the onion and serrano or jalapeño and cook for about 4 minutes, until they are soft and wilted and the edges of the onion are just beginning to brown. Stir in the minced garlic and cook for a minute, then add the tomatoes, tomatillos, and salt. Cook, stirring often, until the tomatoes and tomatillos have softened and released their juices and the mixture has cooked down to a mushy paste, 5 to 10 minutes. Scrape into a medium bowl.

Once the filling mixture has cooled, add the queso fresco and combine well.

To make the tortillas: Combine 2 cups masa harina with the water in a large bowl and mix together. Add the chile puree and stir until well incorporated. If the mixture seems very moist, mix in up to ½ cup more masa. Knead the dough until there are no lumps and it is as soft as Play-Doh.

Cut two 9-inch circles or squares from a thin plastic bag, such as a produce bag or ziplock bag. Line a baking sheet with parchment paper.

Place one piece of plastic on a tortilla press or work surface. Pinch off a 1½-inch piece of dough and roll it into a ball between the palms of your hands. Place the dough round on the plastic. Cover with the other sheet of plastic and press

down with the top of the press—not too hard—or roll with a rolling pin until you have a 4½- to 5-inch tortilla. Peel off the top piece of plastic. Place a tablespoon of the cheese mixture in the center of the tortilla and, using the bottom piece of plastic, fold the tortilla over and press and seal into a half-moon. Press gently with your fingers to spread the filling evenly, with no big bulge in the middle, so that the quesadilla will cook evenly. Remove the plastic and transfer the quesadilla to the baking sheet. Repeat with the remaining dough and filling.

Heat a comal, griddle, or large skillet over medium-low heat for 8 to 10 minutes. Brush with 1 to 2 tablespoons oil. Working in batches, add the quesadillas, without crowding, And cook for 2 to 3 minutes on the first side, until lightly browned and crisped. Turn and cook for 2 to 3 minutes longer. Transfer to individual plates or a platter and serve.

Cook's Notes

► You can substitute dried colorado chiles or guajillo chiles for the anchos. They will make a brick-red masa with a somewhat different taste. Anchos have a sweet-tart edge.

► You can keep the quesadillas at room temperature on a baking sheet or platter covered with foil or plastic for to 8 to 10 hours. Reheat in a 350 degree F oven for 10 minutes or on a hot comal or large skillet.

FRESH MASA AND MASA HARINA

Masa is one of the cornerstones of the Mexican kitchen. The word means dough, and in Mexico, unless otherwise specified, it refers to the corn-based dough used for tortillas.

Fresh masa used to be something you could buy only in Mexico. But, increasingly, U.S. markets catering to Latin cooks carry ready-made dough, and artisanal tortillerias selling both the dough and freshly made tortillas are popping up in cities all over the United States. If you can get fresh masa, wrap it well and refrigerate if not using right away, and use within a couple of days. (It will be difficult to work with if you wait longer, as it tends to dry out.)

If you don't live near a Mexican market, you can make your own tortillas and tamales using **masa harina**. Masa harina is sold in many supermarkets and all Mexican grocery stores. There are many brands. A powdery flour (*harina* means flour) made from dried and nixtamalized corn, it's a very handy ingredient. To make masa dough, all you have to do is mix the masa harina with water: ½ cup masa harina mixed with ½ cup water will make about ⅔ cup masa.

Many supermarkets sell two kinds of masa harina: one for making tortillas and one for tamales, which is slightly coarser. If you can't find the latter, don't worry. Masa harina for tortillas works fine for tamales.

POTATO AND POBLANO SOPES / **SOPES CON PAPAS Y RAJAS**

Makes 12 sopes; serves 6 as an appetizer

Sopes are little edible plates made of masa. They are thicker and smaller than regular corn tortillas, and they are edged with a rim that helps contain their delicious toppings and garnishes. The most popular sopes are covered with a layer of refried beans and garnished with shredded lettuce, white onion, cheese, and salsa (I usually opt for a salsa verde). But when you eat them at street food stands, there are typically many toppings to choose from. These have the beans and the classic garnishes, with even more savory comfort in between—cooked diced potatoes lightly browned in oil with onion and roasted poblano chiles, one of the typical street food offerings and one that I always choose. You can make the sopes ahead before filling them, and once ready, they are quickly assembled (see note).

FOR THE POTATOES AND POBLANOS

1 pound red potatoes, peeled and cut into ½-inch cubes

2 tablespoons vegetable oil

½ white onion, finely chopped

1 teaspoon kosher salt

4 fresh poblano chiles, roasted, sweated, peeled, seeded, and cut into 1-x-¼-inch strips (page 176)

FOR THE SOPES

2 cups masa harina

2 cups water

Pinch of kosher salt

FOR THE TOPPINGS

2 cups Basic Refried Beans (page 158) or Oaxacan Refried Black Beans (page 162), heated

½ cup crumbled Cotija cheese or queso fresco

½ cup shredded romaine lettuce

½ cup chopped white onion

1 cup Cooked Salsa Verde (page 120) or other salsa of your choice

To make the potatoes and poblanos: Bring a medium saucepan of salted water to a boil. Add the potatoes and bring to a simmer, then reduce the heat to medium and cook for 10 minutes, or until tender. Drain.

Heat the oil in a large skillet over medium-high heat. Add the onion and cook for a few minutes, just until softened. Add the potatoes and salt and cook for 3 to 4 minutes, until the potatoes begin to color and the onions soften. Stir in the poblano chile strips and cook for a couple of minutes more to heat them through. Set aside and keep warm.

To make the sopes: Combine the masa harina, water, and salt in a large bowl. Using a circular motion, swish the mixture around the bowl with your hands until well mixed, then knead for a couple of minutes, until the dough is as smooth and pliable as Play-Doh, with no lumps. If it feels too dry, mix in a bit more water a teaspoon at a time.

continued

Cut two 9-inch circles or squares from a thin plastic bag, such as a produce bag or ziplock bag.

Divide the dough into 12 pieces and roll each one into a ball between the palms of your hands.

Place one piece of plastic on a tortilla press or work surface. Place a ball of dough on the plastic. Cover with the other sheet of plastic. If using a press, press down, not too hard, to make a 3-inch round; it will be about ¼ inch thick, much thicker than a tortilla (more like a pancake). Alternatively, you can flatten and shape the sopes by hand. Repeat with the remaining dough balls.

Meanwhile, heat a comal, griddle, or large skillet over medium-low heat until hot, at least 5 minutes.

Working in batches, place the dough rounds on the hot pan, without crowding, and cook for about 2 minutes on each side, until they are opaque and speckled on the bottom and can easily be turned, without sticking to the pan. Turn and cook for about 2 minutes on the second side. The sopes will not be completely cooked through.

As each sope is ready, remove from the pan and place on a cutting board. (Leave the pan over the heat.) Using a kitchen towel to protect your fingers, immediately press and pinch a rim around the edges of the sope. Return to the pan and cook for 1 minute more on each side, or until cooked through.

Transfer the sopes to a platter, rimmed side up, and top each with a generous 2 tablespoons of the refried beans, a couple of tablespoons of the potato and poblano mix, and some of the cheese, lettuce, chopped onion, and salsa. Serve with the remaining salsa on the side for people to add as much as they like.

Cook's Note

► You can keep the cooked sopes at room temperature, wrapped in a clean kitchen towel, for up to 12 hours. They can also be wrapped well and refrigerated for up to 3 days or frozen for up to 6 months. Reheat on a hot comal or skillet for a couple of minutes before assembling; add a bit of oil to the pan before reheating them. You can also make the potato and poblano mixture up to 4 days ahead and refrigerate, covered, until ready to use.

PLANTAIN MOLOTES WITH PICADILLO FILLING / MOLOTES RELLENOS DE PICADILLO

Makes 12 molotes; serves 12 as an appetizer, 6 as a main course

A molote is like a quesadilla, but it's always made with a fresh dough rather than with tortillas. The dough can be a corn masa, but it can also be a potato masa, or, more frequently, a ripe plantain masa. These plantain molotes are my favorite kind. They're among the most festive of all molotes, and they typify a baroque style of Mexican cooking characterized by a complex mix of local and tropical ingredients with ingredients brought from Spain. The picadillo filling contains raisins, almonds, olives, and capers. There's a wonderful set of contrasts happening here—sweet and savory, soft and crunchy, pungent and mild.

The trick to making a plantain dough that isn't overly sticky, dry, or too wet is to simmer the plantains in water until they are mushy. You can use a tortilla press or a rolling pin to shape the plantain mash into rounds. Or you can just pat out the dough between your hands.

The molotes are shallow-fried in oil. They will crisp and brown slightly on the surface, but inside, the luscious dough remains much softer than corn masa dough.

4 ripe plantains (about 2 pounds), not peeled, cut crosswise in half

2 cups Beef Picadillo (page 275; see note), at room temperature

Vegetable oil for shallow-frying

Crema or sour cream for topping (optional)

Crumbled queso fresco for topping (optional)

Place the unpeeled plantains in a large saucepan, cover with water, and bring to a boil. Reduce the heat to medium and simmer for about 30 minutes, or until the plantains are very soft. Remove from the heat and set aside to cool in the water.

Once they are completely cool, drain the plantains, peel, dice, and place in a bowl. Using a potato masher or a large fork, mash until smooth, as if you were making mashed potatoes.

Grease a baking sheet with vegetable oil. Cut two 9-inch circles or squares from a thin plastic bag, such as a produce bag or ziplock bag.

Oil your hands to prevent sticking. Pinch off 3-tablespoon pieces of the mashed plantain dough and roll between your hands into approximately 2-inch balls.

Place one piece of plastic on a tortilla press or work surface. Place a ball of dough on the plastic and cover with the other piece of plastic. Press down with the press, not too hard, to make a ¼-inch-thick round, or roll out with a rolling pin into a round. (Or you can pat the dough flat with your hands.) The round should look like a thick tortilla.

continued

Peel off the top piece of plastic. Place 2 tablespoons of the picadillo in the middle of the round and, using the bottom sheet of plastic, fold over the dough to make a half-moon and enclose the filling. Press the edges together to seal. You can stay with the half-moon shape or, again using the plastic, roll the stuffed molote into a cigar shape. Peel off the plastic and place the molote on the oiled baking sheet. Repeat with the remaining dough and filling.

Fill a large deep skillet with ¼ inch of oil and heat over medium heat until a small piece of dough bubbles actively around the edges when added to the oil. Place a cooling rack on a baking sheet lined with paper towels.

Carefully add 2 to 3 molotes at a time to the oil, without crowding the pan, and fry for 1 to 2 minutes per side, until they are golden brown and the surface is lightly crisped. If you shaped them into cylinders, roll the molotes around as they fry so they brown and crisp evenly on all sides. Remove with a slotted spoon and drain on the cooling rack.

Serve at once, or allow to cool, cover, and then reheat in a low oven when ready to eat. Serve topped with the cream and cheese, if desired.

Cook's Notes

► You can make the picadillo with pork instead of beef, or even with chicken or turkey.

► Once assembled, the molotes can be covered with plastic wrap and refrigerated for up to 12 hours. Fry them when you are ready to eat. The fried molotes can be kept at room temperature, covered, for about an hour, or refrigerated for up to 24 hours; reheat them in the oven.

PLANTAINS: BANANA'S VERSATILE COUSIN

In most regions of Mexico, plantains, which are native to India and the Caribbean, are called *plátanos machos*—macho bananas. They do look like jumbo bananas, but although they come from the same family, plantains are a different food altogether—starchier, meatier, firmer, milder in flavor, with a much thicker, clingier skin. They are not eaten raw, only cooked—steamed, grilled, baked, or fried— and are most often treated like a starchy vegetable.

You can find plantains in many supermarket produce sections. Ripe plantains are almost completely black. They begin to mature as they turn yellow, but they are still not ripe. You know they are ready when they feel soft and give a little, though they shouldn't feel mushy.

To ripen plantains, let them sit in a warm area of your kitchen or in a paper bag at room temperature. They will take 3 to 4 days to go from yellow to almost black. Once they are fully ripened, they will keep in the refrigerator for about 3 days.

SWEET POTATO AND BLACK BEAN TAMALES /
TAMALES DE CAMOTE CON FRIJOL

Makes about 20 tamales; serves 10

I first ate a black bean and sweet potato tamal at Criollo, a restaurant in the city of Oaxaca run by chef Luis Arellano, who is known for his contemporary interpretations of Oaxacan culinary traditions. Since then, I have encountered this combination in various renditions beyond Oaxaca.

In this interpretation, sweet potato moistens the masa and gives it a beautiful orange hue, a rich texture, and a sweet taste that plays off against the refried black bean filling. I like to use the Oaxacan-style refried beans for these because of the added fragrance and anisey taste from avocado leaves, as well as a mild kick from the chile de árbol. We love flavor contrasts, so it is common in Mexico to dress a sweet masa tamal with something savory, tangy, or salty, such as queso fresco. But you could also take a sweeter route and drizzle some agave syrup or honey on top—or top your tamales with both.

2 pounds sweet potatoes

1 cup lard or vegetable shortening

½ teaspoon kosher salt

1 teaspoon baking powder

3 tablespoons dark brown sugar or grated piloncillo

1⅔ cups masa harina, preferably for tamales (page 89)

½ cup chicken or vegetable broth

1 (10-ounce) package dried corn husks for tamales (at least 40)

2 cups Oaxacan Refried Black Beans (page 162) or Basic Refried Beans (page 158), made with black beans

1 cup crema or sour cream for serving (optional)

1 cup crumbled queso fresco and/or honey or agave syrup for serving (optional)

Preheat the oven to 425 degrees F, with a rack in the middle. Pierce the sweet potatoes with a fork, put them on a foil-lined baking sheet, and bake for 50 minutes to an hour, or until they are completely soft. Remove from the oven.

When the sweet potatoes are cool enough to handle, split them open and scoop the cooked pulp into a bowl. Mash until smooth with a potato masher or fork. Set aside to cool completely.

To make the dough: Place the lard or shortening and the salt in the bowl of a stand mixer fitted with the paddle attachment, or put in a large bowl and use a hand mixer. Beat on medium speed until very light, about 1 minute. Reduce the speed to low and beat in the baking powder and brown sugar. Add the masa harina in 3 additions, alternating with the broth. Increase the speed to medium and beat for 6 to 7 minutes, until the dough is homogeneous and light. Add the sweet potato in 4 additions, mixing thoroughly after each addition. Then continue mixing for another 5 to 6 minutes, until the mixture is thoroughly blended and the masa is fluffy.

continued

To assemble the tamales: Place about 40 corn husks in a large bowl of hot water. Soak for a couple of minutes, or until they are pliable. Remove about 30 of the larger and more perfect corn husks from the water, drain in a colander, and pat dry.

Lay out a corn husk on a work surface with the tapering end toward you. If the husk seems narrow, layer a second one on top, fanning the two slightly to get a wider husk. Leaving a 1- to 1½-inch border at the bottom, spread about ⅓ cup of the masa into a 2- to 3-inch rectangle, depending on the size of the husk; it should be a little more than ¼ inch thick; leave a border of at least ½ inch on the sides and more than that at the top. Make an indentation in the middle of the masa and place about 2 teaspoons of the bean filling in it. Bring the two long sides of the corn husk over so they meet in the middle and fold snugly over to one side. Then fold up the empty tapered end, leaving the top of the tamal open. Gently press on the filling from the bottom up to the top to even it out. Repeat with more husks and the remaining masa and filling to make about 20 tamales. If you're not steaming the tamales now, place them seam side down on a plate or baking sheet, cover with plastic, and refrigerate.

To prepare the steamer: Pour enough water into a steamer pot to come to just below the bottom of the steamer basket. To monitor the water so it doesn't evaporate during the long steaming time, place a coin in it (when you no longer hear the coin jingling against the pot, check the water and replenish as necessary). Line the steamer basket with one or two layers of the remaining soaked corn husks.

To cook the tamales: Stand the tamales on end as well as you can in the steamer basket, with the open ends up. If there is space left in the steamer, tuck in some more corn husks so the tamales won't move around. Cover with more soaked corn husks. Set the steamer over high heat and heat, uncovered, until you see steam emerging from the pot. Cover the pot tightly, reduce the heat to medium, and steam the tamales for 55 minutes to an hour. You will know they are ready when the masa comes away easily from the husks. The tamales can be kept warm for about 2 hours in the steamer.

If desired, serve the tamales topped with crema and crumbled queso fresco, and/or honey or syrup.

Cook's Notes

► You can assemble the tamales a day ahead and keep them refrigerated, well covered.

► The tamales can be steamed ahead and refrigerated, well wrapped, for up to 3 days. They can also be frozen for up to 6 months. Reheat in the steamer; refrigerated tamales will take about 20 minutes, frozen ones about 45 minutes.

Lard is as central to Mexican cooking as the pork it is rendered from. It is such an iconic touchstone that our word for it—*manteca*—is also used for other fats, including butter and even vegetable shortening, which we call *manteca vegetal*. Arriving with the Spanish in the sixteenth century, lard became a key ingredient in some of our most traditional foods. It makes tamal doughs fluffy and irresistible, and flour tortillas flaky and addictive. Yes, you can substitute vegetable shortening for lard, or even beef tallow, chicken fat, or coconut oil, but they lack lard's depth of flavor.

There is lard, and there is good lard. The milky-white commercial lard that you find in most supermarkets is hydrogenated to give it a longer shelf life and tends to be bland. If you can find lard at your local butcher shop, it will probably be darker than supermarket lard, and it will certainly have a lot more flavor.

You can also make your own lard. Every time you make a slow-cooked pork dish, such as Brown Sugar Carnitas (page 301), pour off some of the fat from the pot and let it solidify. Or refrigerate the dish overnight, and the next day, lift off some of the fat that has solidified on the top. The fat may have some utterly delicious cracklings in it, which you can strain and add to other dishes, or you can leave them in the lard for great flavor. I suggest straining the melted fat if you want a more neutral flavor— for example, if you are using it for pastry. Store lard in a tightly sealed container in the fridge for up to 4 months or in the freezer for up to a year. It will have a longer shelf life if strained.

TAMALES WITH FRESH CORN, CHEESE, AND GREEN CHILE / **TAMALES DE ELOTE CON RAJAS DE CHILE VERDE Y QUESO**

Makes 15 tamales; serves 6 or 7

When I tasted this Sonoran tamal made with a combination of fresh corn and masa, with a savory filling of softened onions, roasted Anaheim peppers, and cheese, I was instantly smitten. Sonorans are proud of their white corn, which is a starchier, less sweet variety than what you find anywhere else in Mexico, or in the United States, but any tender fresh corn will work here.

Although these tamales can be made with lard or vegetable shortening, in Sonora many cooks make them with butter, with a little evaporated milk to moisten the masa. The dough is textured and just sweet enough to set off the savory filling and melted cheese.

This masa is quite moist compared to that of other tamales. The assembled tamales require about 30 minutes longer in the steamer, and a 15-minute rest once done. Then they will come away from the husks without falling apart. They do end up sticky, and that is one of the things I most like about them.

FOR THE DOUGH

4 cups fresh corn kernels (from 5 to 6 ears; see note)

½ cup evaporated milk

8 tablespoons (1 stick) unsalted butter, at room temperature

1 tablespoon sugar

1¼ cups masa harina, preferably for tamales (page 89)

1 teaspoon baking soda

½ teaspoon kosher salt

1 teaspoon vegetable oil

FOR THE FILLING

1 tablespoon vegetable oil

1 cup slivered white onion

1 pound fresh Anaheim chiles, roasted, sweated, peeled, seeded, and cut into thin strips (page 176)

½ teaspoon kosher salt

1½ cups grated melting cheese, such as asadero, Oaxaca, Monterey Jack, or mozzarella (6 ounces)

30 dried corn husks (from a 10-ounce package), plus more for lining the steamer

To make the dough: Coarsely puree the corn kernels with the evaporated milk in a food processor or blender. The mixture should be a bit chunky, not completely smooth.

Combine the butter and sugar in the bowl of a stand mixer fitted with the paddle attachment, or put in a large bowl and use a hand mixer. Beat at medium speed until very soft and creamy, about 2 minutes. Scrape down the bowl and beater(s).

In a medium bowl, whisk together the masa harina, baking soda, and salt.

continued

On low speed, add the fresh corn puree to the butter, alternating with the masa harina mixture. Once the mixture is homogenous, add the oil, increase the speed to medium, and beat until creamy and fluffy, 7 to 8 more minutes.

To make the filling: Heat the oil in a large skillet over medium heat. Add the onion and cook, stirring often, until it begins to soften, 3 to 4 minutes. Stir in the chiles, sprinkle with the salt, and cook for another 3 to 4 minutes, stirring often, until the onions are very soft and the flavors have combined. Scrape the filling into a bowl.

To assemble the tamales: Place about 40 corn husks in a large bowl of hot water. Soak for a couple of minutes, or until they are pliable. Remove about 30 of the larger and more perfect corn husks from the water, drain in a colander, and pat dry.

Lay out a corn husk on a work surface with the tapered end toward you. If the husk seems narrow, layer a second corn husk on top, fanning the two slightly to get a wider husk. Leaving a 1- to 1½-inch border at the bottom, spread about ⅓ cup of the masa into a 2- to 3-inch square or rectangle, depending on the size of the husk; it should be a little more than ¼ inch thick. Leave a border of at least ½ inch on the sides and a little more than that at the top. Arrange a generous tablespoon of the chile and onion filling lengthwise down the middle of the masa and top with a generous tablespoon of the grated cheese. Bring up the two long sides of the corn husk over to meet in the middle and fold over snugly to one side. Fold up the empty tapered end, leaving the

top of the tamal open. Gently press on the filling from the bottom toward the top to even it out. Repeat with more husks and the remaining masa, filling, and cheese to make 15 tamales. If you're not steaming the tamales now, place them seam side down on a plate or baking sheet, cover with plastic, and refrigerate.

To prepare the steamer: Pour enough water into a steamer pot to come to just below the bottom of the steamer basket. To monitor the water so it doesn't evaporate during the long steaming time, place a coin in it (when you no longer hear the coin jingling against the pot, check the water and replenish as necessary). Line the steamer basket with one or two layers of soaked corn husks.

To cook the tamales: Stand the tamales up as well as you can in the steamer basket, with the open ends up. If there is space left in the steamer, tuck in some corn husks so the tamales can't move around. Cover with more corn husks.

Set the steamer over high heat and heat, uncovered, until you see steam emerging from the pot. Cover tightly, reduce the heat to medium, and steam for 1 to 1½ hours; the tamales should appear firm. Let them rest for 10 to 15 minutes. You know the tamales are ready when they come away easily from the husks. The tamales can be kept warm for about 2 hours in the steamer.

Serve hot or warm.

Cook's Notes

► If fresh corn is not in season, you can use thawed frozen kernels. But do *not* use canned; it is too watery.

► You can assemble the tamales a day ahead and keep them refrigerated, well covered.

► The tamales can be steamed ahead and refrigerated, well wrapped, for up to 3 days. They can also be frozen for up to 6 months. Reheat in the steamer; refrigerated tamales will take about 20 minutes, frozen ones about 45 minutes.

ANAHEIMS, THE SONORAN GO-TO CHILE

Sonora is a major producer of Anaheim chiles, the long bright green chiles that we sometimes call California chiles or New Mexico chiles, and that the Sonorans call *chiles verdes*.

These fresh chiles usually have a very mild heat, though occasionally they can be spicy. They have a flowery, vegetal flavor, with tart, fresh, citrusy notes. They're often served as a vegetable, in the form of rajas (charred, sweated, and cut into strips); stuffed for chiles rellenos; or used as a vegetable component in a dish rather than a spicing ingredient.

The fresh chiles are also allowed to ripen until they become bright red. In Sonora, when they reach this stage, they are called *chiles colorados* (for their red color, not the American state), and they are most often dried and used in a thousand ways.

ACHIOTE CHICKEN TAMALES / **MINI PIBIS DE POLLO**

Makes 16 tamales; serves 8

You find these savory banana-leaf–wrapped tamales all over the Yucatán Peninsula, where they are called mini pibis. They have a saucy, sloppy Joe–like filling of shredded chicken or pork bathed in an achiote sauce. Achiote, which tastes a little bit like saffron, gives the sauce its rich, full flavor and punch.

These tamales are different from the corn-husk sort found in other parts of Mexico, not just because of the wrapping, but also because the masa is unique. Called *colados*, it is lightly cooked before being spread on the banana leaves. Cooking gives it a silky texture, and once steamed, it is stickier, much more dense, and less fluffy than the masa in corn-husk tamales.

Throughout the Yucatán, you also find a gigantic version of these tamales called *mucbi pollo* or *pibi de pollo*. Typically served at large celebrations and fiestas, they are like huge tamal pies, made with the same masa and sauce, but usually with whole chicken pieces (skin, bones, and all) instead of shredded chicken. The tamal is wrapped in banana leaves and cooked in an underground pit, called a *pib* in Mayan, which is why both the large pies and the tamales are known as *pibis*. When I was in Champotón, a small Gulf Coast town nestled on the west coast of the Yucatán in the state of Campeche, I was treated to an unforgettable feast by a charismatic lifelong resident and wonderful cook named Chachi, and pibi de pollo was the centerpiece of the meal.

Although the popular mini-size pibis are cooked in a steamer or cazuela, not an underground pit, the name has stuck. My family and I absolutely adore them. The boys and I stumbled upon the most delicious mini pibis we had ever tasted near Mérida, in a little hut where a cook named Miri sold snacks through a small window. We went back for seconds, and then for thirds.

FOR THE MASA

3¼ cups (about 1 pound) masa harina, preferably for tamales (page 89)

2¾ cups chicken broth

1½ cups water

½ teaspoon kosher salt

1 cup lard, vegetable shortening, or coconut oil

FOR THE FILLING

½ cup chicken broth

3 tablespoons achiote paste

1 pound ripe tomatoes, quartered, or 1 (15-ounce) can whole tomatoes

4 garlic cloves, peeled

¼ cup coarsely chopped white onion

1 teaspoon dried oregano

¼ teaspoon ground allspice

1 teaspoon kosher salt

¼ teaspoon freshly ground black pepper

1 tablespoon vegetable oil

3 cups shredded cooked chicken (page 251) or rotisserie chicken

1 (16-ounce) package banana leaves, thawed if frozen

continued

To make the masa: Combine the masa harina and chicken broth in a large bowl and mix together with your hands, squeezing and kneading the ingredients until they are thoroughly combined and the dough is very smooth.

Combine the water and salt in a medium pot and bring to a boil. Reduce the heat to low and add the masa in batches, working it into the water with a wooden spatula or wide spoon as you go. Add another batch only when the previous batch has been incorporated, and continue until all of the masa has been incorporated. Add the lard and work it in with the spatula or spoon, stirring until it is thoroughly incorporated. After 3 to 4 minutes, the masa should be very thick. It will smell like cooked corn tortillas and be lightly browned. Remove from the heat.

To make the filling: Combine the chicken broth, achiote paste, tomatoes, garlic, onion, oregano, allspice, salt, and pepper in a blender and puree until smooth.

Heat the oil in a large heavy saucepan over medium heat. When the oil is hot, carefully add the puree (it will splatter, so use the pan's lid as a shield), cover partially, and cook, stirring frequently, for about 10 minutes, until the puree thickens and darkens. Stir in the shredded chicken and continue to cook, stirring occasionally, for 8 to 10 minutes, until the chicken has absorbed much of the liquid but the mixture is still moist (like sloppy Joe filling). Remove from the heat and set aside.

To make the tamales: Unfold the banana leaves and cut 16 rough rectangles, about 10 inches on the long sides, from them (set the remaining leaves aside). Turn a gas or electric burner to low and, using tongs, slowly pass both sides of each banana leaf piece over the heat until slightly softened. (This step makes the leaves more pliable, so they won't tear when you shape the tamales.) One by one, set a leaf piece on a work surface with the shiny (outer) side down. Spoon about ¼ cup of the masa onto the center and spread it into an approximately 4-x-3-inch rectangle. With the spoon (or your finger), make a shallow channel down the middle of the masa. Spoon a couple of tablespoons of the chicken filling into the channel and spread it evenly. Gently close the tamal by folding over the longer sides and then the shorter sides to create a flat, tight package. Take care not to press down too hard on the tamal; that could cause the filling to ooze out or the leaf to tear. Repeat with the remaining cut banana leaves and filling to make 16 tamales.

To prepare the steamer: Pour enough water into a steamer pot to come to just below the bottom of the steamer basket. To monitor the water so it doesn't evaporate during the long steaming time, place a coin in it (when you no longer hear the coin jingling against the pot, check the water and replenish as necessary). Cut a few more banana leaf pieces and line the steamer basket with them, just covering the bottom.

To cook the tamales: Add the tamales one by one to the pot, laying them flat with the seam side up and staggering them. Cover with a few more pieces of banana leaf. Set the steamer over high heat and heat, uncovered, until you see steam emerging from the pot. Cover tightly, reduce the heat to medium, and cook for 50 minutes to an hour, until the tamales feel firm. The leaves will darken, wilt, and shrink so that they wrap around the filling like a skin. Remove from the heat and let rest, covered, for 10 to 15 minutes so that the tamales firm up before serving.

Cook's Notes

- You can assemble the tamales a day ahead of steaming; cover and refrigerate.

- The tamales can be steamed ahead and refrigerated, well wrapped, for up to 3 days. They can also be frozen for up to 6 months. Reheat in the steamer; refrigerated tamales will take about 20 minutes, frozen ones about 45 minutes.

- The chicken pibil filling is also delicious in tacos and tortas.

BANANA LEAVES: NATURE'S SWEET-SCENTED WRAPPERS

Banana leaves are a beautiful dark green, and their aroma is fragrant and tropical. When you steam or roast food wrapped in banana leaves, the leaves infuse them with their essence. You can find packaged banana leaves in the produce sections of many international, Mexican, or Latin grocery stores, and in Asian groceries as well. When you take them out of their package, you will find that they are quite long, and they can be a bit unwieldy; you'll usually need to cut them into pieces. When using them for Lamb Barbacoa (page 291), though, make sure the pieces are large enough to wrap the meat; you may have to use several large pieces to do this. One 16-ounce package is enough for any of the recipes in this book.

TRADITIONAL FLOUR TORTILLAS / **TORTILLAS DE HARINA**

Makes 16 tortillas

In the northern states of Mexico, you will find flour tortillas on every table. They are such an integral part of the culture that in many homes, kids learn to make them at a very young age. They vary in size, from huge to large to the most common 5- to 6-inch rounds, and even minis. The type of fat used also varies, from beef tallow to lard to vegetable shortening or even butter. In Sonoran cattle country, beef tallow is the fat of choice, and sometimes beef cracklings are added to the dough. Different liquids are used to moisten the dough; some recipes call for water, some milk, and some for evaporated milk (page 110).

This recipe is for classic flour tortillas for tacos, made with lard or vegetable shortening. You can also use them for burritos or chimichangas, although in that case you might want to make larger tortillas than the 7-inch rounds this recipe describes. Thin and pillowy-soft, they're easy to make and hard to resist.

> 3⅔ cups (1 pound) all-purpose flour
>
> 1 teaspoon kosher salt
>
> ⅔ cup lard or vegetable shortening
>
> 1 cup lukewarm water

Combine the flour and salt in a large bowl. Add the lard or shortening and mix together with your fingertips until the fat is broken up into very small pieces and evenly distributed through the flour. Add the water and mix it into the flour in a circular motion, scraping from the bottom and folding the dough over itself from the center out to the edges of the bowl. At first it will be very sticky and lumpy, but as you continue to knead, it will become more elastic and less wet. When you can turn it out of the bowl in one piece, knead the dough on your work surface until it is as smooth as Play-Doh; it should be springy to the touch.

Divide the ball of dough in half, then divide each half in half again, and continue until you have 16 pieces. Shape each piece into a ball and place on a lightly floured baking sheet or board. Cover with a clean dish towel and let rest for 25 to 35 minutes.

Heat a comal, griddle, or large skillet over medium-low heat for at least 5 minutes (preheating is important so the tortillas don't stick and burn).

Lightly flour a work surface and your rolling pin and, one at a time, roll out each ball into a 7-inch tortilla. Rotate the dough 5 or 6 times as you roll it out, and don't worry if you don't get perfect rounds. As soon as you are finished rolling out a tortilla, put it on the hot pan. You will hear a faint sizzle. After 40 to 50 seconds, there should be brown freckles on the bottom and air bubbles visible on top. Turn the tortilla and cook for another 40 to 50 seconds, until the second side is freckled and the tortilla puffs up even more, like pita bread. Remove and wrap in a clean kitchen towel or place in a tortilla warmer. Continue with the remaining dough, stacking the warm tortillas as you go.

Cook's Note

▸ If you plan to eat the tortillas the same day, you can keep them wrapped in the towel. If you don't use them all, put the remaining stack in a plastic bag, seal it, and refrigerate. The tortillas will keep for 3 to 4 days. Reheat on a hot comal, griddle, or large skillet over medium-low heat for a minute or so per side.

FROM PLOWSHARES
TO TORTILLA GRIDDLES

Huge flour tortillas from northern Mexico are called *sobaqueras,* so named because women pass them from arm to arm when making them, then stretch them the length of their arms, right up to their armpits—*sobacos* in Spanish. Sobaqueras are very thin and used for chimichangas and burritos. Traditionally they were cooked on plowshares, or disks—*discos de arado*—that were no longer in use in the fields and given a second life as comals or griddles. Sobaqueras are also called *tortillas de agua,* because they are made with more water than other flour tortillas. When the *discos de arado* are set over the wood fire, typically mesquite, they are placed curved side up for tortillas, which are stretched thin, set on the hot griddle, and cooked quickly on both sides.

CHUBBY FLOUR TORTILLAS / **TORTILLAS DE HARINA GORDITAS**

Makes 16 tortillas

These luscious tortillas are sweeter and thicker than other flour tortillas. They are made with evaporated milk instead of water, and with more fat, which is why they also go by the name *tortillas gorditas* or *tortillas gorditas de manteca,* whether or not they actually use pork lard. Sonorans adore them, especially as the wrappers for chubby quesadillas or sincronizadas, spread with Fiesta Refried Beans (page 159) and cheese.

This dough is much stickier than the flour tortilla dough on page 108. It's almost like a wet biscuit dough. In fact, the tortillas are so flaky that they remind me of Southern biscuits—if Southern biscuits were thinner and flatter and pliable. You can use a stand mixer fitted with the paddle attachment or knead the dough by hand. At first you won't believe that it will become workable, but after 10 minutes of beating or kneading, it will be. Have faith, enjoy the process, and give yourself time; the tortillas will be incredible, and they're really fun to make.

3⅔ cups (1 pound) all-purpose flour, plus ¼ cup for finishing the tortillas

1½ teaspoons kosher salt

1 cup plus 2 tablespoons vegetable shortening, plus 2 tablespoons for the balls of dough

1 (12-ounce) can evaporated milk

Combine the flour and salt in the bowl of a stand mixer fitted with the paddle attachment, or in a large bowl. Add the vegetable shortening by spoonfuls or chunks, mixing on low speed or with your fingertips, until the fat is broken into very small pieces and evenly distributed through the flour. Add the evaporated milk in 4 or 5 additions, beating on low speed or folding it into the flour in a circular motion with your hands, scraping the flour up from the bottom of the bowl and working from the center out to the edges of the bowl. If using a mixer, increase the speed to medium and beat for 7 to 8 minutes, until the dough is elastic and no longer sticky. If you are kneading by hand, the dough will be very sticky and lumpy at first, but as you continue to knead, it will become smoother, more elastic, and less wet. After 8 to 10 minutes, the dough should be completely smooth and springy to the touch; it will still be a bit sticky.

Gather the dough into a ball, put it back in the bowl, and cover the bowl with a clean kitchen towel. Let rest for 20 to 30 minutes.

Divide the dough in half. Grab one piece and squeeze out 1½-inch balls of dough between your thumb and index fingers; you should get 8 balls. Set them on the counter as you go. Repeat with the other half of the dough. Alternatively, divide the dough in half, then in half again, and repeat until you have 16 pieces. Sprinkle the ¼ cup flour over a work space and grease your palms with 1 tablespoon of the remaining shortening. Roll each ball in your hands to grease it, then roll generously in the flour and return to the bowl, or place the balls on a baking sheet. Repeat with the remaining dough and shortening. Cover the balls with a kitchen towel and set aside to rest for 20 to 30 minutes.

Preheat a comal, griddle, or large skillet over medium-low heat for at least 5 minutes (preheating is important so the tortillas don't stick and burn).

Lightly flour a work surface and your rolling pin and, one at a time, roll out each ball into a ⅛-inch-thick tortilla. Rotate the dough on your work surface 5 or 6 times as you roll it out, and don't worry if you don't get perfect rounds. As soon as you are finished rolling out each tortilla, put it on the pan and cook for about a minute, until you begin to see bubbles forming on top. Check to see if the bottom has become a little freckled and, if so, turn the tortilla and cook on the second side until it puffs up and the bottom begins to freckle. Remove and wrap in a clean kitchen towel or place in a tortilla warmer. Continue with the remaining dough, stacking the tortillas in the towel or tortilla warmer as you go.

Cook's Notes

▶ You may not get your tortillas perfectly round, but that's okay. Be patient and concentrate on the end result: deliciousness rather than exact rounds. The shape can even be an irregular oval; it will still make for good eating, whether as a wrapper or on its own. Have faith that the more you make them, the nicer your rounds will become.

▶ If you plan to eat the tortillas the same day, you can keep them wrapped in the towel. If you don't use them all, put the remaining stack in a plastic bag, seal it, and refrigerate. The tortillas will keep for 3 to 4 days. Reheat on a hot comal, griddle, or large skillet over medium-low heat for a minute or so per side.

Corn tortillas were the only type of tortilla in Mexico before the Spanish arrived. A nutritious staple, they varied in color from place to place, since different types of corn were used—white, blue, pink, yellow, and purple, as well as cacahuacintle (hominy or giant corn). But regardless of variety, the corn was always processed in the same way. The dried kernels were soaked in water with an alkaline ingredient such as ashes or slaked lime, a process called nixtamalization, to loosen the hulls and make the nutrients more available. Then they were ground into a masa, or dough. The masa was made into tortillas and numerous other shapes. The Aztecs called tortillas *tlaxcalli,* and there were many other names for them in other pre-Hispanic civilizations. *Tortilla* became the Spanish word for them.

When the Spanish arrived in the New World in the late fifteenth century, they were unfamiliar with corn. Having brought wheat with them, they adapted the tradition of tortilla making but substituted wheat flour for corn. In the beginning, they prepared their tortillas with just flour, water, and salt, but over time, they began to add lard (another Spanish legacy), because it produced a more malleable dough and allowed the tortillas to remain soft for a longer time.

To the Spanish missionaries, wheat was crucial—and not only because it was a staple. The bread symbolized the body of Christ in the Catholic communion service, and part of the strong push to evangelize the native population of Mexico involved getting them to substitute wheat flour for corn masa in their tortillas.

Today, the flour tortilla is ingrained in the cultural and gastronomic landscape of the country, especially in the northern wheat-producing regions. Flour tortillas are traditionally used there in quesadillas and burritos, and certain kinds of tacos, like the traditional Sonoran Carne Asada Tacos (page 72), are always made with flour tortillas.

There are many unwritten rules about which tortillas are to be used for which dishes. Some of these make a lot of sense, like the use of corn tortillas for deep-fried taquitos, such as the Drowned Crispy Beef and Potato Taquitos on page 69 and the Chicken Codzitos on page 66, or for chilaquiles, because they crisp and crunch so nicely and they're resilient. Mexican cooks always use corn tortillas for enchiladas as well, because corn tortillas will not get as soggy or cardboardy when drenched with sauce. But many rules are really just passed-down traditions, so there is flexibility. The more you make and eat tortillas, the more you will understand these rules and customs.

HOMEMADE CORN TORTILLAS / **TORTILLAS DE MAÍZ**

Makes 12 tortillas

There is nothing, *nothing,* like a freshly made corn tortilla, hot off the comal. It's soft and pliable, with spots of earthy char on the surface and edges. You can't resist eating them plain, with a little salt—what we in Mexico call a *taco de nada.*

Since they are readily available all over Mexico, fresh from *tortillerias,* not many people learn to make corn tortillas at home. I didn't grow up doing it, but I missed fresh tortillas so much when I first came to the U.S. that I learned how. You may mess up a few before you get the technique down (see the tips on the opposite page), but I promise you, eventually you'll nail it.

2 cups masa harina

Pinch of kosher salt

1¾ to 2 cups warm water

Cut two 9-inch circles or squares from a thin plastic bag, such as a produce bag or ziplock bag. Heat a comal, griddle, or large skillet over medium-low heat for 8 to 10 minutes while you mix the dough.

In a large bowl, combine the masa harina and salt. Add 1¾ cups water and, using your hand, mix until smooth, using a circular motion. Once the dough is all mixed together, knead it a little so that it is uniform. It should have the consistency of Play-Doh and should not be wet or sticky. If it feels too dry—if it crumbles when you begin to make the masa balls—add a little more water, a teaspoon at a time. (If you are not making the tortillas right away, cover the masa with a damp kitchen towel. The dough dries out quickly.)

One by one, pinch off pieces of dough and shape into balls about 1½ inches in diameter; you should get 12 balls of dough.

If using a tortilla press, line it with one of the pieces of plastic. Place a dough ball on top. Place the other piece of plastic on top of the dough ball, close the tortilla press, and press down, not too hard. Alternatively, you can roll the plastic-covered dough out with a rolling pin. The tortillas should be about ⅛ inch thick and about 5 inches in diameter. If the edges of the first tortilla you make are cracked and jagged, you need to add a little more water to the dough. If the edges are smooth, you're good to go.

Open the press, if using, and carefully peel off the top piece of plastic, or peel off the plastic from the rolled-out tortilla. Lift the tortilla up, flip it onto your other hand, carefully peel off the plastic, and quickly but gently lay the tortilla on the hot pan. If it isn't perfectly flat, don't worry. Let it sit without moving it for 30 to 40 seconds, or it will tear. Once you can easily lift the tortilla from the pan, with a spatula or your fingers, turn it over. It should be lightly colored, but not browned, on the first side. Leave for a minute on the second side, until opaque and beginning to freckle and brown. If it is opaque but not freckled, leave for another 30 seconds or so, until brown spots appear.

Turn the tortilla once more. After 15 seconds or so, it should begin to puff in places, which means it is cooking internally. If it doesn't puff, gently poke the tortilla in a few places near the center with your finger. Once it puffs, let it cook for about 20 seconds more, until fully cooked and soft. Remove and wrap in a clean kitchen towel or place in a tortilla warmer. Continue with the remaining dough, stacking the tortillas as you go.

If you plan to eat the tortillas the same day, you can keep them in the kitchen towel or tortilla warmer. If not, put the stack in a plastic bag, seal, and refrigerate. They will keep for 3 days. (After that, they will be too hard.) They can also be frozen, well wrapped, for up to 3 months (thaw before reheating). To reheat, heat a comal, griddle, or skillet for at least 5 minutes over medium-low heat and heat the tortillas for about a minute on each side.

TIPS FOR MAKING CORN TORTILLAS

- ► Invest in a tortilla press; they aren't expensive at all. You can roll out the dough with a rolling pin, but the tortilla press makes this process much easier and your tortillas will be uniform.
- ► Make sure that the water you add to the masa harina is lukewarm or warm.
- ► The amount of water may vary a bit, depending on the weather. It's important that you feel the dough: It should be like Play-Doh. If the edges of your first tortilla are cracked, the masa is too dry; add more water, a teaspoon or two at a time, to the remaining masa. If the dough is too wet, it will stick stubbornly to the sheet of plastic. If that is the case, add a bit more masa harina to the dough, or just leave it uncovered for 5 minutes; the dough dries out quickly if left uncovered.
- ► As you make the tortillas, keep the remaining dough covered with a clean kitchen towel so that it doesn't dry out.
- ► Rub the base of the tortilla press with a little bit of water before you line it so the plastic doesn't move around.
- ► Make sure your comal or griddle (or skillet) is hot before cooking the tortillas. Heat it for 8 to 10 minutes over medium heat. If it is not hot enough, the tortillas will stick.
- ► Don't use heat higher than medium. If the pan is too hot, the tortillas will burn.
- ► Let the tortilla sit on the comal for 30 to 40 seconds without moving it. Even if you didn't put it on evenly and there are little folds or wrinkles, it will sort itself out. If you try to move it, it will tear.
- ► You turn corn tortillas not once, but twice. After 30 to 40 seconds on the first side, turn and leave for about a minute, then turn again.
- ► After the second turn, if the tortilla doesn't puff, poke it gently with your finger in several places so it puffs. If the tortillas don't puff, they won't fully cook inside.

SALSAS, PICKLES, AND GUACAMOLES

The world of Mexican salsas is wide and deep, familiar and unfamiliar, local and widespread. Think about how salsa-crazy America has become over the last twenty years or so, then imagine that obsession as a culture that goes back thousands of years. Our salsas are raw and cooked; smooth and chunky; fiery, smoky, and mild; fruity and nutty; made with fresh chiles and with dried. They contain ingredients that were known in Mexico long before the Spanish arrived—chiles and tomatoes, tomatillos and avocados, peanuts, fragrant herbs and seeds—and some that came with the conquistadores or with immigrants who arrived later from other places.

As I've crisscrossed the country over the last decade, I've found certain standard salsas on the tables of taquerias and family eateries everywhere, like tomato and jalapeño salsa, salsa verde, and street-style salsa. But at every turn, I've also found variations that open and multiply the paths that salsa can take. Sometimes the tomatoes, tomatillos, onion, and chile are roasted, while other times they are simmered. In most cases, it's the choice of chiles that ends up setting a salsa apart and stamping it with a regional identity. In Mexico City, jalapeños heat up a salsa, whereas in the northern states, mild-mannered chiles verdes—what we know as Anaheims—define its personality.

Certain salsas are associated with specific dishes. If you are in the Yucatán and eating the grilled pork dish poc chuc (page 319), you will be served the habanero-spiced tomato salsa chiltomate (page 126), with charred red onion pickles alongside. The "drunken" salsa called *borracha* (page 136), typically made with pulque (or beer) and pasilla chiles, goes hand in hand with Lamb Barbacoa (page 291) and slow-cooked lamb (page 287) in the central part of the country, where these dishes prevail.

Just as cooks throughout Mexico have many ways of varying salsa, they take many different approaches to guacamole. In the central part of the country, a mash of roasted chiles, garlic, and onion delivers a smoky undercurrent to the luxurious avocado. In the north, Sonorans mix their guac with roasted Anaheims and diced serranos and are adamant about never using lime juice. In Mexico City, though, guacamole always has lime. Sometimes the avocados are blended with tomatillos and seasonings, with a result that's more like a thick salsa.

But regardless of their regional origins or whether it is classified as a salsa, pickle, or guacamole, or considered a hybrid, the condiments in this chapter will brighten a simple taco, add a wow element to avocado toast, and make that grilled chicken stand out above the rest.

ROASTED SALSA VERDE / **SALSA VERDE ASADA**

Makes about 2 cups

Salsa verde—green salsa—has tomatillos as a base, and there are many versions of it, with one or another type of chile, and with variations on the onion, cilantro, garlic, and sometimes spices. Some are raw, some simmered, and some roasted. The same ingredients will yield a salsa with completely different characteristics depending on how they are cooked, or if they are cooked at all.

Here roasting gives the salsa a fabulously rustic taste and texture, intensifying and sweetening the flavors so they contrast beautifully with the bitterness of the charred bits of the tomatillos, chiles, garlic, and onion. Use this on anything and everything.

1 pound tomatillos, husked and rinsed

2 garlic cloves, not peeled

1 to 2 serrano or jalapeño chiles

1 thick slice medium white onion

1 cup coarsely chopped fresh cilantro leaves and upper stems

¾ teaspoon kosher salt, or to taste

Preheat the broiler, with the rack 2 to 3 inches from the heat source. Put the tomatillos, garlic, chiles, and onion on a baking sheet lined with foil and broil, turning the vegetables halfway through, until they are charred and the tomatillos are mushy, 5 to 7 minutes for the garlic and 10 to 12 minutes for the other ingredients. Remove the garlic when it is charred and softened and, when it's cool enough to handle, peel it. Alternatively, you can toast the vegetables on a comal or large skillet over medium-low heat, turning every 4 to 5 minutes, until charred. Remove from the heat.

Transfer all the vegetables to a blender or molcajete. Add the cilantro and salt and coarsely puree in the blender or mash in the molcajete. Taste and adjust the seasonings.

The salsa will keep, tightly covered, for up to 5 days in the refrigerator or for up to 2 months in the freezer.

Variations

There are many ways to transform tomatillos and chiles into a salsa verde. See the variations on the following page.

continued

RAW SALSA VERDE / **SALSA VERDE CRUDA**

Makes about 2 cups

This is the simplest salsa verde, but the most vivid, because the ingredients are not cooked and their colors and textures remain bright. Tomatillos, onion, lots of cilantro, and chiles are pulsed in a blender to a chunky puree. I never add garlic, since raw garlic would compete with the flavors of the other ingredients. I prefer a coarse texture, but you can also puree it until smooth. *The photo is on page 125.*

1 pound tomatillos, husked, rinsed, and quartered

2 tablespoons coarsely chopped white onion

1 cup coarsely chopped fresh cilantro leaves and upper stems

1 to 2 serrano or jalapeño chiles (to taste; I sometimes use one of each)

¾ teaspoon kosher salt, or to taste

Place all the ingredients in a blender and pulse to a chunky puree. (You may want to add one chile at a time and check the heat level.)

The salsa can be refrigerated, tightly covered, for up to 3 days.

Cook's Notes

▶ Substitute chipotles in adobo sauce for the serranos and/or jalapeños. They will add a sweet, smoky flavor.

▶ Instead of the fresh chiles, use chiles de árbol, gently toasted, for a smoky, spicy flavor.

COOKED SALSA VERDE / **SALSA VERDE COCIDA**

Makes about 2 cups

This salsa verde is smoother than Raw Salsa Verde (at left), but I don't puree it to the point of losing the juicy texture of the tomatillo seeds. It's more versatile than the uncooked version. Not only can you drizzle it over countless foods, but you can also use it as a base for braised dishes, stews, enchiladas, chilaquiles, and more. *The photo is on page 129.*

1 pound tomatillos, husked and rinsed

1 garlic clove

1 to 2 serrano or jalapeño chiles

2 tablespoons coarsely chopped white onion

1 cup coarsely chopped fresh cilantro leaves and upper stems

¾ teaspoon kosher salt, or to taste

Place the tomatillos, garlic, and chiles in a medium saucepan and cover with water. Bring to a boil, reduce the heat to medium, and cook until the color of the tomatillos has changed from bright green to a more muted green and they are soft and mushy, about 10 minutes. Drain.

Transfer the tomatillos, garlic, and chiles to a blender, along with the onion, cilantro, and salt. (You may want to add one chile at a time and check the heat level.) Puree until fairly smooth, but not so smooth that the seeds aren't visible; they give the salsa a nice texture.

The salsa will keep, tightly covered, for up to 5 days in the refrigerator or for up to 2 months in the freezer.

Cook's Note

► Substitute fresh epazote for the cilantro. I usually do this when I am using the salsa for chilaquiles.

TWICE-COOKED SALSA VERDE / **SALSA VERDE SAZONADA OR GUISADA**

Makes about 2 cups without broth, 2¾ cups with broth

When you sear a cooked salsa in hot oil for a few minutes, until it changes color and thickens slightly, the flavors blend and intensify. Chicken broth is often added, which contributes depth and marries all the elements. This heftier, more complex salsa is often used as a base for a chicken *guisado* (stew), as well as for chilaquiles, which may be topped with sunny-side-up eggs, cheese, or chicken.

1 pound tomatillos, husked and rinsed

1 to 2 serrano or jalapeño chiles

1 garlic clove

2 tablespoons coarsely chopped white onion

1 cup coarsely chopped fresh cilantro leaves and upper stems

¾ teaspoon kosher salt, or to taste

1 tablespoon vegetable oil

1 cup chicken broth (optional)

Place the tomatillos, chiles, and garlic in a medium saucepan and cover with water. Bring to a boil, reduce the heat to medium, and cook until the color of the tomatillos has changed from bright green to a more muted green and they are soft and mushy, about 10 minutes. Drain and transfer to a blender, along with the onion, cilantro, and salt. (You may want to add one chile at a time and check the heat level.) Puree until smooth.

Heat the oil in a medium saucepan over medium heat until very hot but not smoking. Pour in the salsa, along with the broth, if using, and cook, stirring occasionally, until the salsa thickens and darkens and the flavors intensify, 5 to 6 minutes. Remove from the heat.

The salsa will keep, tightly covered, for up to 5 days in the refrigerator or for up to 2 months in the freezer.

FIRE-ROASTED SONORAN CHUNKY SALSA / **SALSA TATEMADA NORTEÑA**

Makes about 2 cups

Each region of Mexico has its version of fire-roasted or charred salsa. These go by names such as *tatemada* (charred), in Sonora; *martajada* (mashed), in Oaxaca; or *tamulada*, for the implement used to mash the roasted ingredients, in the Yucatán. The fire-roasted salsa that rules a region is mostly defined by its signature chile. In the northern states of Sonora, Sinaloa, and Chihuahua, that chile is the Anaheim—chile verde—also known as the New Mexico, Fresno, or California chile.

This salsa is a must for a carne asada cookout. The ingredients usually hit the grill before the meat is thrown on. It's a substantial salsa, almost like a roasted vegetable salad, and not spicy at all. I learned it from my friend Jose Luis Lambarri; it's very common in Ciudad Obregón, where he lives. In addition to the traditional chile verde, tomatoes, and onion, he adds roasted garlic and a squeeze of lemon. I was surprised to see the lemon juice, since lemons don't come from the region. I learned that they have become a big export crop over the last decade in Sonora, and so many Sonorans have begun to use them in their own kitchens as well.

1 pound tomatoes (see note)

½ pound fresh Anaheim (aka New Mexico or Fresno) chiles

¼ large white onion, cut in half

1 to 2 garlic cloves, not peeled

1 tablespoon freshly squeezed lemon juice, or to taste

¾ teaspoon kosher salt, or to taste

Preheat the broiler, with the rack 2 to 3 inches from the heat source. Put the tomatoes, chiles, onion, and garlic cloves on a baking sheet lined with foil and broil, turning the vegetables halfway through, until they are charred and the tomatoes are mushy and beginning to release their juices, about 5 to 7 minutes for the garlic and 10 to 12 minutes for the other vegetables. Remove the garlic when it is charred and softened. Alternatively, you can toast the vegetables on a comal or skillet over medium heat, turning them every 4 to 5 minutes, until charred. (And you can grill the vegetables on an outdoor grill if preparing a carne asada or another cookout.) Remove from the heat.

Place the chiles in a plastic bag and seal the bag, or put them in a bowl and cover the bowl tightly with plastic. Allow to sweat and cool. Stem, peel, and seed the chiles under a thin stream of water. Coarsely chop.

While the chiles are cooling, peel the garlic cloves and coarsely chop. Coarsely chop the roasted tomatoes (don't remove the skin, seeds, or cores) and onion. Combine the chiles, garlic, tomatoes, and onion in a bowl and mix together, or mash them together in a molcajete. Add the lemon juice and salt.

The salsa will keep, tightly covered, for up to 5 days in the refrigerator.

Cook's Note

▶ You can substitute 1 (15-ounce) can fire-roasted tomatoes for the roasted fresh tomatoes; add them to the bowl along with the chiles.

STREET-STYLE SALSA / **SALSA CALLEJERA**

Makes a generous 3 cups

Almost every famous taqueria has a secret signature salsa, a *callejera* (which refers to being on the street), a *salsa especial* that they know their customers will like and will associate with their establishment. This one is mine. Slightly chunky, it brings together sweet tomatoes with acidic tomatillos, fresh green chiles with smoky dried ones, and adds onion, garlic, a pinch of cumin, and cilantro to the mix. *The photo is on the opposite page.*

2 dried chiles de árbol, stemmed, or more to taste

1½ pounds ripe tomatoes or 1 (28-ounce) can whole tomatoes

½ pound tomatillos (about 4), husked and rinsed

1 to 2 jalapeños, or to taste

1 garlic clove, peeled

2 tablespoons coarsely chopped white onion

½ cup coarsely chopped fresh cilantro leaves and upper stems

⅛ teaspoon ground cumin

¾ teaspoon kosher salt, or to taste

1 tablespoon vegetable oil

Heat a comal or small skillet over medium-low heat. Add the chiles de árbol and toast for about a minute, turning them once, until toasted and fragrant. Remove from the heat.

Place the fresh tomatoes, if using, tomatillos, jalapeños, and garlic in a medium saucepan, cover with water, and bring to a boil. Reduce the heat to medium and simmer for about 10 minutes, until the tomatoes and tomatillos are mushy and the jalapeños have softened and their color has dulled.

Using a slotted spoon, transfer the tomatoes, tomatillos, jalapeños, and garlic to a blender. Add the canned tomatoes, if using, and the chiles de árbol, onion, cilantro, cumin, and salt and pulse to a chunky puree.

Heat a medium saucepan over medium heat and add the oil. Once the oil is hot, pour in the salsa—be ready to partially cover the pan with the lid, as it will splatter. Cook for 4 to 5 minutes, stirring often, until the salsa has thickened, the color has deepened, and the flavors have come together. Remove from the heat and serve warm or at room temperature.

The salsa will keep, tightly covered, for up to 5 days in the refrigerator.

CHILE DE ÁRBOL—LOTS OF HEAT IN A SMALL PACKAGE

The chile de árbol is a shiny red-orange, delicate-looking dried chile, small (anywhere from 2 to 3 inches long), slender, smooth, and tapering to a point. When toasted and crushed, this chile will not only spice up a salsa or dressing but also add a deeper flavor. The chile de árbol goes by other names, such as *bravo* (aggressive or brave), because of its heat; *pico de paloma* (dove's beak); and *cola de rata* (rat's tail), because of its thin, pointy shape.

I use chiles de árbol to add a spicy punch to all kinds of dishes, from salsas to salad dressings to vegetable dishes to soups and stews.

Clockwise from bottom left: RAW SALSA VERDE / SALSA VERDE CRUDA (PAGE 120); CHIPOTLE PEANUT SALSA / SALSA DE CHIPOTLE Y CACAHUATE (PAGE 132); PICKLED RED ONIONS (PAGE 71); STREET-STYLE SALSA / SALSA CALLEJERA (OPPOSITE PAGE)

YUCATECAN TOMATO-HABANERO SALSA / **CHILTOMATE**

Makes 3 cups

When you taste the fiery but fruity heat of this salsa, you taste the Yucatán. Charring the habaneros tames them a little bit, but to play it safe, you should begin by only adding half of the chile(s) to the molcajete with the other ingredients. Try a bite of the salsa and add more of the chile if you're up for more heat.

> 1½ **pounds tomatoes (see note)**
>
> ¼ **white onion**
>
> 1 **to 2 fresh habanero chiles**
>
> 1 **cup coarsely chopped fresh cilantro leaves and upper stems**
>
> ¾ **teaspoon kosher salt, or to taste**

Preheat the broiler, with the rack 2 to 3 inches from the heat source. Put the tomatoes, onion, and habanero(s) on a baking sheet lined with foil and broil for 10 to 12 minutes, turning the vegetables halfway through, until they are charred and the tomatoes are mushy. The habaneros may be done before the tomatoes and onions; keep your eye on them so they don't burn. Alternatively, you can toast the vegetables on a hot comal or skillet over medium heat, turning them every 4 to 5 minutes, until charred. Remove from the heat.

Chop the charred onion. Chop the tomatoes. Seed and chop the habaneros.

Place the tomatoes in a molcajete or bowl and mash them. Stir in the onion, cilantro, and salt, then add half the habanero, and mash until well mixed. Taste for heat and add more habanero, if desired, and adjust the salt. Alternatively, you can make this in a food processor or blender. Pulse until thoroughly combined but still chunky.

The salsa can be refrigerated, tightly covered, for up to 5 days.

Cook's Note

► You can substitute 1 (28-ounce) can fire-roasted tomatoes for the roasted fresh tomatoes. Mash them with the charred onion and habaneros.

HABANEROS: HOT, HOT, HOT!

Habaneros are so iconic in Yucatecan culture that they even have their own president! The region is the largest producer of the chiles in the world, and they are of such high quality that they were granted a Certification of Origin in 2018, meaning that only Yucatecan habaneros can be exported from Mexico.

My boys and I toured a huge habanero farm on the Yucatán Peninsula and watched incredulously as the president of the habanero association bit into a ripe, red-orange chile as if it were an apple. He didn't even break a sweat.

Habaneros are the hottest chile in traditional Mexican cuisine (300,000 to 350,000 on the Scoville scale, which measures chile pepper heat, compared to 10,000 to 15,000 for the jalapeño). But heat isn't the only thing that stands out with these colorful, shiny chiles that look a little bit like miniature bell peppers. They have a lively aroma and flavor to go along with their spicy taste.

You don't need a lot of habanero to spice up a dish, and I suggest that you begin at the low end of the range with my recipes. And seed them so that the heat isn't overwhelming; you will still get plenty of spice.

PASILLA AND TOMATILLO SALSA / **SALSA DE PASILLA CON TOMATE VERDE**

Makes about 3 cups

The combination of deliciously bitter pasilla chiles with tart tomatillos is characteristic of the food of the northwestern Purépecha region of Michoacán, one of Mexico's most underappreciated and, in my opinion, exquisite, regional cuisines. The sweetness of the roasted onion and garlic is accentuated with a spoonful of piloncillo (or dark brown sugar) and salt. It all comes together in one of the most delicious, easy, and yet complex sauces I have ever tasted. I particularly like it with green vegetables, pinto beans, or grilled meats.

2 pounds tomatillos, husked and rinsed

3 garlic cloves, not peeled

¼ large white onion, cut into chunks

5 dried pasilla chiles, stemmed and seeded

1 tablespoon dark brown sugar or grated piloncillo, or to taste

1 teaspoon kosher salt, or to taste

Preheat the broiler, with the rack 2 to 3 inches from the heat source. Put the tomatillos, garlic cloves, and onion on a baking sheet lined with foil and broil, turning the vegetables halfway through, until they are charred and the tomatillos are mushy, 5 to 7 minutes for the garlic and 10 to 12 minutes for the other vegetables. Remove the garlic when charred and softened and when it is cool enough to handle, peel it. Alternatively, you can toast the vegetables on a hot comal or skillet over medium heat, turning them every 4 to 5 minutes, until charred and softened. Remove from the heat.

Place the pasilla chiles in a small saucepan, cover with water, and bring to a boil. Reduce the heat to medium and simmer for about 10 minutes, until the chiles have softened.

Transfer the chiles to a blender, along with ½ cup of the cooking liquid. Add the charred tomatillos, onion, and garlic, the brown sugar or pilloncillo, and the salt. Puree until smooth. Taste for sugar and salt, and adjust if desired.

The salsa can be refrigerated, tightly covered, for up to 5 days. Stir well before using.

PASILLA CHILES

The pasilla chile is the dried form of the slender, dark green chilaca, the most common chile of Michoacán. In towns across the state, hundreds of chilacas dry on mats in the sun, turning soft, wrinkled, and almost black.

Pasillas have a complex, earthy flavor. Used in salsas and soups, rubs and marinades, stews and moles, they are mildly spicy, with a pleasant bitter edge. The chile sometimes goes by other names, such as *chile negro* (black) or *pasilla negro*. Do not confuse it with the *pasilla ancho*, which is the name ancho chiles often go by in California and some other places, a very confusing development! Anchos are much sweeter than pasillas and have a chubbier, flatter shape, with a greater flesh-to-skin ratio. Nor should the pasilla be confused with the pasilla de Oaxaca, which is a much spicier chile.

COLORADO CHILE RED SALSA / **SALSA ROJA DE CHILE COLORADO**

Makes about 2 cups

Salsa roja (red), like green salsa, comes in many iterations. Sometimes the ingredients are raw, sometimes they are simmered, sometimes they are roasted and charred. The mix of ingredients—onions, chiles, garlic, herbs—can vary, but the base is always tomatoes.

This easy recipe is a great one to have in your repertoire. It's a basic red salsa made with tomatoes, onion, and garlic, but the chiles are dried colorados (guajillos can be substituted), rather than fresh serranos or jalapeños. When these dried chiles stand in for fresh, you get an entirely different type of salsa, just a tad spicy but with a rich, earthy flavor and a thicker texture. It may seem like a small change, but it completely transforms the sauce.

Use this to bathe chiles rellenos, to dress tacos and quesadillas, to drizzle over cornbread or eggs, or in a tasty stewing sauce for meat, chicken, vegetables, or beans. *The photo is on the opposite page.*

1 pound ripe tomatoes or 1 (15-ounce) can whole tomatoes

2 dried colorado chiles, stemmed and seeded

2 garlic cloves, peeled

¼ cup coarsely chopped white onion

1 teaspoon kosher salt, or to taste

½ teaspoon freshly ground black pepper

2 tablespoons vegetable oil

Combine the fresh tomatoes, if using, chiles, and garlic in a medium saucepan, cover with water, and bring to a boil over medium-high heat. Reduce the heat to medium and simmer for 10 to 15 minutes, until the tomatoes are cooked and mushy and the chiles are soft.

Using a slotted spoon, transfer the tomatoes, chiles, and garlic to a blender. Add the canned tomatoes, if using, the onion, salt, and pepper and puree until smooth.

Heat the oil in a medium saucepan over medium heat. Pour in the tomato sauce, cover partially, and simmer for 5 to 6 minutes, stirring occasionally, until the flavors and color have deepened and the sauce has thickened slightly. Serve hot, warm, at room temperature, or chilled.

The salsa will keep, tightly covered, for up to 5 days in the refrigerator or for up to 2 months in the freezer.

Variations

► For a regular cooked salsa roja, I simmer tomatoes, garlic, and serrano or jalapeño until soft and puree them with raw onion and salt, but no cilantro. When I make the salsa for chilaquiles, I add a lot of epazote.

► For a thicker salsa with a deeper tomato flavor, I give it a second cooking in a bit of oil to intensify the taste. Sometimes I add chicken broth and use the salsa as a base for a stew or a soup.

► For a rustic taste, roast the ingredients (except for the herbs) instead of boiling them, either under a broiler or on a comal or skillet. Instead of blending, make the sauce chunky by mashing or pulsing the ingredients.

Clockwise from top left: COOKED SALSA VERDE / SALSA VERDE COCIDA (PAGE 120); COLORADO CHILE RED SALSA / SALSA ROJA DE CHILE COLORADO (OPPOSITE PAGE); SALSA BANDERA WITH JICAMA AND PINEAPPLE / SALSA BANDERA CON JICAMA Y PIÑA (PAGE 138); ROASTED TOMATO AND JALAPEÑO SALSITA / SALSITA ASADA DE JITOMATE Y JALAPEÑO (PAGE 130)

ROASTED TOMATO AND JALAPEÑO SALSITA / **SALSITA ASADA DE JITOMATE Y JALAPEÑO**

Makes a generous 1½ cups

This tasty salsa has only three ingredients (and one of them is salt)—it's amazing how something so simple can be so exquisite. But the devil is in the details. The tomatoes must be ripe, the jalapeños fresh, bright, and hot. Then all they need is a nice char to bring out their sweet, concentrated flavors before being mashed in their entirety, including the burnt skin and the juicy cooked seeds.

This salsita is perfect for almost everything. It's a great topping for tacos, quesadillas, sopes, or tamales, and it's also luscious spooned over beans or eggs. It's at its best right after you mash and mix it. *The photo is on page 129.*

> **1 pound tomatoes (see note)**
>
> **1 to 2 jalapeños**
>
> **¾ teaspoon kosher salt, or to taste**

Preheat the broiler, with the rack 2 to 3 inches from the heat source. Put the tomatoes and jalapeños on a baking sheet lined with foil. Broil for 10 to 12 minutes, turning every 4 to 5 minutes, until the skins are completely charred, the tomatoes and chiles are mushy and soft, and the tomatoes have begun to release their juices. (The tomatoes may take a little longer than the jalapeños.) Alternatively, you can char the tomatoes and jalapeños on a preheated comal or skillet over medium heat for the same amount of time, turning them until charred. Remove from the heat, and when they are cool enough to handle, remove the stems (if any) from the jalapeños.

Place the charred tomatoes and jalapeños in a molcajete, add the salt, and mash to the desired chunkiness. Or put everything in the blender and pulse a few times.

The salsa can be refrigerated, tightly covered, for up to 5 days.

Cook's Note

► You can substitute 1 (15-ounce) can fire-roasted tomatoes for the roasted fresh tomatoes. Combine them with the roasted jalapeños and salt and proceed as directed.

WHEN IS A SALSA A SALSITA?

The answer to this question is very Mexican. We add *ito* or *ita* to things we love. I could be ten feet tall, but if you are fond of me, it is likely that you will call me not Pati, but Patita. A salsa may be a salsita because it has an endearing look, or because it is one that is deeply loved, or just because!

Generally speaking, a cooked salsa that is used as a base for a stew or enchiladas would not be called a salsita. But then again, if you had a very small amount of that serious salsa left on your plate, you'd want to sop it up with a piece of a bread or a tortilla, and you'd use the word *salsita* because there is just a tiny bit left.

But let's say someone presents you with a masterful salsa and you say, "Oh, what is this salsita?" The person might take offense because it sounds like you consider it too little a thing. You can always fix that by saying "*¡Que rica salsita!*" Tone matters.

GUACAMOLE SALSA / **SALSA DE GUACAMOLE**

Makes about 2½ cups

As its name suggests, salsa de guac is a cross between a salsa verde and guacamole. It is a blend of tomatillos that have been simmered with chiles and garlic, onion, and lots of cilantro, with avocado added to the mix, and has the creamy texture of a thin, pourable guacamole. I like the heat of serranos here, but I also like the grassy flavor of jalapeños, so I use one of each. The salsa is fairly spicy, but you can make it more or less picante, to your taste, by cutting back on the chiles. If you want a thicker mixture—more guac than salsa—add more avocado.

- **1 pound tomatillos, husked and rinsed**
- **1 garlic clove, peeled**
- **1 jalapeño chile**
- **1 serrano chile**
- **2 tablespoons coarsely chopped white onion**
- **1 cup coarsely chopped fresh cilantro leaves and upper stems**
- **1 large ripe avocado, halved, pitted, and flesh scooped out**
- **1 teaspoon kosher salt, or to taste**

Combine the tomatillos, garlic clove, and chiles in a medium saucepan, cover with water, and bring to a boil over medium-high heat. Reduce the heat to medium and simmer for 10 to 12 minutes, until the tomatillos are mushy and very soft but have not begun to break apart.

With a slotted spoon, transfer the tomatillos, chiles, and garlic to a blender. Add the onion, cilantro, avocado, and salt and puree until smooth.

Serve at once, or transfer to a container, placing a sheet of plastic wrap directly against the surface before topping with the lid to keep the nice green color. The salsa can be refrigerated for a couple of days. Stir before you use it.

FOR DIRECT HEAT, GO FOR SERRANOS

Serranos are a mainstay in my kitchen. I find them much more reliable than jalapeños when it comes to flavor and heat (and their heat is considerable), so even though I give you a choice in many recipes, serranos are usually my pick.

These smooth, slender, bright, and dark green chiles are usually 1 to 2 inches long, occasionally as long as 3 inches, but they are always only about ½ inch wide at the stem end, and taper to a point. Serranos are not as fleshy as jalapeños, but every bit packs a grassy, fragrant punch. If you want to moderate the heat, remove the seeds and veins, where most of the heat— the capsaicin—resides.

CHIPOTLE PEANUT SALSA / **SALSA DE CHIPOTLE Y CACAHUATE**

Makes about 3 cups

Once considered a specialty, this rich, creamy salsa has slowly but surely migrated to the world of must-have table salsas. Why? One taste and you'll understand. It feels luxurious in the mouth, thick and velvety, crunchy and substantial, with a smoky, spicy, nutty flavor. Plus, it's easy and quick to make.

One of my favorite uses for this salsa is as an accompaniment for Puebla-Style Pork Tacos (page 81). But really, it delivers so much flavor that you can use it to dress just about anything. Serve it as a table salsa with savory dishes, or as a dip for some crusty bread or a tortilla or chips before you start your meal. *The photo is on page 125.*

- 1 pound tomatoes (see note)
- 2 garlic cloves, not peeled
- ¼ large white onion, cut into large chunks
- 6 to 7 dried chipotle chiles, preferably moritas (page 133), stemmed
- ¾ cup raw unsalted peanuts (see note)
- ½ teaspoon dried oregano
- 1 tablespoon unseasoned rice vinegar or white vinegar
- ½ cup water
- 1 teaspoon kosher salt, or to taste

Preheat the broiler, with the rack 2 to 3 inches from the heat source. Put the tomatoes, garlic cloves, and onion on a baking sheet lined with foil and broil, turning the vegetables halfway through, until they are charred and the tomatoes are mushy, 5 to 7 minutes for the garlic, and

10 to 12 minutes for the other vegetables. Remove the garlic when charred and softened and when it is cool enough to handle, peel it. Alternatively, you can toast the vegetables on a hot comal or skillet over medium heat, turning them every 4 to 5 minutes, until charred and soft. Transfer the tomatoes, onion, and garlic to a blender, along with any juices on the baking sheet.

Set a comal or small skillet over medium-low heat. Add the chipotles and peanuts and toast, stirring the peanuts and turning the chiles from time to time, just until the chiles soften, puff, and begin to lightly toast but not burn, 4 to 5 minutes. The peanuts should be slightly toasted, but that will barely show. Transfer to the blender.

Toast the oregano on the hot pan for 10 to 15 seconds, until fragrant and just beginning to darken, and add to the blender.

Add the vinegar, water, and salt to the blender and puree until smooth. Taste and adjust the salt.

The salsa will keep, tightly covered, for up to 5 days in the refrigerator. Stir well before using.

Cook's Notes

▶ If you can only find salted and roasted peanuts, toast them with the chipotles as directed in the recipe, but reduce the salt in the recipe to ½ teaspoon, then season to taste with more salt if necessary.

▶ You can substitute 1 (15-ounce) can fire-roasted tomatoes for the roasted fresh tomatoes. Add them to the blender along with the roasted onion and garlic.

Who doesn't find the smoky, spicy, rich flavor of chipotles addictive? *Chipotle* has become a household word, and not just because of the eponymous restaurant chain.

The word comes from the Nahuatl words *chilli* and *poctli,* meaning chile and smoke, which describe chipotles. Specifically, they are jalapeños that have been allowed to ripen to red and are then smoke-dried, a method that has been used for centuries. It is an efficient way to dry and preserve jalapeños, and the bonus is the wonderful dimension that the smoke gives to the dried chile.

There are two types of chipotle, moritas and mecos. **Mecos** are made with a larger variety of jalapeño. The brittle light brown chiles are about 2½ inches long and wrinkled, sometimes with lighter brown, leathery striations. Their flavor is smoky and complex, quite spicy but not astringent. **Moritas** are made from a smaller, more fragrant variety of jalapeño. They're about 1½ inches long, and they are darker, shinier, and redder, and more fragrant, with a richer, fruitier flavor. They are the chipotles that I prefer. Sometimes the packaging simply labels these chiles as moritas, rather than chipotles. Because dried chipotles are hard and can be quite brittle, it's difficult to seed them without soaking them first.

One of the most common ways Mexicans enjoy chipotles is pickled in vinegar with spices, as well as in adobo, which is probably more familiar to most Americans. These canned chipotles are pickled and preserved in a luscious adobo sauce made with tomatoes, vinegar, spices, and piloncillo or brown sugar, sometimes with other dried chiles like anchos. The layers of flavor—smoky, sweet, deep, rich, chocolaty, fruity, spicy—come together in a truly unforgettable way.

Chipotles in adobo are one of my favorite Mexican ingredients, not just because I love the chiles—which I add to just about any type of dish, from tacos to quesadillas to sandwiches to soups to grilled meats—but because I also can't resist the adobo sauce, which has many uses. The chiles and sauce have a wonderful symbiotic relationship, the flavors of the sauce soaking into the dried chiles and the smoky heat from the chiles adding their own dimension to the sauce. One spoonful can infuse so much personality into a soup, mole, pot of beans, salsa, stew, mayonnaise, or even mashed potatoes.

MIXED NUT SALSA MACHA / **SALSA MACHA CON MUCHAS NUECES**

Makes about 3 cups

Salsa macha defies any preconception you may have about salsas. There are no tomatoes or tomatillos, no onion, no fresh chiles. What it has are nuts—tons of them. The chiles in the salsa are dried, and they are fried in oil rather than being toasted, simmered, or roasted as in other salsas. All salsa machas have a combination of nuts, seeds, and dried chiles, and all are cooked in oil and with a splash of something sweet and something tangy. The type of nuts and seeds and the type of chiles can vary. In this one, I use some of my favorites: walnuts, pistachios, and pine nuts, and both chocolaty anchos and feisty chiles de árbol. I love the addition of both pumpkin seeds and amaranth seeds—the tiny nutrient-packed seeds that are popular in Mexican sweets, irresistible. The result is toasty, nutty, a little bit spicy and sweet, with a chunky consistency and a satisfying crunch. You can experiment with salsa macha. Choose the dried chiles and nuts that you like, cook in oil until the ingredients change color and smell toasty, then season with vinegar and your favorite sweetener.

Salsa macha will make a dish shine, from breakfast through dinner, soup to dessert. Use it to top guacamole, omelets, or even ice cream.

1 cup olive oil

½ cup vegetable oil

5 dried ancho chiles, stemmed, seeded, and cut with scissors into small pieces

4 to 5 dried chiles de árbol, stems removed (keep seeds), cut into small pieces

6 garlic cloves, sliced

⅓ cup raw unsalted walnuts

⅓ cup raw unsalted pistachios

⅓ cup raw unsalted pine nuts

¼ cup apple cider vinegar

1 tablespoon dark brown sugar or grated piloncillo, or to taste

2 teaspoons kosher salt, or to taste

⅓ cup hulled raw pumpkin seeds

⅓ cup amaranth seeds

Heat both oils in a medium skillet over medium heat. Add the chiles, garlic, and all the nuts and cook, stirring, until lightly toasted and fragrant, 2 to 3 minutes. Turn off the heat, add the vinegar, brown sugar, and salt, and mix. Stir in the pumpkin and amaranth seeds. Let the mixture sit for 10 to 15 minutes. Scrape into the bowl of a food processor and pulse a few times until coarsely ground.

The salsa will keep, tightly covered, for at least a month in the refrigerator.

DRUNKEN SALSA / **SALSA BORRACHA**

Makes about 1½ cups

Salsa borracha (*borracha* means drunken) is so named because one of its main ingredients is alcohol. Traditionally this was pulque, an alcoholic beverage fermented from the agave plant, but today, it is mostly beer. The salsa is thick and dark—almost black—with a smooth texture and intricate flavor with hints of bitterness that fascinate me. In addition to the alcohol, the key elements in this classic version are pasilla chiles—they give the salsa its dark color and complex taste—onion, roasted garlic, and orange juice. Some versions include fruit, such as apricots, plums, and prunes, and/or crumbled salty queso añejo.

This salsa is common in the central states of Mexico, where it goes hand in hand with another specialty of the region, Lamb Barbacoa (page 291). Simply put, you cannot have barbacoa without salsa borracha. You may see other salsas as well, but there will always be salsa borracha. Salsa borracha is also often the salsa of choice for Wrapped Slow-Cooked Lamb (page 287), and it's a popular choice with Brown Sugar Carnitas (page 301).

2 garlic cloves, not peeled

4 dried pasilla chiles, stemmed and seeded

½ cup water

½ cup beer of your choice (preferably light)

½ cup freshly squeezed orange juice

¾ teaspoon kosher salt, or to taste

3 tablespoons coarsely chopped white onion

Heat a comal or large skillet over medium-low heat. Add the garlic cloves and chiles and toast the chiles for a minute or two, turning them, until they change color and begin to smoke. Remove and set aside. Continue to toast and char the garlic cloves for about 10 minutes longer, turning occasionally, until the garlic has softened and the skin has charred. Remove from the heat and set aside, then peel off the blackened skin when cool enough to handle.

Place the chiles and garlic cloves in a medium saucepan. Cover with the water, beer, and orange juice and bring to a boil. Reduce the heat to medium and simmer for about 10 minutes, until the chiles have completely softened.

Transfer the contents of the saucepan to a blender. Add the salt and onion and puree until smooth.

The salsa will keep, tightly covered, for up to 5 days in the refrigerator.

Variations

There are many ways to vary or dress up your salsa borracha. In fact, there are just about as many variations as there are cooks, and each cook will tell you that his or hers is the one true salsa borracha. See which twist on the salsa is the right one for you.

► Add 3 tablespoons coarsely chopped pitted prunes to the saucepan along with the chiles if you'd like a sweeter salsa borracha. Other fruit options include fresh apricots, plums, and green apple.

- Substitute dried guajillo or ancho chiles for the chile pasillas.

- Grate, dice, or cut queso añejo into matchstick pieces and sprinkle over the salsa. If you can't find queso añejo, you can substitute crumbled Cotija or queso fresco. The cheese makes for a lovely contrast between the bitter and the salty.

- Top the salsa with diced or sliced ripe avocado, along with the queso or not. With its smooth texture and mild flavor, avocado is a comforting addition.

- Top the salsa with additional chopped white onion, about 2 tablespoons, a refreshing, moist, and crunchy add-on.

PULQUE: DRINK OF THE GODS AND HIPSTERS

Pulque is an ancient alcoholic beverage, made by fermenting aguamiel, the sap extracted from the heart of the agave plant. Highly nutritious, and considered a curative by indigenous peoples, it has a texture that is both sticky and viscous, a foam on top, and an alcohol content similar to that of beer, usually between 4 and 8 percent. For many, the milky-white drink is an acquired taste. It's a bit like a light beer, but tangier and with a mild sweetness, or like kombucha, but effervescent and more acidic.

Pulque's fortunes have risen and fallen throughout Mexico's history. In pre-Hispanic times, the drink was considered sacred and reserved for priests to use in rituals, mainly as an offering to the goddess of maguey, Mayahuel. Its production continued after the Spanish Conquest, when it became hugely popular as the beverage of the people, although the church tried to brand it as the cause of degenerate behavior. During the early part of the twentieth century, beer companies, especially foreign breweries, began to flex their marketing muscles and pretty much knocked out pulque. It was deemed unsanitary and unhealthy, scorned as a low-class beverage. It vanished into the hills, surviving mostly in rural and poor areas of Mexico, where it was made only in small batches.

Today, as young Mexicans search for the roots of their cuisine, the 2,000-year-old drink is new again. Pulqerias that serve artisanal batches to hipsters are springing up everywhere in urban centers, particularly in central Mexico, where the tradition has always been strongest. Pulque does not travel well, though, and, unfortunately, good fresh pulque is not available in the U.S.—at least not yet.

SALSA BANDERA WITH JICAMA AND PINEAPPLE /
SALSA BANDERA CON JICAMA Y PIÑA

Makes about 3½ cups

Pico de gallo, the chunky, raw salsa made with tomatoes, onion, jalapeño, and cilantro, is known as salsa bandera in northern states like Sonora (*bandera* means flag, and the colors in the salsa are the colors of the Mexican flag, red, white, and green). This fruity, crunchy variation adds jicama and pineapple to the mix. It's very nice with fish and seafood—I love it with Sonoran Shrimp and Scallop Tostadas (page 52)—but it's also great as a dipping salsa with chips. *The photo is on page 129.*

½ pound tomatoes, cored, seeded, and finely diced

½ cup finely chopped white onion

1 cup finely diced fresh pineapple

1 cup finely diced peeled jicama

1 to 2 jalapeño or serrano chiles, finely chopped

½ cup coarsely chopped fresh cilantro leaves and upper stems

2 tablespoons freshly squeezed lime juice

1 teaspoon kosher salt, or to taste

1 tablespoon olive oil

Combine all the ingredients in a medium bowl and toss well. Let sit for at least 5 minutes before serving.

The salsa will keep, tightly covered, for up to 2 days in the refrigerator.

MANGO-HABANERO SALSA / **SALSA DE MANGO Y HABANERO**

Makes 2 cups

The combination of mango and habanero chiles is classic in salsas, especially in the Yucatán Peninsula, where the habanero reigns. Thick and silky, rich, and bright orange, this salsa delivers oh-so-much sweetness while packing a punch with its chile heat. It makes the perfect dipping sauce for Coconut Shrimp (page 221). I prefer the salsa made with mangoes that are ripe and juicy, but if you want more tartness, go for less ripe ones. If you can find Champagne mangoes (also called Ataulfo), I recommend them for their smooth texture and sweet, full taste. Thawed frozen mangoes will work in a pinch.

> 3 large mangoes (about 3 pounds), peeled, pitted, and cut into chunks (see sidebar; about 4½ cups)
>
> ¾ cup coarsely chopped white onion
>
> ½ cup unseasoned rice vinegar or white vinegar
>
> ½ cup water
>
> ¼ cup packed dark brown sugar or grated piloncillo
>
> ¼ teaspoon ground allspice
>
> 1 teaspoon kosher salt, or to taste
>
> 1 to 2 fresh habanero chiles, quartered and seeded
>
> 2 tablespoons olive oil

Combine the mangoes, onion, vinegar, water, brown sugar, allspice, and salt in a blender and puree until smooth. Add one habanero, blend, and taste to see if you want to add more heat. If it isn't too hot for you, add the second one—or part of it—and blend until smooth. Keep in mind that cooking the salsa tames the heat a bit, and it will calm down a little more as it sits.

Heat the oil in a medium saucepan over medium heat. Add the mango mixture, cover partially (the salsa will splatter a lot), and cook, stirring occasionally and scraping the bottom of the pan to prevent scorching, until the salsa resembles a thick pudding and coats the back of a wooden spoon quite heavily, 15 to 18 minutes. Remove from the heat and allow to cool before serving.

The salsa will keep, tightly covered, for 5 to 7 days in the refrigerator.

THE EASIEST WAY TO DICE MANGOES

Lay the mango on its side and cut down one broad side of the fruit, slightly off center, from the stem end to the tip, following the pit. The knife should slide against the flat side of the pit. Repeat on the other side, again cutting as close to the pit as possible. Then cut the flesh from the two narrow sides of the pit, following the curve.

Lay each half on your cutting surface and score the flesh with the tip of your knife in a crosshatch pattern, down to but not through the skin. Lift the mango half and press on the skin side with your thumbs to turn the mango inside out. The little squares will pop out like porcupine quills, and you can easily cut them away from the skin. Repeat with the other half, then dice the flesh you cut from the two narrow sides of the mango.

APPLE CHILTEPÍN SALSITA / SALSITA DE MANZANA CON CHILTEPÍN

Makes about 1½ cups

Some of my favorite Mexican salsas are both fruity and spicy, and this is one of them. It's a tomato-based salsa, the tomatoes simmered with garlic until mushy, then blended to a puree with a Granny Smith apple, cinnamon, allspice, and oregano, a nice mix of sweet and savory seasonings. Apple cider vinegar adds to the tartness that begins with the apple, and the spice comes from feisty chiltepín chiles. Many cooks in Sonora and Sinaloa told me that one of their favorite ways to use this chile is in fruit-based salsas like this one. It's great with grilled meats or vegetables, with tostadas or quesadillas or tacos, or spooned over eggs or even an avocado salad.

> **¾ pound ripe tomatoes or 1 (15-ounce) can whole tomatoes**
>
> **3 garlic cloves, peeled**
>
> **1 Granny Smith apple, peeled, cored, and diced**
>
> **1 teaspoon dried oregano**
>
> **¾ teaspoon kosher salt, or to taste**
>
> **¼ teaspoon ground canela or cinnamon**
>
> **¼ teaspoon freshly ground black pepper**
>
> **¼ teaspoon ground allspice**
>
> **2 tablespoons apple cider vinegar**
>
> **1 teaspoon dried chiltepín chiles (see note), or to taste**
>
> **1 tablespoon vegetable oil**

Place the fresh tomatoes, if using, and garlic cloves in a medium saucepan, cover with water, and bring to a rolling boil over high heat. Reduce the heat to medium and simmer for 10 minutes, or until the tomatoes are cooked and mushy and their skins are starting to peel off. If using canned tomatoes, just simmer the garlic in a small saucepan of water until soft.

Transfer the tomatoes and garlic to a blender, along with ¾ cup of the cooking liquid. Add the apple, oregano, salt, canela or cinnamon, black pepper, allspice, cider vinegar, and chiles, then add the canned tomatoes, if using, and puree until smooth.

Drain and dry the saucepan and set over medium heat. Add the oil, and when it is hot and starting to ripple, add the puree. The mixture will jump and splatter initially, so use the lid of the saucepan to shield yourself, holding it slightly above the pan. Cook for 3 to 4 minutes, until the salsa has thickened and the flavors have ripened and melded together. Scrape into a bowl and serve, or allow to cool, cover, and refrigerate.

The salsa will keep, tightly covered, in the refrigerator for at least 5 days.

Cook's Note

► If you can't find chiltepínes, you can substitute dried chiles de árbol or chiles piquín, which may be a bit easier to come by.

With its chubby round shape, searing heat, and, most important, its flavor, the chiltepín chile is a charmer. It is such a key ingredient in the gastronomy of Sinaloa and Sonora that you would be hard-pressed to find a household kitchen without it. Although almost everyone has a bush or two in their backyard or in a planter, they typically use more of the chiles than they can grow. And with good reason. Despite its heat, the chile somehow manages to accentuate the flavors of whatever foods it consorts with.

Although the chiltepín is not easy to find in other parts of Mexico, it is thought to be the mother of all chiles. There are no substitutes—the chile de árbol comes close, but it is rare to find so much intensity of flavor and heat in one tiny chile.

Though some chiltepínes are harvested when green and pickled in a light brine of vinegar, salt, and, sometimes, garlic, for the most part, they are left to mature and turn red on the bush. Then the chiles are harvested and dried in the sun. They can be expensive, since they're delicate and must be hand-picked, but a little goes a long way.

Chiltepínes are always sold whole and then ground just before using. Because they are so small, they can be hard to chop, as they tend to jump around on the cutting board. In Sonora, Sinaloa, and Arizona, cooks grind them in a special small hand-carved wooden container, sometimes animal shaped, a sort of mortar and pestle that is used exclusively for grinding chiltepínes. But you can put them in a little bag and mash them on a board with a meat mallet or the bottom of a small heavy skillet.

The chile piquín is larger than the chiltepín and more oblong in shape, and its surface can be more wrinkled. It too is packed with heat, though it's less intense than the chiltepín, and has a subtler flavor that is a bit toastier and more woody, with a slightly citrusy edge. Chile piquín is very common throughout Mexico. You find it ground and sprinkled onto the fresh fruits and vegetables that are dressed with lime and salt and sold as street snacks. It is often the ground chile of choice for street-style corn. Just like the chiltepín, piquines are green when unripe, red when ripe, and usually dried.

ALL-PURPOSE SEASONING SAUCE / **SALSA PREPARADA MILUSOS**

Makes 1⅔ cups

Talk about a multipurpose sauce! *Mil usos* means thousands of uses, and in Mexico, that's a real compliment. We Mexicans pride ourselves on being adaptable. We even use the word for people, calling a jack-of-all-trades *el mil usos* (or *la mil usos*).

You'll find this sauce at just about every seafood stand and restaurant in Sonora. It's made with not one but three intensely flavored dark seasoning sauces—soy, Maggi, and Worcestershire. You may wonder whether these sauces that are generally used on their own compete with each other, but each has a different character, and when they're whisked with plenty of freshly squeezed lime juice and a punch of hot sauce, the salty, citrus, and heat converge and work together. You can dress all kinds of ceviches and seafood with this sauce. Try splashing some onto chicken or beef right at the end of cooking when you make fajitas. It's a favorite for drizzling over grilled vegetables or snacks like potato chips, chicharrones, Japanese peanuts, and even raw fruits and vegetables. It also can be a base for Michelada cocktails.

¼ **cup soy sauce**

¼ **cup Maggi sauce**

¼ **cup Worcestershire sauce**

⅔ **cup freshly squeezed lime juice**

¼ **cup hot sauce, such as Cholula or Valentina, or a combination**

Freshly ground black pepper to taste

Combine all the ingredients in a medium bowl and mix together well. The sauce can be refrigerated, covered, for up to 5 days.

PUEBLA TAHINI SAUCE / **TAHINI PREPARADO**

Makes about 1½ cups

This delicious tahini sauce, which is much like its Middle Eastern counterpart, with lime juice standing in for the lemon juice, was adapted by the families of Lebanese immigrants to Puebla for drizzling onto their Puebla-Style Pork Tacos (page 81). But also try it as a dip with cut-up sticks of jicama, chayote, cucumber, and other vegetables, or drizzled over Seared Nopalito Salad with Radishes and Oregano (page 331).

½ **cup tahini**

½ **cup freshly squeezed lime juice, or more to taste**

½ **cup water**

1 **tablespoon olive oil**

1 **garlic clove, finely chopped**

½ **teaspoon dried oregano**

¼ **teaspoon ground cumin**

¼ **teaspoon ground allspice**

¼ **teaspoon chipotle chile powder**

1 **teaspoon kosher salt, or to taste**

Pinch of freshly ground black pepper

Whisk together all the ingredients in a small bowl. If the sauce isn't smooth and thin enough to be drizzled over the tacos, add a bit more water to thin it out, or more lime juice if you'd like it a bit more sour.

The sauce can be kept, tightly covered, in the refrigerator for up to 5 days.

PICKLED CHIPOTLES WITH BABY POTATOES, ONIONS, AND CARROTS / CHIPOTLES EN VINAGRE Y PILONCILLO CON PAPITAS Y CEBOLLITAS

Makes about 8 cups

Not many people outside of Mexico know about this combination of vegetables and smoky dried chipotles in a vinegary brine. You find it in small towns and cities there, produced in home kitchens rather than factories, and sold in local markets and general stores. Unlike the more common chipotles in adobo, these are marinated in a brine rather than a thick adobo sauce, but unlike pickled jalapeños, they have a pronounced sweetness because of the brown sugar, which suits their smokiness nicely.

Tuck them inside a quesadilla, taco, or sandwich, or serve them alongside grilled meats and other main or side dishes. If you have any of that brine left over, it makes an incredibly flavorful vinegar that can be used to dress any kind of salad, including chicken or tuna.

About 3 ounces dried chipotle chiles, preferably moritas (page 133; 30 moritas or 15 mecos)

4 cups boiling water

Kosher salt

1½ pounds tiny baby potatoes

6 tablespoons vegetable oil

10 garlic cloves, peeled

20 scallions or 10 spring onions, white and light green parts only, cut crosswise in half

5 medium carrots, peeled and sliced about ¼ inch thick on the diagonal

5 cloves, stems removed and discarded, crumbled

½ teaspoon ground allspice

1½ cups white vinegar

1½ cups unseasoned rice vinegar

¼ cup packed dark brown sugar or grated piloncillo

4 bay leaves

5 sprigs fresh thyme

5 sprigs fresh marjoram or 1 teaspoon dried

Place the chiles in a medium bowl and cover with the boiling water. Let them sit for 45 minutes to an hour, until they plump and soften. Drain in a strainer set over a bowl; reserve 3 cups of the soaking water.

Fill a medium saucepan with salted water, bring to a boil, and add the potatoes. Reduce the heat to medium and cook for 15 minutes, just until they are barely cooked through and can be sliced; they should not be falling apart. Drain and set aside.

Heat the oil in a large pot or skillet over medium-high heat. Add the garlic cloves, scallions or spring onions, and carrots. Sprinkle them with 1 tablespoon salt, the crumbled cloves, and allspice, and cook until the garlic begins to brown, the carrots start to soften, and the onions wilt, 3 to 4 minutes. Stir in the drained potatoes and cook until the potatoes color slightly, 3 to 5 minutes.

continued

Add the chiles, along with the reserved soaking water, both vinegars, and the brown sugar or piloncillo. Stir well and bring to a boil. Stir in the bay leaves, thyme, and oregano, reduce the heat to medium, and simmer for 5 minutes. Turn off the heat and allow the mixture to cool completely.

Remove the bay leaves and thyme and oregano sprigs and discard. Divide the chiles, vegetables, and brine among a couple of large lidded jars or containers (or several small jars). Transfer to the refrigerator and allow the vegetables and chiles to marinate for at least 24 hours before serving.

The pickled vegetables will keep in the refrigerator, tightly covered, for up to 3 weeks.

Cook's Note

► When using cloves, I remove and discard the stems and use only the tops. The stems are too hard for many blenders and are also not good to bite into if they make it into the final dish. You can easily crumble the tops between your fingers and add to whatever you may be cooking.

YUCATECAN PICKLED RED ONIONS / **CEBOLLAS ENCURTIDAS YUCATECAS**

Makes 2 cups

These smoky, tangy pickled red onions are always served with Yucatecan Grilled Citrus Pork (page 319). I learned to make them at Kinich, a restaurant in the town of Izamal that specializes in traditional dishes from the Yucatán. Whatever you wish to call it—condiment, pickle, or salsa—you will be seduced, as I was, by its simplicity, its color, and its pungent taste.

You can serve these onions with other Yucatecan dishes, like Yucatecan Pork and Black Beans (page 305), Slow-Cooked Pork Loin with Caramelized Tomatoes (page 307), and Chicken Codzitos (page 66).

2 medium red onions, quartered

¼ cup freshly squeezed lime juice

Splash of white vinegar (optional)

3 tablespoons chopped fresh cilantro leaves and upper stems, or to taste

1 teaspoon kosher salt, or to taste

Prepare a hot fire in a charcoal or gas grill and oil the grill. Grill the onions, turning often, until they soften and the skins have blackened. Remove from the heat, and when they are cool enough to handle, peel and cut into 1-inch pieces.

Place the onions in a bowl and toss with the lime juice, vinegar, if using, cilantro, and salt. Taste for salt and add more if desired. Let sit for at least 15 minutes before serving.

The pickled onions will keep, tightly covered, in the refrigerator for up to 3 days.

Cook's Note

► You can also char the onions on a comal or griddle or under a broiler. If using a broiler, place on a foil-lined baking sheet and roast for 10 to 12 minutes, turning every 4 to 5 minutes, until charred and softened.

CHUNKY CHILE MANGOES / **CHILE DE MANGO**

Makes about 3½ cups

Mexicans love the combination of mango and chile. For sheer pleasure, nothing can match chile de mango, a concoction that hails from the state of Guerrero.

Similar to a chutney or spicy marmalade, it's made with slices of ripe mango that are seared in oil over high heat until the natural sugars caramelize, and then a thick guajillo, garlic, and scallion sauce is added to the pan. The sauce coats the mango pieces, the mangoes begin to fall apart as they continue to caramelize and cook down, and the sauce melds into a delicious sticky mess, sweet with a touch of acid and spicy with a sprinkling of salt. If you're like me, you'll want to eat it as a side with grilled meats or sautéed fish or seafood; as a topping for rice; as a chunky salsa; or spread on toast and sprinkled with any type of cheese. Or just enjoy it with a spoon—it's like candy. It makes a great topping for ice cream!

I prefer to use ripe mangoes for this, but if you want more contrast in the flavors, go for mangoes that are still a bit green and unripe. The result will be a firmer, more acidic salsa.

5 dried guajillo chiles, stemmed and seeded

3 garlic cloves, peeled

6 to 8 scallions or 3 to 4 spring onions, white and pale green parts only, sliced

1 tablespoon white vinegar

¾ teaspoon kosher salt, or to taste

2 tablespoons vegetable oil

4 pounds ripe mangoes, peeled, pitted, and sliced ¼ inch thick on the diagonal

Place the guajillos in a small saucepan, cover with water, and bring to a boil. Reduce the heat to medium and simmer for about 10 minutes, until the chiles are puffed and soft.

Transfer the chiles, along with ⅔ cup of their cooking liquid, to a blender. Add the garlic, scallions or spring onions, vinegar, and salt and puree until smooth.

Heat the oil in a large heavy skillet over high heat. Add the mango slices and cook until lightly browned, stirring once or twice, 5 to 6 minutes. Pour in the chile puree, stir well, reduce the heat to medium, and cook for 15 to 20 minutes, stirring and scraping the skillet from time to time, until the sauce has thickened and some of the mango slices are beginning to fall apart but most still hold their shape. Remove from the heat.

Scrape into a bowl or jar and serve hot, warm, or cold. The chile mangoes will keep, tightly covered, for up to a week in the refrigerator.

SMOKY GUACAMOLE / **GUACAMOLE AHUMADO**

Makes about 2 cups

This rustic guacamole, popular in Mexico City and throughout central Mexico, is made with mashed charred fresh chiles, garlic, and onion, adding a layer of rich smoky flavor to the avocado.

1 serrano or jalapeño chile, or more to taste

2 garlic cloves, not peeled

1 (½-inch-thick) slice white onion

1 tablespoon freshly squeezed lime juice

1 teaspoon kosher salt, or to taste

3 tablespoons coarsely chopped fresh cilantro leaves and upper stems

3 ripe avocados, halved, pitted, and flesh scooped out

Preheat the broiler, with the rack 2 to 3 inches from the heat source. Put the chile, garlic cloves, and onion slice on a baking sheet lined with foil and broil for 5 to 8 minutes, turning the vegetables halfway through, until charred on all sides. Alternatively, you can toast the vegetables on a comal or large skillet over medium heat, turning them every 3 to 4 minutes, until blackened. Remove from the heat.

When they are cool enough to handle, peel the garlic cloves and cut the stem from the chile. Coarsely chop the chile, garlic, and onion. Place in a molcajete or bowl, add the lime juice and salt, and mash and mix with a pestle, fork, or wooden spoon until pasty. Add the cilantro and avocados and mash together until the mixture has reached the desired consistency (some people prefer a chunkier guacamole, others like it smooth). Taste for salt and serve.

Cook's Note

▶ Some versions of guacamole ahumado are made with just roasted chiles and salt.

INCREDIBLE, VERSATILE GUACAMOLE— BUT PLEASE, HOLD THE TOMATOES

A condiment, dip, salad, stuffing, and topping, guacamole is an all-around crowd-winning item on any menu. The most classic version consists of mashed ripe avocados mixed with one or another type of fresh green chile (most commonly jalapeños and serranos), one kind of onion or another, cilantro, salt, and often a squeeze of lime juice, but there are infinite versions. The word comes from the Nahuatl *ahuacamulli*, which means mashed avocado or a mashed mixture made with avocado (*ahuacátl* from avocado and *mulli* from mashed). Being the opinionated person that I am, I will say that I don't like diced tomatoes in my guacamole. For me, they water down the fabulous experience.

GUACAMOLE WITH CHILE VERDE / GUACAMOLE CON CHILE VERDE

Makes about 2 cups

When it comes to adding lime juice to guacamole or not, nowhere are people more adamantly against it than in Sonora. "Never!" protest my friends there if I even suggest it. Although I grew up making guacamole with lime, I must admit that it isn't missed in this very northern rendition. The Anaheim chile brings its own tart citrus taste, the serrano packs a punchy kind of heat, the onion adds some nice brightness, and the cilantro rounds out the flavors for a guacamole that can compete with your current favorite.

1 serrano chile, finely chopped

½ cup coarsely chopped fresh cilantro leaves and upper stems

¼ cup finely chopped white onion

¾ teaspoon kosher salt, or to taste

3 ripe avocados, halved, pitted, and flesh scooped out

1 fresh Anaheim chile, roasted, sweated, peeled, and diced (page 176)

Combine the chile, cilantro, onion, and salt in a molcajete or bowl and mash and mix together. Add the avocados and mash and mix. Add the roasted chile and stir and mash until the ingredients are thoroughly incorporated. Taste for salt and serve.

The molcajete, Mexico's version of the mortar and pestle, dates back to ancient civilizations, long before the Spanish arrived. For thousands of years, this tool has been used to pound, smash, grind, and mix ingredients. Yes, blenders and food processors can do many of these tasks more quickly, but they can't match the molcajete when it comes to the texture and the overall character that it brings to food. And molcajetes can double as handsome serving dishes, especially for salsas and guacamole, and for dishes that need to stay warm.

The name *molcajete* refers to the bowl itself; the heavy oblong pestle is called the *tejolote*. The bowls, which come in various sizes, stand on three short legs. Sometimes they are carved in the shape of an animal, most typically a pig, which can look friendly or scary. Some cooks use smaller molcajetes to make pastes and to grind spices, and larger ones for salsas and guacamoles.

Molcajetes are traditionally made of the country's basalt volcanic rock, which is heavy, very porous, and rough, the perfect material for grinding foods, as the bumpy texture brings out the essential oils of the ingredients. The surface also gives the molcajete a remarkable memory. It seasons with time and use, storing within it the essences, oils, smells, and flavors of all that has been served or made in it as it passes from one generation to the next. That's why people say that a guacamole, sauce, rub, or paste made in a molcajete always tastes better than one made in a blender, and why some people are adamant about using a molcajete for Mexican cooking.

If you want a molcajete for your kitchen, you can bring one back from Mexico, but it will make your bag super-heavy, so be ready to pay an extra fee. Fortunately, you can increasingly find molcajetes not only at Latin markets but also at some mainstream kitchen and cookware stores, as well as online.

Curing a Molcajete Before Using

Before you use a molcajete for the first time, you must "cure" it to remove any grit. There are different ways to do this. Some people grind raw white rice in the bowl with the pestle, washing it out with soapy water and rinsing, and grinding again for a few rounds, until there is no more visible grit. Others cure it by grinding peeled garlic cloves. I like to do both. The rice is a good way to clean the bowl, and the garlic seasons it.

Take a handful of rice and/or several peeled garlic cloves and grind to a powder or paste with the pestle. Then wash the bowl and pestle with a soapy sponge and rinse under cold water. Repeat several times, until you no longer see any bits of grit.

BEANS, RICE, AND PASTA

We eat beans in one form or another, at one meal or another, every single day in my house. I make a big pot of *frijoles de olla* (beans from the pot) two or three times a week, and I can still hardly keep up with the demand. We eat the brothy beans in soup bowls as soon as they are made, or enjoy them under fried eggs or as a side or dip, or slather them on crusty bread for tortas and on warm tortillas for tacos.

When I was growing up in Mexico City, my bean universe was limited to the light brown pintos and creamy-colored Flor de Mayo and Peruano (Peruvian) beans that simmered almost every day in a giant pot in our kitchen. As I've traveled throughout the country, I've tasted many more kinds bubbling on stoves in many kitchens: black beans in the south, little white beans in the Yucatán, fat lima beans in the north. And that is just the beginning: There are more than 200 varieties native to Mexico. Beans have been part of our culinary heritage for thousands of years.

The simplest pot of beans can express itself in many different ways, depending on the kind of bean. Even when you use the same type, you can get a very different dish. Simmer them with epazote and you get one thing, with cilantro and you get another.

I'd always considered refried beans, Mexicans' favorite way to repurpose simmered beans, to be a small subcategory. But I've realized that the dish of *frijoles refritos* has itself evolved into a giant family with many branches. In Jalisco, refried pintos incorporate olives and pickled jalapeños into a hearty mix with bacon and chorizo. At a carne asada cookout in Sonora, the same beans are enriched with pureed colorado chiles and so much cheese that they are called *frijoles maneados* (handled), because you need to use a lot of elbow grease to stir constantly with a wooden spoon in order to mix all that cheese into the beans.

The Spanish brought rice and pasta, and it didn't take long before Mexicans couldn't live without either of them. Rice settled in as if it had always been here, ready to soak up all the wonderful sauces, broths, and juices in a typical Mexican meal. We love it plain and we love it soupy, and as with so many of the other foods that came to Mexico with the Spanish, we love to enrich it with our native tomatoes or tomatillos, chiles, and herbs, for red rice and green rice.

You would be hard-pressed to find many of the local treasures in this chapter outside of their immediate regions—except of course in your own kitchen, because now you have the recipes.

BASIC SIMMERED BEANS / **FRIJOLES DE OLLA**

Makes about 5 cups cooked beans and 3 to 4 cups broth; serves 4 to 6

Simple simmered beans like these can be eaten as a meal on their own with warm tortillas, as they are throughout Mexico. Sprinkle on a little queso fresco and serve them with avocado and salsa, if you wish. Or they can be the base for countless dishes, from soups to stews to enchiladas to tacos to tamales to refried beans and other sides.

Lighter-colored beans—brown pintos, pinkish Flor de Mayo, and pale yellow-beige Peruanos, also known as Mayocoba—are most popular in the northern states. They are softer and creamier than black beans, which are the choice in Veracruz and other southern states. Both black beans and lighter-colored beans are popular in central Mexico, and in certain areas—the Yucatán, Oaxaca, and parts of the north—you find white beans such as navy and limas.

Although canned beans can almost always be substituted for home-cooked, a comforting pot of savory simmered beans requires very little work and yields much more in the way of texture and flavor, with the bonus of the tasty broth to enjoy as a soup or to use for refried beans. Plus, your kitchen will welcome the fragrant aroma of simmering beans. You may think that you don't have the time for cooking them, because you've heard they need an overnight soak before cooking. That is really a myth. Soaking reduces the cooking time by only about a quarter, and it makes no difference in the flavor and texture of the cooked beans. All you need to do is give them a good rinse, and you're ready to go. The cooking itself is hands-off. Put them into a good-size pot, cover them by a few inches with water, add half of a white onion—you don't even need to chop it, just peel away the outer layer and leave the root end intact so you can easily remove it later. Some people also add a few garlic cloves, though I don't, but I do often toss in a few fresh epazote or cilantro sprigs.

I don't add salt until the beans have softened, generally after about an hour. I find that salt can toughen the beans if added too early, before the skins have softened. And if the liquid in the pot looks like it's running low, add hot water rather than cold, because adding cold water can slow down the cooking.

> 1 pound (about 2⅓ cups) dried black, pinto, Flor de Mayo, or Peruvian beans
>
> ½ large white onion
>
> 3 to 4 garlic cloves, peeled (optional)
>
> 1 tablespoon kosher salt, or more to taste
>
> A couple of sprigs of fresh epazote or cilantro (optional)

Put the beans in a colander and rinse with cold water. Drain well and place in a large pot. Cover with at least 3 inches of water (about 14 cups). Add the onion and garlic, if using, and bring to a boil. Reduce the heat to medium-low, cover partially, and simmer until the beans are cooked through and soft, 1¼ to 1½ hours, depending on the age of the beans.

Add the salt and cilantro or epazote, if using, and cook for 15 minutes more, or until the broth has thickened to a soupy consistency and the beans are so soft that they fall apart if you press one between your fingers. If the beans are not quite there, continue to simmer until they are. Add warm water if necessary to keep the beans covered with water.

Taste and adjust the salt. Remove the onion, garlic, and herbs with a slotted spoon before serving. The cooked beans will keep for 4 days, tightly covered, in the refrigerator, and they freeze well in their broth.

EPAZOTE, THE MAGICAL INGREDIENT (DON'T ASK ABOUT THE NAME)

The herb epazote is a deeply Mexican ingredient that has no substitute. It has a clear, somewhat astringent flavor that lends a lot of character to a pot of beans or a soup, stew, or sauce. You can't mistake the distinct dimension it contributes, although you may not be able to put your finger on what exactly that is.

Epazote is best added judiciously (three to five sprigs are usually enough for most dishes). It is most often used for beans, and some cooks consider it essential not only because the flavor combination is divine but also because the herb is said to aid digestion.

The name comes from the Nahuatl word for smelly animal or stinky sweat. (Other names include skunk weed, pigweed, and Mexican tea.) The long serrated dark green leaves do have a distinctive aroma, penetrating and pungent. Because it grows wild almost everywhere in Mexico, epazote is also known as the poor man's herb. You can find it in many Mexican and Latin markets, as well as some farmers' markets. It's easy to grow from seed, but if you do, contain it in a pot, or it will spread like crazy.

In some dishes that call for epazote, you can substitute cilantro, although it has a very different flavor. But if you don't have epazote and want something herbal and green, go for cilantro. If you want something earthier and more astringent, try a small amount of fresh sage. Or just leave out the herbs.

BASIC REFRIED BEANS / **FRIJOLES REFRITOS**

Serves 6

Refried beans can be a base, a spread, an accent, a filling, or a topping. They can also be a side or even the main event. They can be a companion to rice and eggs, as well as an essential spread for tortas and an important ingredient in tacos, tostadas, and sopes. They can fill a tamal or a burrito, and they can be thinned out for soups, stews, and sauces. They're welcome just about any time of day, at breakfast, lunch, or dinner.

The traditional way to make refried beans is to smash the beans as they cook along with some of their broth and other seasonings—typically onion and an herb or chile—in sizzling oil or lard. The beans thicken and concentrate to a chunky finish. As they say in the Yucatán, you know that the consistency is right when the beans "can walk out of the pan." There are various special tools, similar to a potato masher, for mashing refried beans in Mexico. But a lot of cooks just use anything handy, even the bottom of a coffee mug (count me as one of them).

A more streamlined way to mash the beans is to throw them in the blender or food processor. Then you have a pre-mashed mixture before you add them to the hot oil, so that you don't have to wait so long or use so much elbow grease to get them to thicken in the pan. Pulse them or blend them to whatever texture you want, from chunky to really smooth.

3 tablespoons vegetable oil

½ cup chopped white onion

Basic Simmered Beans (page 156), plus 3 cups of the cooking liquid, or 5 cups canned beans, drained and rinsed, plus 2 cups water

1 teaspoon kosher salt, or more to taste

Heat the oil in a large skillet over medium heat until very hot but not smoking. Stir in the onion and cook until softened and browned around the edges, 4 to 5 minutes.

For the traditional method, add about 1½ cups of the beans to the skillet, with some of the liquid, and mash with a potato masher. Add the salt. Continue to add the beans and a total of 2 cups liquid, mashing after each addition. To use a food processor or blender, first coarsely puree the beans with the liquid, pulsing until they are the consistency you like, then add them to the hot oil. Continue to cook, stirring frequently, until the beans are smooth, fragrant, and the consistency of thick mashed potatoes, 15 to 20 minutes. Add up to 1 cup more broth or water if they seem too dry. Taste and adjust the salt.

The beans can be covered and refrigerated, for up to 4 days. Add more liquid when you reheat them to loosen them.

FIESTA REFRIED BEANS / **FRIJOLES MANEADOS DE FIESTA**

Serves 8

These refried pinto beans are mixed with a considerable amount of cheese, chipotle chiles, and dried colorado chiles. Chef Francisco Roberto Ramírez García, of Hermosillo, Sonora, introduced me to this version on my first visit to the city. He uses them to fill quesadillas made with Chubby Flour Tortillas (page 110). The beans also make a wonderful spread for crusty bread or for tortas and a great side with eggs or grilled meats. They are traditionally served at Sonoran quinceañera celebrations, along with barbacoa, and they are always present at carne asada cookouts.

You will find that you need to stir these more than traditional refrieds because of all the cheese. That's why they're called *maneados,* which means stirred a lot with the hands.

3 to 4 dried colorado chiles, stemmed and seeded

Basic Simmered Beans (page 156), made with pinto beans, plus 2 cups of the cooking liquid

2 to 3 chipotles in adobo sauce

3 tablespoons lard or vegetable oil

1½ cups grated melting cheese, such as asadero, Oaxaca, Monterey Jack, or mozzarella (6 ounces)

Kosher salt if needed

Place the dried chiles in a small saucepan, cover with water, and bring to a boil. Reduce the heat to medium and simmer until softened, 10 to 12 minutes. Drain.

Puree the cooked beans with the 2 cups cooking liquid, the soaked colorado chiles, and the chipotle chiles in a food processor or blender.

Heat the lard or oil in a large skillet over medium heat. Add the bean puree and cook for about 15 minutes, stirring and scraping the bottom of the pan as it begins to thicken. Stir in the cheese and continue to cook, stirring and scraping, until the beans have thickened to a soft puree and the cheese is completely incorporated and melted. Taste for salt and serve.

PIGGY BEANS / **FRIJOLES PUERCOS**

Serves 6 to 8

The combination of green olives and pickled jalapeños is a common one in Mexican cooking, but I'd never seen them in a bean recipe until I tasted this dish in Jalisco, where it is a popular appetizer served with tortilla chips in restaurants and bars. I was surprised and then delighted by the way the brininess of the olives and the heat of the pickled jalapeños contrasted with the creamy mild-flavored pintos.

Bean and pork dishes are found in one form or another throughout Mexico, especially in the north. The type of pork can vary and may include ham, sausage, carnitas, and/or chicharrones. Feel free to make these beans as piggy as you desire.

These make a great side for grilled meats, as well as for lazy breakfasts that include eggs cooked any way. If you have leftovers, use them to make soft tacos, or as a spread for molletes, open-faced sandwiches slathered with refried beans and topped with melted cheese and salsa, guacamole, or pickled chiles.

Basic Simmered Beans (page 156), made with pinto beans, drained, broth reserved

6 slices thick-cut bacon, coarsely chopped

½ pound Mexican chorizo, casings removed and coarsely chopped

¼ cup coarsely chopped white onion

⅓ cup chopped pimiento-stuffed green olives

⅓ cup chopped pickled jalapeños, plus 1 tablespoon of the brine

Kosher salt

¼ cup grated Cotija or añejo cheese or crumbled queso fresco

Measure out 2 cups of the bean broth. Set the rest aside for moistening the refried beans as they cook. Combine the 2 cups broth with the beans in a food processor or blender and pulse to a coarse puree.

Heat a Dutch oven or large deep skillet over medium heat. Add the bacon and cook for a couple of minutes, until it begins to render its fat. Add the chorizo and cook, using a couple of wooden spoons or spatulas to break up the chorizo into smaller pieces, until the bacon and chorizo are browned and crisp, about 8 minutes. Remove the bacon and chorizo with a slotted spoon and drain on a plate lined with paper towels.

Add the onion to the fat left in the pot and cook until it softens and the edges begin to brown, 4 to 5 minutes. Add the pureed beans and cook for 4 to 5 minutes, until the puree begins to thicken and the flavor intensifies; add a little more broth if the beans seem dry. Stir in the olives and pickled jalapeños, with the tablespoon of brine, and cook for 5 to 6 more minutes, until the mixture has the consistency of mashed potatoes. Moisten with more of the reserved broth if necessary. Taste and season with salt.

Scrape the beans into a serving bowl and sprinkle the crispy bacon and chorizo on top. Garnish with the cheese and serve.

Cook's Note

▶ You can substitute 3 (15-ounce) cans pinto beans for the home-cooked beans. Puree with 2 cups water or chicken or vegetable broth. As they cook, moisten with more water or broth as needed. You can also use 3 (15-ounce) cans refried beans, moistening them as needed.

OAXACAN REFRIED BLACK BEANS / **FRIJOLES OAXAQUEÑOS**

Serves 6 generously

Every region of Mexico has its own spin on refried beans. This one is unmistakably Oaxacan. Avocado leaves add an anise-like, floral dimension that is different from any other ingredient I know, and the chiles de árbol have a rustic, smoky kick. Toasting unlocks the flavors, oils, and aroma of both. The black beans are cooked in the classic way, simmered with onion until they are soft, salted, and then simmered some more, until they are luxuriously soft and the broth is inky and delicious. I go full-speed Oaxacan for this dish and use lard for the frying when I have some handy, but you can also use vegetable oil.

Serve this as a side with grilled meats or with just about any egg dish, like the Oaxacan Eggs in Roasted Tomato Salsa (page 183). Or wrap warm corn tortillas around the frijoles, sprinkle on some queso, and make a meal of them.

> 5 dried avocado leaves (optional but strongly recommended)
>
> 3 dried chiles de árbol
>
> Basic Simmered Beans (page 156), made with black beans, drained, broth reserved
>
> 2 tablespoons lard or vegetable oil
>
> ½ cup finely chopped white onion
>
> Crumbled queso fresco for garnish
>
> Sliced avocado for garnish

Heat a comal or large skillet over medium-low heat. Toast the avocado leaves, if using, and the chiles until fragrant and lightly colored, turning them often, 1 to 2 minutes, or a little less time for the avocado leaves; take care not to burn them. Remove from the heat.

Break the leaves into pieces and discard the stems. Remove the stems of the chiles and break them into pieces, with the seeds.

Working in batches if necessary, transfer the beans and 2 cups of their broth to a food processor or blender, add the avocado leaves, if using, and chiles, and pulse to a chunky puree, adding more broth if necessary.

Heat the lard or oil in a Dutch oven or large deep skillet over medium-high heat. Add the onion and cook, stirring, until it is translucent and the edges are beginning to brown, stirring occasionally, 4 to 5 minutes.

Stir in the pureed beans, reduce the heat to medium, and cook, stirring and scraping the bottom and sides of the pot occasionally, until the beans thicken to your liking (I cook them for 10 to 12 minutes).

Transfer to a serving dish, sprinkle with queso fresco, and garnish with avocado slices.

AVOCADO LEAVES

The long, slender leaves of avocado trees are used as an herb in Mexican cooking. They resemble large bay leaves and, like bay leaves, they infuse their flavor, which is anise-like, into stews, soups, tamales, beans, slow-cooked meats, and more. Most often dried, avocado leaves are briefly toasted to help unlock their aroma and essence. They are particularly popular in southern Mexico, especially in the cuisines of Oaxaca and Pueblo. You can find avocado leaves in Latin markets or online. If a recipe calls for dried leaves and you have fresh, toast them on a comal or griddle for a minute or so on each side.

BORDER PINTOS / FRIJOLES FRONTERIZOS

Serves 6 to 8

Creamy, mild, and almost sweet, these pinto beans are simmered until tender, then finished with chopped crisp bacon and chorizo, strips of roasted poblano chile, and chopped tomato to brighten and balance the dish. Served with salty queso fresco crumbled over the top, they make a perfect side for the Northern-Style Seared Meat Platter (page 278) or Sonoran Carne Asada Tacos (page 72), or accompaniment to any breakfast-brunch.

I first had them on the border (*frontera*) between Tijuana and San Diego, where this is a common way to prepare pintos, the bean of choice in Baja California Norte.

2 tablespoons vegetable oil

½ pound Mexican chorizo, casings removed and chopped

½ pound thick-sliced bacon, chopped

½ cup finely chopped white onion

1 ripe tomato or 1 canned tomato, finely chopped

3 fresh poblano chiles, roasted, sweated, peeled, seeded, and cut into strips (page 176)

Basic Simmered Beans (page 156), made with pinto beans, with their cooking liquid

1 teaspoon kosher salt, or more to taste

1 cup crumbled queso fresco, for garnish

Heat the oil in a Dutch oven or large deep skillet over medium-high heat. Add the chorizo and cook for about 4 minutes, stirring occasionally, until it has started to brown and has rendered its fat. Add the bacon, stir, and cook for about 4 minutes, until it begins to brown and render its fat. Add the onion, stir, and cook for a couple of minutes, until it softens. Stir in the tomato and poblanos and cook for a couple of minutes, until the tomato softens and the flavors of the poblanos begin to infuse the mixture.

Stir in the cooked pintos, along with their cooking liquid and the salt, and bring to a boil, then reduce the heat to medium and simmer for 7 to 8 minutes, until all the flavors have come together. There should be some puddles of red fat on the top. Taste and adjust the salt.

Scatter the queso fresco over the top before serving.

Cook's Note

► You can substitute 3 (15-ounce) cans pinto beans for the home-cooked beans. Add 2 cups water or chicken or vegetable broth to the pot when you add the beans.

NORTHERN-STYLE LIMA BEANS / **PATOLES DURANGUENSES**

Serves 6 to 8 as a side; 4 to 6 as a main course

In this hearty, humble dish, pillowy lima beans drink up the flavors of several different meats—chorizo, with its vinegary heat, as well as smoky bacon; ham; and turkey sausage, which is popular in Mexico. The effect is almost like a Mexican deli meat platter turned into a cassoulet. As its name suggests, patoles Duranguenses comes from Durango, a northern state that loves its meat. It can be served as a one-dish meal, but, unbelievable though it may seem, it's also popular as a side at carne asada gatherings.

Patol is the name given to large white lima beans. You can substitute other large white beans like cannellini, but I prefer limas here for their size and their starchy texture, which is almost like that of a creamy potato.

1 pound dried lima beans

5 garlic cloves, not peeled

1 tablespoon kosher salt, or to taste

4 slices thick-cut bacon (about 5 ounces), chopped

½ pound Mexican chorizo, casings removed and coarsely chopped

1 cup finely chopped white onion

4 turkey sausages, cut on the diagonal into ½-inch slices

4 slices ham of your choice (about 3 ounces), diced

½ cup light beer (optional)

1 cup pickled blond chile peppers (see sidebar), pickled banana peppers, or peperoncini, or more to taste, plus ¼ cup of the brine

Rinse the lima beans and pick over for stones and broken beans. Place in a large pot and cover with at least 3 inches of water (about 14 cups). Add the garlic cloves and bring to a boil, reduce the heat to medium, partially cover, and cook until the beans are soft, 40 minutes to an hour, depending on the age and size of the beans.

Season with the salt and cook for 10 more minutes, or until the beans are thoroughly cooked and soft but not falling apart. Remove from the heat and remove and discard the garlic cloves. Set aside.

Heat a Dutch oven or large deep skillet over medium heat. Add the bacon and cook until it starts to render its fat and brown, 4 to 5 minutes. Add the chorizo and cook, breaking it apart with two wooden spoons or spatulas, until it starts to render its fat and brown, 4 to 5 minutes. Add the onion, stir to coat it with the rendered fat, and cook, stirring a few times, for 3 to 4 minutes, or until very soft. Add the sausage and cook, stirring, for a couple of minutes, until it begins to brown. Add the ham and cook for another minute.

continued

Drain the lima beans in a sieve set over a bowl; reserve the broth. Add the beans to the Dutch oven or skillet, along with the beer, if using, and bring to a boil, then reduce the heat to medium and simmer for 5 minutes. Add 1 cup of the bean broth, the pickled chiles, and the ¼ cup brine and continue cooking at a medium simmer until the broth has thickened and the ingredients are well blended, 4 to 5 minutes. Remove from the heat.

You can serve the beans right away or refrigerate them and reheat later over medium heat, stirring occasionally. The flavors of the beans will be even better if you reheat them.

Cook's Note

► You can substitute 3 (15-ounce) cans lima beans for the dried beans; skip the first simmering step and omit the whole garlic cloves. You may want to cook a chopped garlic clove along with the onion, adding it after the onion has begun to soften. Add 1 cup of chicken broth or water to the pot when you add the beans.

PICKLED BLOND PEPPERS (TORNACHILES)

Blond peppers are known in Mexico as *chiles güeros,* and there are different kinds. The very small ones that are pickled in northern Mexico are called *tornachiles*; they are smaller and slightly spicier than other blond chiles. Tornachiles are pickled in vinegar with salt and sometimes a sweet element like piloncillo. If you can't find them, you can use the light yellow ones generally labeled as hot chili peppers in brine, or pickled banana peppers, or peperoncini. Or substitute pickled jalapeños.

SEARED WHITE BEANS WITH PUMPKIN SEEDS /
TOK SEEL

Serves 6 to 8

Tok seel, from the state of Quintana Roo, is unlike any of the other bean dishes we associate with Mexico. It's not soupy, and it's not mashed. The beans are simmered just until cooked, drained, and then seared with ground pumpkin seeds, cilantro, and chives. With its toasty nuances, generous amounts of fresh herbs, and the contrasting textures of the soft beans and the crunchy pumpkin seeds, it's unforgettable. You won't find anything like it outside the Yucatán.

In the traditional Mayan cooking process, small white beans called *ibes blancos* are cooked in a large pot over an open fire. Sizzling-hot stones are added directly to the pot toward the end to intensify the heat (*tok* means burned). To get the depth of flavor reminiscent of the original, I use a mix of olive, peanut, and toasted sesame oils and do the final searing in batches so that the beans don't steam or get mushy.

You can top this with other garnishes from the region, like Yucatecan Pickled Red Onions (page 147) and/or Yucatecan Tomato-Habanero Salsa (page 126). Serve as a side or as a light main dish or lunch, along with corn tostadas or crusty bread.

1 pound dried white beans, such as navy beans, cannellini, or great northern

3 garlic cloves, not peeled

½ red onion

3 sprigs fresh epazote or cilantro

1 tablespoon kosher salt

½ pound raw hulled pumpkin seeds

2 tablespoons toasted sesame oil

2 tablespoons peanut oil

2 tablespoons olive oil

½ teaspoon freshly ground black pepper, or more to taste

1 cup coarsely chopped fresh cilantro leaves and upper stems, plus 1 tablespoon for garnish

1 cup coarsely chopped fresh chives, plus 1 tablespoon for garnish

3 to 4 scallions, white and light green parts only, thinly sliced

3 or 4 limes, halved

1 fresh habanero or serrano chile, minced, for garnish

Rinse the beans in cold water and pick over for stones and broken beans. Drain and place in a large pot. Cover with at least 3 inches of water (about 14 cups). Add the garlic, onion, and epazote or cilantro and bring to a boil, then reduce the heat to medium-low, cover partially, and simmer for 1 hour.

Add the salt and cook for 15 to 30 minutes more, or until the broth has thickened to a soupy consistency and the beans are cooked through and soft but not falling apart. Turn off the heat.

With a fork or a pair of tongs, remove the onion, garlic, and herb sprigs and discard. Drain the beans in a colander and set aside in the colander in the sink or set over a bowl so the beans continue to drain.

continued

Heat a small skillet over medium-low heat. Add the pumpkin seeds and toast, stirring constantly, until they brown lightly, smell toasty, and some of the seeds pop like popcorn, 4 to 5 minutes. Take care not to let them burn, as they can turn bitter quickly. Transfer the seeds to a food processor and pulse until they are ground to a medium-fine consistency.

Heat 1 tablespoon each of the three oils in a Dutch oven or large deep skillet over high heat. Add half of the cooked beans, season with ¼ teaspoon of the pepper, and sear for a couple of minutes, stirring. The skins of the beans should begin to brown. Add half of the ground pumpkin seeds, half the cilantro, and half of the chives and cook for a minute or two. Scrape onto a serving platter. Heat the remaining tablespoons of the three oils and repeat with the second batch of beans, seasoning the beans with the remaining ¼ teaspoon pepper and then adding the remaining pumpkin seeds, cilantro, and chives. Scrape out over the first batch. Top with the scallions and the cilantro and chives for garnish.

Serve, giving everyone a half lime to squeeze over their serving. Pass the chopped serrano or habanero for those who want some heat.

Cook's Note

► You can use 3 (15-ounce) cans white beans instead of the home-cooked (omit the simmering step). Cannellini beans will hold their shape best, followed by great northern, and then navy beans.

PUMPKIN SEEDS

Pumpkin seeds, aka pepitas, which are the seeds of several varieties of pumpkin and winter squash, have been a vital part of Mexican cooking since pre-Hispanic times. They thicken moles, salsas, soups, and stews, enriching them with their mellow, nutty flavor. They're also one of our favorite snacks, sold hulled or unhulled; raw, toasted, or fried; salted or unsalted; or spiced, everywhere from street stands to grocery stores.

Packed with fiber, vitamins, minerals, and antioxidants, pepitas were prized by pre-Columbian civilizations. It is thought that the Maya were the first to grind the seeds to use as a base for sauces, and the ground seeds are still a key ingredient in the cuisine of the Yucatán, home to the Maya. In fact, one of the most basic Yucatecan seasoning pastes is a light green pumpkin seed paste that is sold ready-made in markets and used for, among other dishes, Enchiladas with Hard-Boiled Eggs and Two Sauces (page 191).

Pepitas are not difficult to find; look for them in health food stores, Latin markets, and larger supermarkets. In the recipes in this book, I always have you toast them as a first step, but if you buy them already toasted or roasted, there is no need to toast them again. If you buy them salted, though, be careful about how much salt you add.

RICE WITH LENTILS AND CARAMELIZED ONIONS / **ARROZ CON LENTEJAS**

Serves 8

You find this dish in Lebanese, Syrian, Turkish, and Jewish communities throughout Mexico, especially in the Yucatán, Puebla, and Mexico City. It is very much like its Middle Eastern counterpart, with lots of onions that are cooked in a generous amount of olive oil until golden and caramelized, then cooked some more with rice and lentils. It's the spoonful of ancho chile powder added with the cumin that makes it clear that this is firmly part of the Mexican repertoire.

1 cup lentils, rinsed and picked over

3 bay leaves

6 tablespoons olive oil

2 large white onions, coarsely chopped

2 cups extra-long-grain white rice or jasmine rice

1 teaspoon ground cumin

1 teaspoon dried oregano

½ teaspoon ground ancho chile, or more to taste

¼ teaspoon ground turmeric

¼ teaspoon ground coriander

1 teaspoon kosher salt, or more to taste

6 cups chicken or vegetable broth or water

Combine the lentils, bay leaves, and 4 cups water in a medium saucepan and bring to a boil. Reduce the heat to medium, cover partially, and cook for 15 to 20 minutes, or until the lentils are just cooked and soft but not mushy. Drain, remove the bay leaves, and set aside.

Heat ¼ cup of the olive oil in a Dutch oven or large heavy saucepan over medium heat. Add the onions and cook, stirring occasionally, for about 20 minutes. The onions will first soften and become translucent and then they will brown, which is what you want.

Clear a space in the middle of the pot, add the remaining 2 tablespoons olive oil, and then add the rice. Cook for 2 to 3 minutes, stirring gently with a wooden spoon. The rice will change from grayish white to bright white and feel heavier in the spoon. Don't let it brown. Make room in the middle of the pot once again, add the cooked lentils, all the spices, and the salt and stir well. Add the broth or water and bring to a boil, then reduce the heat to the lowest possible setting, cover, and cook for 20 to 25 minutes, until most or all of the liquid has been absorbed and the rice is tender. Remove the lid and check to see that the rice is cooked. If it is still a bit al dente, add a couple more tablespoons of water if necessary, cook for a few more minutes, and test again. When the rice is ready, remove from the heat and let rest, covered, for 5 minutes.

Fluff with a fork, taste and adjust the salt, and serve.

RICE WITH POBLANOS AND CORN / **ARROZ CON ELOTE Y POBLANO**

Serves 6

If there is a rice dish that makes my mouth water and fills me with nostalgia for the food from my childhood, it's this one. My mother served it whenever she wanted a side that was special but homey, and many of my friends' moms did the same.

When there are corn and poblanos in a dish, I usually add butter. I also use a bit of ground allspice here; it brings out the exuberance of the poblanos. The traditional rice for this is extra-long-grain white. I've started using jasmine rice instead, because its fragrance is heavenly. The grains of jasmine cling together a bit when they are cooked, and I like the contrast between the soft little clumps and the juicy chunks of corn and poblano.

It's said that this kind of rice preparation has its origins in the kitchens of Puebla, where the combination of corn, onion, and poblano is widespread. Wherever it comes from, I can think of no main dish that doesn't love its company.

- 3 tablespoons vegetable oil
- 2 cups extra-long-grain white rice or jasmine rice
- 1 tablespoon unsalted butter
- ⅔ cup finely chopped white onion
- 1½ cups corn kernels (from about 2 ears)
- 1¼ teaspoons kosher salt, or more to taste
- ½ teaspoon ground allspice
- 4 cups chicken broth or water, plus more if needed
- 4 fresh poblano chiles, roasted, sweated, peeled, seeded, and cut into 1-x-¼-inch strips (page 176)

Heat the oil in a large saucepan over medium-high heat until very hot but not smoking. Add the rice and cook, stirring often, until it starts to become milky white, crackles, and feels heavier as you stir it, 2 to 3 minutes.

Clear a space in the center of the pan and add the butter. Once it melts, add the onion and corn and cook, stirring and mixing them with the rice, for 2 to 3 minutes, until the onion begins to soften. Add the salt and allspice, stir well, and stir in the broth. Bring to a boil, add the poblanos, stir once, cover, and reduce the heat to the lowest setting. Simmer for 12 to 15 minutes, until most of the liquid has been absorbed but there is still some moisture in the pan. The rice should be tender; if it is not but all the liquid has been absorbed, add 2 tablespoons or so of broth or water, cover again, and cook for a couple more minutes. Remove from the heat and let rest, covered, for 5 minutes.

Fluff the rice with a fork, taste and adjust the salt, and serve.

The medium-to-large shiny, dark green, curvy chiles, which originally came from Puebla, are a star in the Mexican kitchen. These are the chiles we use most often for chiles rellenos and for rajas, those strips of roasted chile that appear in all sorts of dishes.

Poblanos are robust and meaty, with a matchless flavor and versatile nature. But their rich, fruity taste and lush texture have to be coaxed out through cooking, most often roasting, either on a comal or skillet or under the broiler. Once the chiles are charred, they're sweated in a plastic bag or a tightly covered bowl until their thin skins can be peeled away easily.

While the heat of most poblanos is quite mild, they can be a bit capricious, and every so often you may get a moderately hot or even a very hot one. But the heat is always mollified by roasting, and if the chile is still too hot, you can soak it, once it's peeled and cleaned, in a solution of warm water mixed with 1 tablespoon of dark brown sugar or grated piloncillo for about 10 minutes, then rinse.

Roasting, Sweating, Peeling, and Seeding Poblano (or Anaheim) Chiles

TO ROAST: The process is the same as for red bell peppers. I usually use the broiler method because I can do several peppers at a time that way. But you can also roast the peppers directly over an open flame on a gas stove, on a comal or skillet, or on an outdoor grill.

Preheat the broiler, with the rack 2 to 3 inches from the heat source. Put the peppers on a baking sheet lined with foil. Broil the peppers for 10 to 12 minutes, turning them every 3 to 4 minutes, until blistered and completely charred on the outside. The flesh should be cooked, not burnt. Anaheims will roast a bit more quickly, since they are thinner than poblanos. Roast them for about 8 minutes, turning them every 2 to 3 minutes.

TO SWEAT AND PEEL: Place the roasted chiles in a plastic bag and seal it, or put them in a bowl and cover tightly with plastic wrap. Let them sweat for at least 10 minutes (you can do this up to 12 hours ahead). Holding the peppers under a thin stream of cold running water, or working in a bowl filled with water, remove the charred skin with your fingers.

TO SEED: Make a slit down one side of each pepper and remove the cluster of seeds and veins. Pat dry with paper towels. Remove the stems unless you are making stuffed chiles. The prepared chiles can be stored in the refrigerator, tightly covered, for up to 5 days or frozen for up to 6 months.

TO MAKE RAJAS: Cut the chiles lengthwise into thin strips, ¼ to ½ inch wide. The length may vary depending on the recipe, but it's usually 1½ to 2 inches.

MEXICAN-STYLE PASTA WITH THREE-CHILE SAUCE /
FIDEO SECO A LOS TRES CHILES

Serves 6

In Mexico you are as likely to find the comforting pasta dish *fideo seco* on the table as beans or rice, especially in central Mexico, where it is very popular. We cook fideos not as the Italians do, but like the Spanish, who brought them to Mexico, first frying them in oil until they are toasty and nutty-tasting, then simmering them in a tomato-based sauce or broth until the sauce thickens considerably and coats the noodles. Forget al dente—our pasta is soft, and that's the way we love it. The dish is called fideo seco—dry noodles—because it is not saucy at all. It's also very convenient, because you can make it ahead. You can get packages of fideo pasta, thin noodles broken into pieces, in stores that sell Mexican ingredients, but you can also use thin Italian noodles such as vermicelli, angel hair, thin spaghetti, or spaghetti, and break them up yourself.

I include three different kinds of dried chiles—ancho, guajillo, and chipotle—here in addition to tomatoes, onion, and garlic. For one more layer of complexity—a bit of sweetness in addition to smoky heat—I add some adobo sauce from chipotles in adobo. Top with a drizzle of crema and a sprinkling of tangy cheese, with some sliced avocado to counterbalance the heat of the chiles, and I guarantee that you'll make it again and again.

1½ pounds ripe tomatoes or 1 (28-ounce) can whole tomatoes

1 garlic clove, peeled

1 dried guajillo chile, stemmed and seeded

1 dried ancho chile, stemmed and seeded

1 dried chipotle chile, preferably morita (page 133)

¼ cup coarsely chopped white onion

1 tablespoon sauce from chipotles in adobo

½ teaspoon crumbled dried oregano

1½ teaspoons kosher salt, or more to taste

¼ teaspoon freshly ground black pepper

3 tablespoons vegetable oil

1 pound fideos, or vermicelli, angel hair, or spaghettini, broken into smaller pieces

3 cups chicken or vegetable broth

2 bay leaves

½ cup crema or sour cream

½ cup crumbled queso Cotija or añejo, or, for a milder, moister cheese topping, queso fresco, feta, or farmers' cheese

1 ripe avocado, halved, pitted, and sliced, for garnish

Place the fresh tomatoes, if using, garlic, and guajillo, ancho, and chipotle chiles in a medium saucepan and cover with water. Bring to a boil, reduce the heat to medium, and simmer until the tomatoes are soft and the chiles are softened, about 10 minutes. Remove the chipotle and allow it to cool until you can handle it, then remove the stem and seeds.

continued

Using a slotted spoon, transfer the tomatoes, garlic, and chiles (including the chipotle) to the blender, then add ½ cup of the cooking liquid. Add the canned tomatoes and their juice, if using, the onion, adobo sauce, oregano, salt, and pepper and puree until smooth.

Heat the oil in a Dutch oven or large deep skillet over medium heat. Add the pasta pieces and cook, stirring constantly, until they are nicely browned and smell toasty, 4 to 8 minutes. Take care not to burn them.

Pour in the tomato-chile puree, using the lid to shield yourself, as it will sizzle and splatter. Stir to combine with the noodles and cook, stirring often, until the sauce thickens and darkens, 5 to 6 minutes.

Stir in the broth and bay leaves. Continue to cook, uncovered, stirring occasionally to keep the pasta from sticking, until the pasta is soft and the tomato sauce has thickened, 10 to 12 minutes. The mixture should be quite dry. Remove and discard the bay leaves.

Serve garnished with the cream, cheese, and avocado slices.

Cook's Note

▸ The variety of dried chiles you use for this dish is not set in stone. If you don't have one or the other of the chiles listed, use two of the same kind, or choose another chile. You could also substitute a canned chipotle in adobo for the dried one.

COTIJA AND AÑEJO

Crumbly, dry, and salty, Cotija and añejo cheese are among the most popular Mexican cheeses.

Cotija, named after the city of Cotija in the state of Michoacán, has become fairly easy to find in the United States in recent years. A grating or crumbling cheese, it has a tangy, assertive flavor and a granular texture. It's perfect as a finish for enchiladas, tacos, chilaquiles, refried beans, grilled corn, and salads, or sprinkle it over fideos or another pasta. It also makes a wonderful contrasting partner with fruits like watermelon or with cucumbers, jicama, or tomatoes. It isn't a melting cheese, but it will soften when grated or crumbled over something hot.

Queso añejo (*añejo* means aged) used to be made exclusively from goat's milk, but now you can find cow's-milk and goat's-milk añejos. It's drier and saltier than Cotija, and a welcome garnish for all the same types of food. You can find añejo in most markets where Mexican cheeses are sold.

If you can't find Cotija or añejo, you can substitute Romano or Parmesan, although both Mexican cheeses are slightly acidic and sharper than Parmesan.

EGGS

It's no secret in my house that I'm obsessed with eggs. I eat them for break-fast in one form or another every day of the week. Growing up, I watched my mother do the same, and I will never forget how much pleasure she took in her breakfasts. Egg-based breakfasts rule in Mexico. They range from simple—ham and cheese scramble, eggs cooked sunny-side up and dressed with a salsa or served with a side of chorizo, bacon, or queso fresco—to more complex—layers of scrambled eggs smothered in chunky roasted tomato salsa, or eggs scrambled with cured beef or grilled marinated pork, or with seared nopalitos, which is what we call succulent cactus paddles (this last version is so delicious that its nickname is "morning caviar"). We are serious about our breakfasts and construct them so that they are sure to get us through until lunchtime.

Eggs were the first thing I was allowed to cook solo as a child. I was eight or nine years old, and my paternal grandfather had come to brunch as he did every Sunday. That day, for the first time, my mother let me, the youngest of four girls, make the scrambled eggs. She set up a stool and a bowl next to the stove, put a pan over low heat, set the eggs, salt, and butter on the counter, and let me go to work. She suggested the only thing the eggs needed was a sprinkle of salt, and I could choose between butter and oil. Then, because it was right in front of me, I opened the door of the spice cabinet. So many choices, so many colors, and so many shapes, all begging to be thrown into my scrambled eggs! I added what I thought was a judicious amount of all of them—oregano, paprika, cinnamon, marjoram, and thyme. I even threw in a whole star anise. The more the merrier!

Since that day, I have learned to tame my enthusiasm for seasonings, but not for eggs themselves. They are such a perfect food, accessible to everybody, whether you live in the country and get your eggs from your own chickens, or in the city and buy your eggs at a market or supermarket. In this chapter, you will find some egg dishes that began as local sensations but have become national treasures. Some provide messy and irresistible vehicles for our other favorite food, corn tortillas. Check out the scrambled eggs with fried tortillas and guajillo salsa from Guerrero that goes by the unforgettable name of "Dance with Your Wife" Migas (page 185). And I promise you that all of these egg dishes are judiciously but exquisitely seasoned.

OAXACAN EGGS IN ROASTED TOMATO SALSA / HUEVOS EN SALSA MARTAJADA

Serves 4 or 5

This is one of the most popular breakfasts in the city of Oaxaca. It's a simple combination of scrambled eggs and a chunky salsa. The salsa has two ingredients, tomatoes and roasted fresh chiles. The name *martajada* comes from a word meaning to mash something without pureeing it, the way you would with a molcajete. The salsa should be good enough to eat on its own with a spoon, so it's essential that you use very ripe tomatoes and season with a generous amount of salt.

It's also important not to overcook the eggs. Cook them just until they set, then add them to the salsa and spoon some salsa over the top. These are typically served with Oaxacan Refried Black Beans (page 162) and warm corn tortillas on the side.

2 pounds very ripe tomatoes

5 fresh banana chiles or jalapeños

1 teaspoon kosher salt, plus more for seasoning the eggs

2 tablespoons plus 2 teaspoons vegetable oil

8 to 10 large eggs

Preheat the broiler, with the rack 2 to 3 inches from the heat source. Put the tomatoes and chiles on a baking sheet lined with foil and broil, turning them halfway through, until both are completely charred and the tomatoes are mushy, 7 to 8 minutes for the chiles and 10 to 12 minutes for the tomatoes. Alternatively, you can roast them on a comal or skillet over medium heat, turning them every 4 to 5 minutes, until charred. Remove from the heat.

Place the chiles in a plastic bag, close it tightly, and let them sweat; or put them in a bowl and cover tightly with plastic wrap. After 10 to 15 minutes, remove the chiles and remove their skins under a thin stream of water or in a bowl of water. Make a slit down the side of each chile with a knife and remove the seeds. Slice the chiles horizontally in half.

Transfer the tomatoes and their juices to a blender or a food processor and add one of the chiles and the salt. Process or pulse for only a few seconds, until chunky; you don't want a smooth puree. Alternatively, you can mash everything in a molcajete.

Heat 2 tablespoons of the oil in a large deep skillet over medium-high heat. Add the salsa (protect yourself with the lid if it splatters), stir in the remaining sliced chiles and cook, stirring often, for 5 to 6 minutes, until the salsa has thickened and the flavors have intensified. Set aside.

continued

Beat the eggs in a bowl and season with salt. Heat the remaining 2 teaspoons oil in a large nonstick skillet over medium-high heat. Add the eggs and cook, tilting the pan and lifting the edges so the uncooked eggs run underneath. When the eggs are just set—somewhere between scrambled eggs and a runny omelet, which should take 2 to 3 minutes—transfer to the skillet with the salsa, pushing some of the salsa to the sides and spooning some of it over the top. Don't worry if the eggs break apart or fold over themselves in places.

Serve hot.

Cook's Note

► You can substitute 2 (15-ounce) cans fire-roasted tomatoes for the fresh (skip the broiling step). Add them to the blender with the roasted chile.

Variation

In Oaxaca, there's a version of this dish called *queso in salsa martajada*. You can make it using cheese instead of the eggs, or with half cheese and half eggs. Heat a thick slice of queso Oaxaca, queso fresco, or queso panela in the pan and cover with the warm salsa.

MEXICO'S BEAUTIFUL BLONDS

Güero means blond in Spanish, and that's what these fresh chiles are—pale yellowish, or sometimes pale green. In U.S. markets, they are often called banana peppers, though true banana peppers are longer, narrower, and much milder than güeros.

The güeros that I use are shaped like jalapeños, 2½ to 3 inches long, and tapering to a blunt point. They have a similar fresh, juicy taste, with a heat level that is usually moderate. They are used in many Oaxacan dishes, where they are called *chiles de agua*, and they are also popular in Veracruz.

One of my most memorable güero-eating experiences was in Tucson, Arizona, where chef Daniel Contreras roasts the chiles and serves them alongside his Sonoran hot dog at his James Beard Award–winning hot dog stand, El Güero Canelo. (Contreras's nickname is Güero, after his favorite chile.)

Another blond chile, this one from the Yucatán, is the xcatic, whose Mayan name means blond. It is commonly used in the Yucatán for pickles and for stuffing as well as in salsas. The chile resembles a güero, but it's longer and more tapered, like a banana pepper. Its heat level is moderate. It is often roasted, but when it is roasted, it is not peeled. The tornachile is another blond chile, found in the north of Mexico and typically pickled as well.

"DANCE WITH YOUR WIFE" MIGAS / **BAILA CON TU MUJER**

Serves 4 or 5

The only explanation I could find for the colorful name of these equally colorful migas (crispy tortillas mixed with eggs) from Guerrero is that they are the best thing to eat after you've been out dancing all night, presumably with your wife—or if you are hung over after a night out with friends and want to make peace with her.

The dish couldn't be easier. You make a simple blended salsa with guajillo chiles, tomatoes, garlic, and cilantro; fry tortillas in oil until they are crisp; scramble everything together in a skillet; and garnish with cilantro, scallions, and avocado. It's a great way to use stale corn tortillas, but you don't have to wait for them to dry out in order to make this.

1 pound ripe tomatoes or 1 (15-ounce) can whole tomatoes

4 dried guajillo chiles, stemmed and seeded

2 garlic cloves, peeled

Vegetable oil for deep-frying

12 corn tortillas, cut into strips or bite-size pieces

1 teaspoon kosher salt, plus more for seasoning the tortilla chips

1½ cups coarsely chopped fresh cilantro leaves and upper stems, plus ¼ cup chopped leaves for garnish

6 large eggs, lightly beaten

3 scallions, white and light green parts only, thinly sliced

1 ripe avocado, halved, pitted, and sliced

Place the fresh tomatoes, if using, chiles, and garlic in a saucepan, cover with water, and bring to a boil. Reduce the heat to medium-high and cook for 10 minutes, until the tomatoes are mushy and the chiles are soft. Remove from the heat.

Meanwhile, place a cooling rack on a baking sheet lined with paper towels. Fill a large deep skillet with 1 inch of oil and heat over medium heat for 5 minutes. Test the heat of the oil with a tortilla piece; if the oil actively bubbles right away, it is ready. If the tortilla doesn't bubble, wait for a few more minutes and test again.

Add a batch of the tortillas, without crowding the pan, and fry for 2 to 3 minutes, until crisp and golden (don't let them brown, or they will taste burnt). Remove with a slotted spoon and transfer to the cooling rack to drain; immediately sprinkle with salt to taste. Continue with the rest of the tortilla pieces, making sure the oil is hot enough before you add each batch. Pour off all but about a tablespoon of the oil from the skillet and discard; set the skillet aside.

Using a slotted spoon, transfer the cooked tomatoes, chiles, and garlic to a blender. Add the canned tomatoes, if using, salt, and cilantro and puree until smooth.

Heat the reserved oil in the skillet over medium heat. Add all of the tortilla chips and let them reheat for a minute or two. Stir in the beaten eggs. As soon as they begin to set, pour in the salsa and gently begin to fold until all of the tortilla pieces are covered with sauce and the eggs are cooked, just a couple of minutes. Remove from the heat.

Garnish with the scallions, cilantro, and avocado and serve.

SCRAMBLED EGGS WITH NOPALITOS / **CAVIAR MAÑANERO**

Serves 4

I love nopalitos (aka nopales, or cactus paddles) so much that I have this signature Mexican breakfast at least once a week. We call it morning caviar, not because there is any actual caviar in it, but because to us, the mix of seared nopalitos, chiles, onion, and tomatoes stirred into creamy scrambled eggs is just as luxurious. Sometimes I serve the eggs over multigrain toast with slices of ripe avocado, other times with a side of refried beans and warm corn tortillas. You can also sandwich or taco them. Or you can enjoy them just as is.

3 tablespoons vegetable oil

¾ pound nopalitos, cleaned (page 332) and cut into ⅛-inch dice

1¼ teaspoons kosher salt, or more to taste

½ cup finely chopped white onion

1 to 2 serrano or jalapeño chiles, finely chopped

1 pound ripe tomatoes, finely chopped, or 1 (15-ounce) can crushed tomatoes

8 large eggs

¼ teaspoon freshly ground black pepper

Heat 2 tablespoons of the oil in a large skillet over medium-high heat until shimmering. Add the nopalitos. When they release their juices, add ½ teaspoon of the salt, stir, and cook for 4 to 5 minutes, until the juices begin to thicken and dry up a bit but there is still moisture in the pan.

Clear a space in the center of the pan, add the remaining 1 tablespoon oil and then the onion and chiles, and cook for 1 to 2 minutes, until softened. Stir everything together and cook for another couple of minutes.

Make room in the center once more, add the tomatoes, and cook for 7 to 8 minutes, stirring occasionally but keeping them in the middle of the pan, until they cook down and are soft and mushy.

Meanwhile, beat the eggs in a bowl with the remaining ¾ teaspoon salt and the pepper.

Stir the tomatoes into the nopalitos and cook for another minute. The mixture should be barely moist. Reduce the heat to medium-low. Add the eggs and cook, stirring and scraping the bottom of the pan for 3 to 4 minutes; take care not to overcook the eggs. As soon as they are set, remove from the heat and serve.

Cook's Note

► You can cook the nopalito mixture ahead of time. Let it cool, cover, and refrigerate for up to 4 days, then reheat when you are ready to make the eggs.

YUCATECAN HUEVOS RANCHEROS / **HUEVOS MOTULEÑOS**

Serves 4

There are many terrific egg dishes in the Yucatán Peninsula, but probably the most famous is this one-stop breakfast. Yucatán's rendition of huevos rancheros has a lot more going on than your regular rancheros. Corn tortillas are slathered with refried black beans and topped with sunny-side-up eggs that are dressed with a rich tomato sauce spiced with the signature chile of the region, the habanero. Diced ham, peas, and crumbled fresh cheese are scattered over the top. For the final touch, slices of caramelized ripe plantains are served on the side.

The *Motuleños* in the name refers to Motul de Carrillo Puerto, the town where this classic was born. But the eggs have become much more famous than their namesake, with the result that most people will tell you that *Motuleños* means the dressed and saucy eggs from the region.

2 pounds ripe tomatoes or 2 (15-ounce) cans whole tomatoes

1 to 2 fresh habanero or serrano chiles, to taste

2 garlic cloves, peeled

1 (1-inch-thick) slice large white onion (about 2 ounces)

1 teaspoon kosher salt, or more to taste

½ teaspoon freshly ground black pepper

3 tablespoons plus 1 teaspoon vegetable oil, or as needed, plus more for the tortillas if desired

1 large very ripe plantain, peeled and cut on the diagonal into ¼-inch-thick slices

1 cup diced deli ham

8 corn tortillas

8 large eggs

2 cups Oaxacan Refried Black Beans (page 162), warmed

1 cup fresh or thawed frozen peas, cooked just until tender

½ cup crumbled queso fresco

Combine the fresh tomatoes, if using, chiles, and garlic in a medium saucepan, cover with water, and bring to a boil. Reduce the heat to medium and simmer for 10 to 15 minutes, until the tomatoes are cooked and mushy and the chiles and garlic are soft.

Using a slotted spoon, transfer the tomatoes, chiles, and garlic to a blender. Add the canned tomatoes, if using, onion, salt, and pepper and puree until smooth.

Heat 1 tablespoon of the oil in a medium saucepan over medium heat. Pour in the tomato puree, shielding yourself with the lid, cover partially, and simmer for 5 to 6 minutes, stirring occasionally, until the flavors and color have deepened and the sauce has thickened slightly. Set aside and keep warm.

Heat 2 tablespoons of the oil in a medium skillet over medium heat. Add the plantain slices and cook for about 2 minutes per side, until softened, cooked through, and starting to brown. Drain on a paper towel–lined plate.

continued

Return the skillet to medium-high heat, add the diced ham, and cook, stirring occasionally, for a couple of minutes, until the pieces begin to color. Scrape into a bowl and set aside.

You can cook the tortillas by shallow-frying them in a couple of tablespoons of oil, or you can heat them for a few minutes on a comal or large skillet over medium heat until hot; set aside.

Heat the remaining 1 teaspoon oil in a large nonstick skillet over medium-low heat. Crack 4 of the eggs into the pan, season with salt to taste, and cover with the lid. Cook until the egg whites are set but the egg yolks are still runny, 2 to 2½ minutes. You can cook the eggs over easy, if you prefer. Transfer to a platter and keep warm while you cook the remaining eggs, adding more oil to the pan if necessary.

To serve, place 2 corn tortillas on each plate and cover them with ½ cup of the refried beans. Top the beans with 2 of the fried eggs and cover the eggs with the tomato sauce. Garnish with the ham, peas, and queso fresco. Arrange the plantains on the side and serve at once.

QUESO FRESCO

There is something comforting about queso fresco, the ubiquitous soft, crumbly fresh white cheese that is found throughout Mexico and increasingly in American supermarkets. It's tangy but mild, salted but not salty, and it rounds out a bowl of brothy beans or refried beans, soups, egg dishes, and salads. You can also serve it as a side with guacamole, or with chips, along with a salsa. The cheese crumbles easily but it can also be cut into sticks or squares. It is not a melting cheese like Oaxaca cheese or mozzarella; it softens and remains deliciously chewy when heated. It is usually added to dishes just before serving.

In Mexico, queso fresco is sometimes sold wrapped in banana leaves, occasionally still in the small basket molds that the cheese is made in. It also goes by the names *queso de pueblo*, *queso ranchero* or *de rancho*, and *queso blanco*. If you can't find it, substitute a mild feta or farmers' cheese.

ENCHILADAS WITH HARD-BOILED EGGS AND TWO SAUCES / **PAPADZULES**

Serves 6

These enchiladas, filled with chopped hard-boiled eggs and topped with two zesty sauces, one green and one red, have been popular for centuries in the Yucatán. The green sauce is very different from a traditional salsa verde. It's a hefty, velvety puree with a ground pumpkin seed base, lots of earthy epazote, and habanero chile. It makes an intense backdrop for the red sauce that goes on top.

The name for this dish is Mayan, but there are various explanations for its meaning. One links it to the Maya words *papa* (food) and *dzul* (gentleman), translated as gentleman's food, and indeed it is elegant and old-fashioned. Another theory is that the name derives from *papak,* which means slathered, and *zul,* which comes from the word for soak. Either works for me!

FOR THE EGGS

12 large eggs

¾ teaspoon kosher salt, plus a pinch

¼ teaspoon freshly ground black pepper

FOR THE RED SAUCE

1 pound ripe tomatoes, coarsely chopped, or 1 (15-ounce) can crushed tomatoes

½ green bell pepper, coarsely chopped (about ¾ cup)

½ cup coarsely chopped white onion

1 fresh habanero chile, seeded

1 teaspoon kosher salt, or to taste

½ cup water

1 tablespoon vegetable oil

FOR THE GREEN SAUCE

4 cups chicken broth

3 cups (about 4 ounces) fresh epazote leaves or coarsely chopped fresh cilantro leaves and upper stems

½ pound tomatillos, husked and rinsed

¼ medium white onion

1 fresh habanero chile, halved and seeded

1¾ cups hulled raw pumpkin seeds

Kosher salt

¼ teaspoon freshly ground black pepper

12 to 14 corn tortillas

To make the eggs: Place the eggs in a medium saucepan and cover with water by a couple of inches. Bring to a boil, reduce the heat to medium-high, and cook for 1 minute. Cover the pot, turn off the heat, and let the eggs stand for 10 minutes. Remove from the water and let cool.

Peel the eggs. Finely chop 9 of them and place in a bowl. Cut the remaining 3 eggs in half, remove the yolks, and add the yolks to the bowl. Add the salt and pepper and mix and mash well. Grate the whites from the 3 eggs into a small bowl and season with a pinch of salt. Set aside for the garnish.

To make the red sauce: Combine the tomatoes, bell pepper, onion, habanero, salt, and water in a blender and puree until smooth.

continued

Heat the oil in a medium saucepan over medium-high heat. Add the tomato puree and cook, stirring occasionally, until it cooks down and darkens to a much deeper red, 12 to 14 minutes. Set aside.

To make the green sauce: Combine the chicken broth and epazote or cilantro in a medium saucepan and bring to a boil. Reduce the heat to medium and simmer for 7 to 8 minutes. Add the tomatillos, onion quarter, and habanero and simmer for another 5 to 6 minutes. Remove from the heat and let cool slightly.

Remove the tomatillos, onion, and habanero from the broth with a slotted spoon and reserve. Strain the broth into a bowl and discard the herb leaves. You should have 2¾ to 3 cups broth. If you have less, add water as necessary.

Heat a medium skillet over medium-low heat. Add the pumpkin seeds and toast, stirring constantly, until they brown lightly, smell toasty, and some of the seeds begin to pop like popcorn, 4 to 5 minutes. Remove from the heat and transfer to a blender.

Add 2¾ cups of the reserved broth to the pumpkin seeds and puree until smooth. Season with salt to taste and the pepper. Pour into a saucepan.

Heat a comal or skillet over medium-low heat for at least 5 minutes. One or two at a time, heat the tortillas for about a minute per side, until both sides color slightly but the tortillas are still very soft and malleable. Wrap in a clean dish towel, stacking them as you go, to keep warm, or use a tortilla warmer.

Meanwhile, bring both sauces (separately) to a simmer over medium-low heat.

Top each tortilla with about 3 tablespoons of the mashed egg mixture, roll up, and place seam side down on a platter. Cover with the green sauce, spoon the red sauce over the top, and garnish with the grated egg whites. Serve right away.

Cook's Notes

► Be careful not to burn the pumpkin seeds when you toast them; they should be very lightly browned. If you toast them for too long and they become dark, the sauce will be bitter.

► You can make both sauces up to 3 days ahead and refrigerate, tightly covered. Reheat just before serving.

SEAFOOD

SCALLOPS IN CHILE WATER / **AGUACHILE DE CALLO DE HACHA** 197

"COME BACK TO LIFE" SEAFOOD COCKTAIL / **VUELVE A LA VIDA** 198

PICKLED POBLANOS STUFFED WITH TUNA / **CHILES RELLENOS DE ATÚN** 201

ACHIOTE ADOBO FISH / **TIKIN XIC** 204

SAUCY BEACHSIDE SNAPPER / **PESCADO ZARANDEADO** 208

HALIBUT IN TOMATO-TOMATILLO SAUCE WITH ALMONDS AND OLIVES / **PESCADO AGRIDULCE** 210

SEARED POMPANO IN GREEN SAUCE / **PÁMPANO EN VERDE** 211

PANFRIED FISH WITH GARLIC, ALMONDS, AND GUAJILLOS / **PESCADO AL AJILLO CON ALMENDRAS Y GUAJILLOS** 212

CRISPY FRIED FISH FINGERS WITH CHIPOTLE MAYO / **PESCADO EMPANIZADO** 215

CLAMS WITH DIRTY RICE / **ALMEJAS CON ARROZ** 217

COCONUT SHRIMP / **CAMARONES AL COCO** 221

Often when I search for local foods in Mexico, I end up finding a charismatic person behind them. When I was in Sinaloa researching aguachile, a raw seafood dish that has its origins there, I kept hearing about Don Beto and his restaurant, Mariscos Beto. Beto began selling seafood from a wooden plank he balanced over rocks on the beach, then he had a seafood stand, and now he owns one of the most popular seafood restaurants in Mazatlán. When I finally got there, I found a long line. Some of the customers lounged at the bar, others sat at tables, and others waited to pick up orders to take along on boat trips or back to their homes or offices. They had come for his aguachiles, made primarily with shrimp; for the incredible patés he makes with smoked marlin and shrimp; and for his cheesy shrimp dishes. They had also come for the oysters, shrimp tacos, and platters of octopus and shellfish. Beto, who is a humble chef with a great personality, will be the first to tell you that his success is all about the quality of the seafood itself.

When I saw the mountains of gleaming shrimp in the markets of Sinaloa and tasted Don Beto's shrimp aguachile, I instantly understood why Sinaloa is the home of this dish and of so many other spectacular shrimp dishes—ceviches, shrimp cocktails, and all kinds of tacos and tostadas. The shrimp there are simply the best I have ever tasted.

Beto has his counterparts in just about every seaside town, city, or village in Mexico. The country's 5,800 miles of coastline stretch along the Pacific Ocean, the Gulf of Mexico, and the Caribbean Sea. Our seafood dishes run the gamut from the simplest sliced raw scallops enjoyed at informal beachfront stands to gorgeous plated dinners served in upscale restaurants.

All up and down the coasts, Mexicans grill freshly caught fish in the hinged baskets called *zarandas* as quickly as they can get them off the boat and clean them, or fry the fish, sometimes filleting them first and dipping crisp nuggets into chipotle mayonnaise. They bury shellfish in rice, infusing the grains with its aromatic flavors as it cooks. The rubs, marinades, salsas, and sauces—and the fish themselves—change from region to region. Whether you're at the fancy tourist resort of Cabo San Lucas on the Baja Peninsula or at a shack in the little town of Champotón on the Gulf, one thing's for sure: Whatever you order will be stunningly fresh, and cooks continuously find ways to dress their seafood bounty in the best possible way.

SCALLOPS IN CHILE WATER / AGUACHILE DE CALLO DE HACHA

Serves 4 as an appetizer

Aguachile (which means chile water) is a dish of super-fresh raw seafood splashed with lime juice and sprinkled with smoky chiltepín chiles. Its home is Sinaloa, where it's traditionally made with raw shrimp, so good and fresh, chased by the tang of the lime and bite of the chiltepín. The most common way to present aguachile is on a simple platter. My seafood of choice here is scallops, arranged over cucumber slices, garnished with sliced red onion, and drizzled with a mix of lime juice, crushed chiles, salt, and pepper. Freshness is key, so talk to your fishmonger and be sure to use only what has been shipped fresh and has just arrived.

1 cucumber, peeled, cut lengthwise in half, seeds scooped out, and thinly sliced

1 pound very fresh large sea scallops, tough side muscles removed

¼ red onion, slivered

½ to 1 teaspoon crushed dried chiltepín chiles, chiles piquín, or chiles de árbol, or more to taste (see note)

¾ teaspoon kosher salt, or more to taste

Freshly ground black pepper

¼ cup freshly squeezed lime juice

2 tablespoons olive oil

Tortilla chips, saltine crackers, or other crackers for serving (optional)

Arrange the cucumber slices on a platter. Slice the scallops very thin—no more than ¼ inch thick, preferably thinner. Arrange the slices on top of the cucumber, overlapping them. Garnish with the red onion.

In a molcajete or other mortar and pestle, grind together the chiles, salt, and pepper to taste. Or crush the chiles with the salt and pepper in a small bowl with the back of a spoon; make sure the chiles are finely crushed. Add the lime juice and olive oil and mix well.

Pour over the scallops, taste, and add more salt and/or crushed chile if desired. Serve with tortilla chips, saltines, or other crackers on the side.

Cook's Note

► You can also make this dish with very thinly sliced fresh jalapeños or serranos to taste. Don't grind the chiles with the salt, just stir them together with the salt, pepper, lime juice, and olive oil and drizzle over the sliced scallops.

"COME BACK TO LIFE" SEAFOOD COCKTAIL / **VUELVE A LA VIDA**

Serves 6 to 8 generously as an appetizer, 4 to 6 as a light main course

One of Mexico's most famous pick-me-ups after a long night out, this very saucy, almost soupy, mixed seafood cocktail gets its name because it is tossed with a bracing mix of tart, pungent, and spicy ingredients. In restaurants all along the Gulf and Pacific Coasts, vuelve a la vida is usually made to order. Many people will ask for the dish *con todo*, with every possible seafood in the kitchen. Others will request their favorite mix.

The cocktails play around with different chile concoctions, including fresh and pickled, and various seasonings and hot sauces. It's essential that the fish be very fresh, not thawed from frozen, because it's just cold-cooked in a lime juice marinade, as in a traditional Mexican ceviche.

Here's my favorite take. The seafood is a combination of lime-marinated fish, cooked shrimp, and crabmeat. Olive oil seasoned with garlic and chile de árbol gives the saucy mix added depth and a hefty punch.

1 pound firm, mild white fish fillets, such as flounder, snapper, or sea bass, cut into ½-inch dice

2 cups freshly squeezed lime juice (from 12 to 14 limes)

6 tablespoons olive oil

2 garlic cloves, peeled

2 dried chiles de árbol

Kosher salt

1 pound large shrimp, peeled and deveined

2 tomatoes, finely chopped

1 to 2 jalapeños, finely chopped

2 pickled jalapeños, finely chopped, or to taste

⅔ cup finely chopped white onion

½ cup chopped fresh cilantro leaves and upper stems

⅓ cup pimiento-stuffed green olives

¼ cup chopped drained capers

1½ cups ketchup

1½ teaspoons dried oregano

1 pound jumbo lump crabmeat, picked over for shells and cartilage

¼ teaspoon freshly ground black pepper, or to taste

1 to 2 ripe avocados, halved, pitted, and sliced or diced

Corn tostadas, tortilla chips, or saltine crackers for serving

Place the diced fish in a bowl, add the lime juice, and gently mix. Cover with plastic wrap and marinate for at least an hour, and for up to 12 hours, in the refrigerator.

Heat the olive oil in a small skillet over medium-low heat. Add the garlic cloves and chile de árbol and cook until the garlic is golden, 10 to 15 minutes, stirring occasionally; take care not to burn the garlic and chiles. Turn off the heat and allow the oil to cool, then remove and discard the garlic cloves and chiles.

Bring a medium saucepan of water to a boil, salt generously, and add the shrimp. Cook for 1 minute, or just until pink. Immediately drain the shrimp and transfer to a bowl. Let cool.

continued

In a large bowl, combine the tomatoes, fresh and pickled jalapeños, onion, cilantro, olives, capers, ketchup, and oregano and mix well. Stir in the seasoned olive oil.

Drain the fish, reserving the marinade, and add the fish, shrimp, and crabmeat to the bowl, along with 1½ cups of the marinade from the fish. Gently mix together, then season with 2 teaspoons salt and the black pepper. Taste and adjust the salt and pepper.

Serve in small bowls or martini or other stemmed glasses, topped with the avocado and with tostadas, chips, or crackers on the side.

Cook's Note

► You can play around with the fish (marinate any fresh fish in lime juice as instructed) and seafood combinations, substituting or adding other varieties of shellfish, such as raw oysters and/or clams, raw conch, and/or raw scallops, as well as cooked lobster, squid, and/or octopus, to equal 3 pounds total.

PICKLED POBLANOS STUFFED WITH TUNA / CHILES RELLENOS DE ATÚN

Makes 8 stuffed chiles; serves 4 or 5 as a light meal

These stuffed pickled chiles are common in central Mexico, where I grew up. Chiles rellenos of all kinds—poblanos, Anaheims, and even jalapeños, stuffed with cheese or picadillo—are beloved in Mexico. Sometimes they're battered and fried, sometimes they're just covered in a rich tomato sauce. But we also like to pickle the chiles and stuff them with all sorts of salads, like this tuna salad studded with tiny cubes of lightly cooked potatoes and carrots. We serve them cold or at room temperature as a light meal, often with a side of rice or toast. These are perfect for days when you're not sure what time you're going to eat. I have lots of those times, since my husband often comes home from work quite late. Because Daniel loves them, I buy extra poblanos at least once a month, roast them, and cover them with the pickling marinade so they're ready to be stuffed on a moment's notice.

The most time-consuming part of the dish—the pickled chiles—can be held in the refrigerator for days; they keep on getting better the longer they sit. You need to start pickling the chiles at least a day ahead.

FOR THE PICKLED POBLANOS

8 fresh poblano chiles, roasted, sweated, peeled, and seeded but stems left intact (page 176)

½ cup olive oil

2 cups thinly sliced white onions

3 garlic cloves, thinly sliced

3 bay leaves

5 cloves, stems removed and discarded, tops crushed

1 teaspoon freshly ground black pepper

1 teaspoon ground allspice

1 teaspoon dried oregano

1 teaspoon dried thyme

1 tablespoon kosher salt

1 teaspoon dark brown sugar or grated piloncillo

⅔ cup unseasoned rice vinegar

⅔ cup white vinegar

FOR THE TUNA STUFFING

Kosher salt

½ pound yellow potatoes, peeled and cut into small dice (about ¼ inch)

2 medium carrots, peeled and cut into small dice (about ¼ inch)

3 (5-ounce) cans tuna in oil or water, drained

¼ cup mayonnaise

1 tablespoon freshly squeezed lime juice

2 tablespoons finely chopped white onion

2 tablespoons finely chopped celery

2 tablespoons finely chopped fresh parsley leaves

To pickle the poblanos: Place the roasted poblanos in a baking dish large enough to hold them in a single layer.

continued

Heat the oil in a large deep skillet over medium heat. Add the onions and cook, stirring occasionally, until they are soft and the edges are beginning to brown, 8 to 10 minutes. Stir in the garlic and cook for a minute, or until it is fragrant. Add the bay leaves, cloves, black pepper, allspice, oregano, thyme, salt, and brown sugar, stir, and cook for another minute. Add both vinegars, increase the heat to medium-high, stir, and bring to a boil. Boil for 3 to 4 minutes to blend the flavors. Pour the hot pickling marinade over the poblanos and allow the marinade to cool. Cover the dish with plastic wrap and refrigerate for at least 24 hours.

To make the stuffing: Bring a medium saucepan of salted water to a boil over high heat. Add the potatoes, reduce the heat to medium-high, and cook until tender, about 5 minutes. Remove with a slotted spoon and transfer to a small bowl. Add the carrots to the boiling water and cook for 3 to 4 minutes, until just tender. Transfer to the bowl with the potatoes.

Mash together the tuna, mayonnaise, and lime juice in a bowl with a fork. Add the onion, celery, parsley, and ½ teaspoon salt and mix well. Gently stir in the cooked potatoes and carrots. Taste for salt and adjust if desired.

One at a time, open the chiles at the slit and stuff each one with about ½ cup of the tuna salad. It may look as if that is too much stuffing, but you want chubby chiles. It doesn't matter if they don't fully close. Top with some of the pickled onions.

Serve the stuffed poblanos at room temperature or chilled.

Cook's Notes

► The pickled chiles will keep in the refrigerator for at least 7 days, and the tuna salad keeps for 2 to 3 days tightly covered. It's best to stuff the chiles shortly before you serve them, but the stuffed chiles can be refrigerated for up to 2 days.

► When I'm in a hurry, I leave out the potatoes and carrots.

ACHIOTE ADOBO FISH / **TIKIN XIC**

Serves 6

The entire Yucatán peninsula claims this Mayan dish as its own, and people love it so much that it has migrated from fish stands to home kitchens. At the beach, the fish is grilled over coals after being rubbed with a mix that always includes achiote paste and bitter orange juice. Roasting it makes for a quick and easy dinner.

The sauce, which defines the dish, is a brick-red combination of guajillo chiles, achiote paste, and citrus. After being drenched with it, the fillets are cooked just until the sauce begins to crust on the surface. Serve the fish with rice on the side, or tuck the fillets into tacos.

2 tablespoons vegetable oil, plus more for the baking sheet

2 to 2¼ pounds skin-on red snapper, tilapia, or sea bass fillets

2 dried guajillo chiles, stemmed and seeded

1 cup bitter orange juice or Bitter Orange Juice Substitute (page 206)

2 tablespoons achiote paste

9 garlic cloves, peeled

¼ cup coarsely chopped white onion

5 cloves, stems removed and discarded

¼ teaspoon ground allspice

1 teaspoon kosher salt, plus more for seasoning the fish

¼ teaspoon freshly ground black pepper

Preheat the oven to 450 degrees F, with a rack in the middle. Cover a large baking sheet with aluminum foil. Brush the foil with vegetable oil. Place the fish on the baking sheet, skin side down, and let come to room temperature while you make the sauce.

Heat a comal or large skillet over medium-low heat. Add the guajillo chiles and toast for about 30 seconds per side, until the color darkens; be careful not to let them burn.

Transfer the chiles to a small saucepan, cover with water, and bring to a boil. Reduce the heat to medium and simmer for 10 to 12 minutes, until the chiles are softened.

Transfer the chiles to a blender, along with 2 tablespoons of their cooking water. Add the bitter orange juice, achiote paste, garlic, onion, cloves, allspice, salt, and pepper and blend until smooth.

Heat the 2 tablespoons oil in a medium saucepan over medium-high heat. Add the chile sauce, shielding yourself from splatters with the lid. Cover partially and cook, stirring often, until the sauce thickens and darkens and the flavors bloom, 8 to 10 minutes. Remove from the heat. Set ½ cup of the sauce aside for serving.

Season the fish with a little salt and top with the remaining sauce. Roast for 10 to 15 minutes, or until the fish is opaque and the sauce is just beginning to crust.

Serve the fish with the reserved sauce.

ACHIOTE PASTE

Achiote paste gets its vivid orange-red hue from the seeds of a shrub native to Mexico. Also called annatto, the ground seeds give the paste a pungency somewhat reminiscent of saffron. Charred garlic, herbs, toasted spices (typically cloves, cumin seeds, black peppercorns, allspice, and coriander seeds), and bitter orange contribute to the multi-leveled taste. Achiote paste (labeled *pasta de achiote* or *recado rojo*) can be found in many Latin stores, large grocery stores, and online. It keeps for months stored in a cool, dark place. The brands that I go for are those that come from the Yucatán, such as Anita and El Yucateco.

Don't substitute ground achiote seeds for the paste. Achiote seeds are just one of the ingredients that make the paste. Also, get the achiote paste that looks like a little red brick; don't go for the wet rub, which is not the Mexican kind.

BITTER ORANGE JUICE

The bitter orange, *naranja agria*, looks like a misshapen, bumpy orange, but if you were to bite into one, you'd get a surprise: The juice has a distinctive sour and bitter taste. Its high acid content makes the juice particularly good for tenderizing meats and seafood.

You can find bitter oranges in some Mexican markets and also some Asian markets. It isn't always easy to find them, though, and you can't simply substitute regular orange juice, because bitter orange has a unique flavor, which brings out the subtleties in Yucatecan dishes, especially those that contain achiote paste. But if you put together equal parts lime juice, orange juice, and grapefruit juice and pump up the acidity with a little white vinegar, you're there. You get sweetness from the orange, acidic punch from the lime, bitterness from the grapefruit, and a bit more edge from the vinegar.

BITTER ORANGE JUICE SUBSTITUTE

Makes 2 cups

½ cup freshly squeezed lime juice

½ cup freshly squeezed orange juice

½ cup freshly squeezed grapefruit juice

½ cup white vinegar

Combine all the ingredients in a jar or bowl and shake or stir well. The juice can be refrigerated, covered, for up to 2 weeks. Shake or stir well before using.

Cook's Note

► You can also make this without grapefruit juice, using ⅔ cup each lime juice, orange juice, and vinegar.

SAUCY BEACHSIDE SNAPPER
/ PESCADO ZARANDEADO
(PAGE 208)

SAUCY BEACHSIDE SNAPPER / **PESCADO ZARANDEADO**

Serves 6 to 8

You'll feel like you're at a beachside stand in Sinaloa or Sonora when you taste this incredibly moist snapper. The sauce that smothers the delicate fish, insulating it from the high heat of the oven (or, on the coast, the grill), is a concoction of unexpected ingredients that may seem surprising but taste amazing together. The creamy base of the sauce is like a cross between a Caesar and green goddess dressing. It gets so much *sazón* from yellow mustard, soy sauce, and Worcestershire mixed with roasted garlic, onion, tomatoes, and green chiles. When I have the time, I add a garnish of sliced bell peppers and onion tossed with some of the sauce.

In the northern states of Sonora and Sinaloa, the sauces for the zarandeado are usually creamy, like this one. As you move south from Sinaloa, you will find adobo marinades and chile rubs. In the Yucatán, achiote is part of the formula. But no matter where you are, the fish is cooked on a *zaranda,* a flat-hinged grilling basket, from which it gets its name.

Because grilling a sauced fish can be tricky and not everyone has this type of grilling basket, like many cooks, I've adapted this coastal-inspired version to a hot oven. I still like to use whole sides of fish, though, as they do on the beach. I buy a whole snapper and have it cleaned, split in half, and boned.

You can eat the fish as is, topped with the vegetable garnish or not. Or do as they do in Sonora and Sinaloa and once it comes out of the oven, taco everything in warm corn tortillas, with splashes of hot sauce, a squeeze of lime, and a sprinkling of salt. *The photo is on page 207.*

FOR THE SAUCE

1 medium tomato

6 garlic cloves, not peeled

½ white onion, quartered

2 fresh Anaheim chiles

¼ cup freshly squeezed lime juice

¼ cup mayonnaise

2 tablespoons crema, crème fraîche, or heavy cream

3 tablespoons yellow mustard

2 tablespoons soy sauce

1 tablespoon Worcestershire sauce

2 tablespoons unsalted butter, softened

1 teaspoon kosher salt

½ teaspoon freshly ground black pepper

FOR THE FISH

Vegetable oil for the baking sheet

1 (4½- to 5-pound) whole snapper, split in half and deboned by the fish market (see note)

Kosher salt

1 red bell pepper, cored, halved, seeded, and cut into 2-inch matchsticks

1 yellow bell pepper, cored, halved, seeded, and cut into 2-inch matchsticks

1 green bell pepper, cored, halved, seeded, and cut into 2-inch matchsticks

½ red onion, cut into slivers

FOR SERVING (OPTIONAL)

2 or 3 limes, quartered

Hot sauce

10 to 12 warm corn tortillas

To make the sauce: Preheat the broiler, with the rack 2 to 3 inches from the heat source. Put the tomato, garlic, onion, and chiles on a baking sheet lined with foil and broil, turning the vegetables halfway through, until they are charred and the tomato has begun to release its juices, 5 to 7 minutes for the garlic and about 10 minutes for the other ingredients. Remove the garlic when it is charred and softened and, when it's cool enough to handle, peel it. Alternatively, you can char everything on a preheated comal or skillet over medium-low heat. Remove from the heat.

Transfer the Anaheims to a plastic bag and seal, or place in a bowl and cover tightly with plastic wrap. Allow to sweat for 10 minutes, then halve, peel, and seed.

Place all the roasted vegetables, including any juices, in a blender. Add the remaining sauce ingredients and puree until smooth.

To roast the fish: Preheat the oven to 450 degrees F, with a rack in the middle. Cover a large baking sheet with foil. Brush the foil with vegetable oil.

Pat the fish dry and place skin side down on the baking sheet. Reserve ½ cup of the sauce if making the garnish, and spread the rest generously over the fish.

Roast the fish for 20 to 30 minutes, depending on thickness, until it is cooked through and pulls apart when a fork is inserted; the sauce should be nicely browned and a little crusty on top.

Meanwhile, make the optional garnish, if desired: Combine the bell peppers, onion, and the reserved sauce in a medium bowl, tossing to coat the vegetables.

Give the fish a sprinkling of salt and serve with the garnish, if using, and, if you like, with limes, hot sauce, and warm tortillas on the side.

Cook's Note

▸ You can substitute 3 pounds red snapper fillets for the boned whole snapper. Or you can use other firm white fish fillets, like tilapia or sea bass. Fillets will take less time to roast than a whole fish.

HALIBUT IN TOMATO-TOMATILLO SAUCE WITH ALMONDS AND OLIVES / **PESCADO AGRIDULCE**

Serves 4 to 6

Pescado agridulce, pan-cooked halibut in a colorful tomato and tomatillo salsa, is one of the quickest and easiest recipes in this collection. The sauce is a classic marriage of ingredients from Spain—almonds, olives, olive oil, sweet spices—with ingredients native to Mexico—tomatoes and tomatillos. Ideal for a weeknight dinner, the dish is also elegant enough for a dinner party. All you need is rice or slices of Potato Crown (page 344) to go alongside. Ironically, the simple sauce was originally served with one of the most complex moles I've ever tasted. I learned it from Ixchel Ornelas, the amazing chef-owner of El Patio in Tlaxiaco, Oaxaca, who taught me how to make it when I visited her to learn more about the local cuisine of la Mixteca, a region in the northwestern part of the state.

¼ cup olive oil

1 cup very thinly sliced white onion

4 garlic cloves, finely chopped

1 pound ripe tomatoes, finely chopped, or 1 (15-ounce) can crushed tomatoes

1 pound tomatillos, husked, rinsed, and finely chopped

1 teaspoon dark brown sugar or grated piloncillo

1 teaspoon kosher salt, plus more for seasoning the fish

¼ teaspoon ground allspice

¼ teaspoon ground canela or cinnamon

¼ cup slivered almonds

¼ cup sliced pimiento-stuffed green olives

4 to 6 halibut fillets, preferably skin-on, (about 2 pounds)

Heat 2 tablespoons of the oil in a large skillet over medium heat. Add the onion and cook for a couple of minutes, until it begins to wilt. Add the garlic and cook for another minute, or until fragrant. Stir in the tomatoes, tomatillos, brown sugar, salt, allspice, and canela or cinnamon and cook, stirring occasionally, for 5 minutes, or until the vegetables have softened.

Stir in the almonds and olives and cook for another 7 to 8 minutes, stirring occasionally, until the tomatoes have cooked down a little more and the flavors have blended. Turn off the heat.

Season the fish with salt.

Heat the remaining 2 tablespoons olive oil in a Dutch oven or a large deep skillet with a lid over medium-high heat. Add the fish, skin side down, and cook for 1 to 2 minutes, until the bottom side begins to brown. Scrape the chunky sauce over the fish, cover, and reduce the heat to low. Cook for 10 minutes, or until the fish is opaque throughout.

Serve hot.

SEARED POMPANO IN GREEN SAUCE / **PÁMPANO EN SALSA VERDE**

Serves 2

This is one of the most celebrated items on the menu of La Pigua, a restaurant in Campeche in the Yucatán, whose owner, Francisco Hernández Romero, is a proud spokesman for the cuisine of his city. Francisco's choice for the dish is pompano, a meaty white-fleshed fish that is abundant in the Gulf of Mexico. He marinates the fish briefly in a mix of lime juice, cilantro, and garlic, then sears it and spoons over a silky-smooth emerald-green sauce, made by heating a blend of olive oil, bitter orange juice, and fresh herbs, enriched with a bit of broth. The dish is herbal, citrusy, and slightly acidic.

FOR THE MARINADE AND FISH

¼ cup chopped fresh cilantro leaves and upper stems

¼ cup water

¼ cup freshly squeezed lime juice

3 garlic cloves, peeled

1 teaspoon kosher salt, or to taste

½ teaspoon freshly ground black pepper

1 pound meaty white fish fillets, such as pompano, snook, halibut, or sea bass

FOR THE SAUCE

½ cup olive oil

¼ cup bitter orange juice or Bitter Orange Juice Substitute (page 206)

1 cup chopped fresh cilantro leaves and upper stems

½ cup chopped fresh parsley leaves

1 cup chopped fresh chives

½ teaspoon kosher salt, or more to taste

Freshly ground black pepper

½ cup chicken or vegetable broth

2 tablespoons olive oil

To marinate the fish: Combine the cilantro, water, lime juice, garlic, salt, and pepper in a blender and puree until smooth. Place the fish in a baking dish and pour the marinade over it. Turn over a few times to coat and let sit for 5 minutes.

Meanwhile, make the sauce: Combine the olive oil, bitter orange juice, cilantro, parsley, chives, salt, and a pinch of pepper in a blender and blend until smooth. Pour into a small saucepan and bring to a boil. Stir in the broth and adjust the seasonings. Keep warm.

To cook the fish: Heat the olive oil in a large skillet over medium-high heat. Sear the fish fillets in batches until golden and cooked through, 2 to 3 minutes per side. Transfer to plates and spoon the warm sauce over the top. Serve.

PANFRIED FISH WITH GARLIC, ALMONDS, AND GUAJILLOS / PESCADO AL AJILLO CON ALMENDRAS Y GUAJILLOS

Serves 4

There is a very Spanish feel to this dish, but it is Mexican through and through, and you will find variations on it up and down the coasts. Similar dishes are standard offerings in every beachside seafood hut: fish, octopus, or shrimp sautéed with abundant garlic. Different cooks and establishments add their own spin, typically with one kind of dried chile or another. Here thinly sliced guajillos and slivered almonds supplement the abundance of sautéed sliced garlic that tops the delicate fish, adding a crunchy, nutty texture and heat. I always add a generous squeeze of lime juice to my serving.

The dish comes together in minutes. Fillets of flounder or sole require only a couple of minutes to cook, and the garlic, chiles, and almonds brown almost instantly in the hot pan. I usually have a batch of steaming white rice ready on the side and I call my hungry eaters to the table before I begin frying the fish.

2 pounds flounder or sole fillets or other skinless mild-tasting white-fleshed fish, such as sea bass, snapper, or tilapia

1 teaspoon kosher salt, or to taste

Freshly ground black pepper

4 tablespoons unsalted butter

¼ cup vegetable oil

15 garlic cloves, sliced (about ½ cup)

2 dried guajillo chiles, stemmed, seeded, and thinly sliced or snipped with scissors (see note)

⅓ cup slivered almonds

2 limes, halved

Season the fish with the salt and black pepper to taste. Heat 2 tablespoons of the butter and 2 tablespoons of the oil in a large skillet, preferably nonstick, over medium-high heat. Once the butter melts and bubbles, add half the fillets in a single layer without crowding the pan. Sear for 1 to 2 minutes on the first side. Before turning, run a spatula under the fish to make sure that the fillets aren't sticking. Turn and cook for 1 or 2 minutes on the other side, until the fish can be flaked with a fork. Transfer to a platter. Heat the remaining 2 tablespoons each butter and oil and cook the remaining fillets. Transfer to the platter.

Add the garlic and guajillo chiles to the pan, stir, and cook for about 30 seconds, until fragrant and beginning to color. Add the almonds and stir as everything browns and crisps, no more than a minute.

Scrape the garlic mixture over the fish. Serve with the halved limes.

Cook's Note

► Since the dried chiles can be a bit hard, it's easier to cut them with scissors. Stem and seed them, then hold them over a bowl and snip.

CRISPY FRIED FISH FINGERS WITH CHIPOTLE MAYO / **PESCADO EMPANIZADO**

Serves 6 to 8

Fried fish in the crispiest of coatings is savored hot from the pan at practically every beach stand and restaurant along the Mexican coasts. But it's not just a seaside classic, it's a beloved dinner throughout the country, especially during Lent. Pescado empanizado was one of our favorite fish dishes when I was growing up. We drizzled the crusty pieces with lime juice and dunked them in chipotle mayo. Alongside, we had mashed potatoes, or we tucked the fish into warm corn tortillas with a slice of ripe avocado.

Marinades for the fish vary. Lime juice, salt, and pepper is the simplest. Some cooks, like my mom, take the milk route, as I do here. The milk tenderizes the fish and also acts as a subtle vehicle for additional flavors.

In restaurants or beach joints, the fish is usually accompanied with rice and a simple green salad, with tortillas on the side so people can taco it if they feel like it. You can bread, fry, and serve the fish whole, or you can cut it into strips as in this recipe, so you get more bang for your crunch.

FOR THE FRIED FISH

1 cup milk

5 garlic cloves, peeled

½ cup coarsely chopped white onion

3 chipotle chiles in adobo sauce

1 teaspoon dried oregano

½ teaspoon dried marjoram

½ teaspoon dried thyme

2 teaspoons kosher salt

1 teaspoon freshly ground black pepper

2 pounds mild white fish fillets, such as red snapper or tilapia, cut into 2- to 3-inch pieces

1 cup all-purpose flour

3 large eggs

2 cups bread crumbs

Vegetable oil for frying

FOR THE CHIPOTLE MAYO

1 cup mayonnaise

2 to 3 tablespoons sauce from chipotles in adobo

Juice of 1 lime

Kosher salt and freshly ground black pepper

Warm corn tortillas for serving (optional)

Sliced avocado for serving (optional)

Quartered limes for serving

To marinate the fish: Combine the milk, garlic, onion, chipotles, oregano, marjoram, thyme, 1 teaspoon of the salt, and ½ teaspoon of the pepper in a blender and puree until smooth.

Place the fish in a bowl and cover with the marinade. Toss and turn a few times to be sure all the pieces are coated. Cover and refrigerate for at least 2 hours, and up to 24 hours.

To make the mayo: Mix the mayonnaise, adobo sauce, and lime juice in a bowl. Season to taste with salt and pepper. Cover and refrigerate until needed.

continued

When ready to fry the fish: Remove the fish from the marinade; discard the marinade.

Place the flour on a wide plate. Crack the eggs into a wide bowl, lightly beat them, and whisk in ½ teaspoon of the salt and ¼ teaspoon of the pepper. Place the bread crumbs on a wide plate and toss with the remaining ½ teaspoon salt and ¼ teaspoon pepper.

One at a time, dip the fish pieces in the flour to lightly coat, tapping off the excess flour, dip in the beaten eggs, turning to coat, and then dip in the crumbs to coat; place on a baking sheet. Place a cooling rack on a large platter or baking sheet lined with paper towels.

Heat 1 inch of oil in a large skillet over medium heat for at least 5 minutes. Test to see if the oil is hot by inserting a piece of a tortilla or fish fillet; the oil should bubble around it enthusiastically. Add the breaded fish pieces in batches, without crowding, and cook for 3 to 4 minutes per side, turning with rubber-tipped tongs or a slotted spoon or spatula, until golden brown and crisp. Remove from the oil and drain on the cooling rack.

Serve the fish with the chipotle mayonnaise on the side and some warm corn tortillas and sliced avocado, if desired. Pass lime wedges at the table.

CLAMS WITH DIRTY RICE / **ALMEJAS CON ARROZ**

Serves 4 to 6

Because the huge state of Sonora is so well known for its beef, it's easy to forget that its extensive coastline along the Sea of Cortez has produced a rich array of seafood dishes. In this one, rice is infused with an earthy tomato-chile sauce blended with clam broth, becoming rust-red and fragrant in the process. To cook the clams and get that wonderful broth for the rice, a mix of aromatic vegetables—onion, red bell pepper, leeks, and carrots—is sautéed in butter and olive oil, and a little beer is poured in and cooked down before adding the clams. The clams release their juices into the sauce as they open.

5 dozen littleneck clams

2 dried colorado, New Mexico, or guajillo chiles, stemmed and seeded

1 pound ripe tomatoes or 1 (15-ounce) can whole tomatoes

3 garlic cloves, peeled

1 teaspoon dried oregano

½ teaspoon ground cumin

2½ teaspoons kosher salt

5 tablespoons olive oil

2 tablespoons unsalted butter

⅔ cup finely chopped white onion

⅔ cup finely chopped red bell pepper

⅔ cup finely chopped well-washed leeks (white and light green parts only)

⅔ cup finely chopped peeled carrots

⅔ cup beer of choice

1 to 2 cups water or chicken, vegetable, or seafood broth, as needed

2 cups extra-long-grain white rice or jasmine rice

Chopped fresh parsley and/or cilantro leaves for garnish

Rinse and scrub the clams, discarding any that are broken. Set aside.

Put the chiles, fresh tomatoes, if using, and garlic in a medium saucepan, cover with water, and bring to a boil. Reduce the heat to medium and simmer for 10 to 12 minutes, until the chiles have softened and the tomatoes are cooked and mushy but not falling apart.

Using a slotted spoon, transfer the vegetables to a blender and add 1 cup of the cooking liquid. Add the canned tomatoes, if using, oregano, cumin, and 1 teaspoon of the salt to the blender and puree until smooth. Set aside.

Heat 2 tablespoons of the olive oil and the butter in a Dutch oven or large deep skillet with a lid over medium-high heat. When the butter begins to foam, add the onion, bell pepper, leeks, and carrots and cook, stirring often, for 5 to 6 minutes, until the vegetables have fully softened and begun to lightly brown along the edges. Stir in the beer and ½ teaspoon of the salt and simmer until the alcohol has just about evaporated, 4 to 5 minutes. The vegetables should be quite soft and still moist but not wet.

Pour the tomato puree over the vegetables, bring to a boil, and add all the clams. Cover, reduce the heat to medium, and cook for 7 to 8 minutes, until the clams open. Turn off the heat and let sit for 5 minutes.

continued

Using a slotted spoon or tongs, transfer the clams to a bowl, discarding any that haven't opened. Transfer the sauce and vegetables to a bowl or large Pyrex measuring cup and wipe the Dutch oven or skillet clean. Add enough water or broth to the sauce to measure 5 cups.

Remove about 3 dozen clams from the shells; discard the shells.

Heat the remaining 3 tablespoons olive oil in the Dutch oven or skillet over medium-high heat until very hot but not smoking. Add the rice and cook, stirring often, until it crackles, becomes milky white, and feels heavier as you stir it, 3 to 4 minutes; don't let it brown. Add the reserved sauce and vegetables and the remaining 1 teaspoon salt and stir well. Add all the clams (both shelled and still in the shells) and bring to

a boil, then cover and reduce the heat to low. Cook for 15 minutes, until most of the liquid has evaporated and the rice has cooked. Taste the rice, and if it isn't fully cooked but the liquid has almost evaporated, add another ¼ to ½ cup water or broth, scrape the bottom of the pot, cover, and cook for a few more minutes, until the rice is tender. Remove from the heat and let stand, covered, for 5 minutes.

When ready to serve, fluff the rice with a fork, garnish the dish with parsley and/or cilantro, and dig in.

COCONUT SHRIMP / **CAMARONES AL COCO**

Serves 6 as a main course, 10 to 12 as an appetizer

Imagine the most gigantic, moist shrimp you've ever seen, tails still on, enrobed in a crisp, golden brown coconut coating, and you'll get the picture of this festive but fast dinner or amazing appetizer. It's one of the many memorable dishes I tasted in Campeche, a state in the Yucatán with a long coastline along the Gulf of Mexico. Though Campeche is not as well known as other parts of the Yucatán Peninsula, it boasts stupendous seafood and many charming towns and villages.

For the coating, some cooks use sweetened shredded coconut, others use unsweetened. I choose both, because I love the chewy texture and moist sweetness of the sweetened coconut, but I also like the fragrance and drier crunch of unsweetened. I combine them with bread crumbs. Buy the biggest shrimp you can get. Take care not to overcook them, so they remain plump and juicy inside the crunchy coating. They're perfect with fruity, fierce Mango-Habanero Salsa.

1 cup shredded or flaked unsweetened coconut (not chips)

1 cup shredded or flaked sweetened coconut (not chips)

1 cup bread crumbs

1 teaspoon kosher salt

½ teaspoon freshly ground black pepper

1 cup all-purpose flour

4 large eggs

Vegetable oil for deep-frying

2 pounds extra-large shrimp, peeled, tails left on, and deveined

Mango-Habanero Salsa (page 139) for serving

Mix the coconut, bread crumbs, ½ teaspoon of the salt, and the pepper in a baking dish or wide bowl. Put the flour on a large plate or in a wide bowl. Combine the eggs and the remaining ½ teaspoon salt in a shallow bowl and beat well with a whisk or fork.

Heat 1 inch of oil in a large deep skillet over medium heat to 350 degrees F, at least 5 minutes. Place a cooling rack on a baking sheet lined with paper towels.

Meanwhile, dredge each shrimp in the flour so it is completely coated, tapping or shaking off the excess flour, dip into the beaten eggs, turning to coat, and then place on the coconut mixture and press down while patting and pressing the coconut onto the shrimp with your hands so it is completely coated; gently set on a plate or cutting board.

When you have finished coating the shrimp, check the oil temperature and if it is not yet at 350 degrees F, increase the heat to medium-high. If you don't have a thermometer, dip the tail of a shrimp into it; it should actively bubble.

Fry the shrimp in batches, taking care not to overcrowd the pan, until they are golden brown and cooked through, 1 to 2 minutes per side; use rubber-tipped tongs or a slotted spoon or spatula to turn them. Be careful not to overcook. Transfer to the cooling rack to drain.

Serve the shrimp with the salsa for dipping.

CHICKEN AND TURKEY

GARLIC, CHILE, AND CUMIN ROAST CHICKEN / **POLLO AJOCOMINO** 224

OAXACAN OREGANO ROAST CHICKEN / **POLLO AL ORÉGANO OAXAQUEÑO** 227

ORANGE AND ANAHEIM CHICKEN / **POLLO A LA NARANJA Y CHILE VERDE** 228

CHORIZO CHICKEN TINGA / **TINGA DE POLLO CON CHORIZO Y PAPA** 231

CHICKEN POZOLE WITH PINTO BEANS / **GALLINA PINTA** 232

CHICKEN IN PECAN AND ANCHO CHILE SAUCE / **POLLO CON SALSA DE NUEZ Y CHILE ANCHO** 236

ALMOND CHICKEN / **POLLO ALMENDRADO** 237

CHICKEN MOLE WITH MUSHROOMS / **ATÁPAKUA DE POLLO CON HONGOS** 240

COLORADITO MOLE WITH CHICKEN / **MOLE COLORADITO CON POLLO** 245

MOLE POBLANO WITH CHICKEN / **MOLE POBLANO CON POLLO** 248

PLAZA CHICKEN AND ENCHILADAS / **ENCHILADAS PLACERAS CON POLLO** 252

CHIPOTLE TURKEY MEAT LOAF / **ALBONDIGÓN DE PAVO** 257

FIESTA TURKEY WITH CHORIZO AND CASHEW STUFFING / **PAVO DE FIESTA CON CHORIZO Y NUEZ DE LA INDIA** 258

When I was growing up, my mother shopped every weekend at a big market in Mexico City called Mercado de Prado Norte. In the middle, visible from all sides, was Doña Lucy's poultry stand. A loud, hardworking woman who always wore a spotless white apron, Doña Lucy knew my mother's weekly orders by heart, as she did those of all her other customers.

When my mother arrived, Doña Lucy would have three whole chickens ready, and also chicken livers, ground chicken for meat loaf, and boneless, skinless breasts that she pounded thin with a tremendous mallet and layered between sheets of plastic so they could be frozen for *milanesas*. In addition to chicken in every form, Doña Lucy sold holiday turkeys, which we always ordered in advance.

Like Doña Lucy, most food purveyors in Mexico work hard to build their fan base, and once you are a customer, they become devoted to you. And you become devoted to them. My grandmother Lali was also Doña's Lucy's long-time customer, and ever since they got married, my sisters have been as well. After my wedding, when I still lived in Mexico City, I shopped there too. It was Doña Lucy who taught me how to deftly break down a chicken into serving pieces. At the beginning of each week, I make chicken broth with a whole cut-up chicken so I'll have the tasty broth for soups, salsas, sauces, stews, and rice dishes, as well as a ready supply of shredded chicken for tacos, tamales, and chicken tinga, the Puebla classic with its chipotle-laced sauce.

In this chapter, you will find a playlist of such favorites, including the simplest but tastiest oregano roast chicken from Oaxaca and a creamy, luxurious chicken mole with mushrooms from Michoacán. Some are weeknight specials, like roast chicken rubbed with garlic, chile, and cumin. Others, like mole coloradito, are dishes that we might make several times a year when we have company. A few more, like mole poblano, are reserved for very special occasions.

We celebrate Christmas and New Year's in a major way in Mexico, and turkey is a vital part of those holidays. The classic way of cooking it is in an adobo sauce that brings together spicy and sweet flavors, always with some fruit, which can be in the stuffing or the sauce, or both. Now that I live in the U.S., I've moved our family turkey tradition to Thanksgiving, since it fits into that menu so well. In fact, Thanksgiving has become my favorite holiday of the year, not the least because it allows immigrants to bring flavors from our old homes to our new one.

GARLIC, CHILE, AND CUMIN ROAST CHICKEN / **POLLO AJOCOMINO**

Serves 4 or 5

Rubbed and marinated in a spicy adobo-like sauce of dried chiles, abundant garlic, toasted cumin, and olive oil, this easy roast chicken is packed with flavor. Some of the rub chars a little as the bird roasts, adding another wonderful dimension.

The dish is from the state of Hidalgo in central Mexico, and you'll find versions with different names in other parts of the country as well. In San Luis Potosí, Hidalgo, and Oaxaca, it goes by *pollo ajocomino* (garlic cumin chicken), the name I use. In Guerrero, it's called *chileajo* (chile garlic). I guess it would be a tongue twister to call it *chileajocomino* (chile-garlic-cumin), but chiles are at the heart of the marinade, with each seasoning in perfect harmony and none overpowering.

The types of chiles vary according to the region. I use a mix of anchos and dried chipotles, which gives the sauce a smoky and adobo-like flavor.

The chicken is delicious hot, at room temperature, or cold. You'll like having leftovers; they are great for sandwiches and tortas.

4 dried ancho chiles, stemmed and seeded

2 dried chipotle chiles, preferably moritas (page 133), stemmed

2 teaspoons cumin seeds

15 garlic cloves, peeled

2 teaspoons kosher salt, or more to taste

⅓ cup olive oil, plus more for the baking sheet

3½ to 4 pounds bone-in chicken pieces (8 to 10 legs, thighs, and/or halved breasts)

1 cup chicken broth

Place the ancho and chipotle chiles in a saucepan, cover with water, and bring to a boil. Reduce the heat to medium and simmer for 10 to 15 minutes, pushing the chiles down into the water from time to time to submerge, until they soften. Remove from the heat and fish out the chipotles from the saucepan. When they are cool enough to handle, remove the seeds.

Heat a small skillet over medium-low heat. Add the cumin seeds and toast, stirring or shaking the pan constantly, until fragrant and very slightly darkened, 45 seconds to 1 minute. Immediately transfer to a small bowl or plate.

Place the ancho and chipotle chiles in a blender, along with ½ cup of their cooking liquid. Add the garlic, cumin seeds, salt, and olive oil and puree until smooth. Scrape into a large bowl and let cool slightly.

Add the chicken to the chile-garlic marinade and turn to coat each piece thoroughly; set aside while you preheat the oven.

Preheat the oven to 450 degrees F, with a rack in the middle. Generously oil a large baking sheet. Place the chicken skin side down on the baking sheet and coat with any marinade remaining in the bowl. Sprinkle with a little salt. Roast for 15 minutes.

continued

Reduce the temperature to 375 degrees F, turn the chicken pieces over, and spoon on any marinade and juices from the baking sheet. Pour the chicken broth onto the baking sheet and return to the oven. Roast for 45 to 50 more minutes, or until the chicken is cooked through and juices, if any, run clear when pierced with a knife.

Serve hot, at room temperature, or cold.

Cook's Notes

► Ancho chiles are easy to seed, but chipotle chiles are easier to seed after they have been simmered.

► You can marinate the chicken for up to 2 days, covered and refrigerated.

OAXACAN OREGANO ROAST CHICKEN / **POLLO AL ORÉGANO OAXAQUEÑO**

Serves 4 or 5

In this traditional Oaxacan dish, which is a weekly dinner in my home, chicken is rubbed with a paste made with a generous amount of fresh oregano, lots of garlic, lime juice, olive oil, and salt—a kind of pesto, but more earthy and tart—and roasted. You'll be surprised that despite all the garlic, the chicken does not taste sharp, just beautifully seasoned. I find it fascinating that Oaxaca, a region known for its complex and laborious moles, also produced such a deliciously simple dish.

⅓ cup extra-virgin olive oil, plus more for the baking sheet

30 garlic cloves, peeled

1 cup tightly packed fresh oregano leaves

⅓ cup freshly squeezed lime juice

1½ teaspoons kosher salt, or more to taste

½ teaspoon freshly ground black pepper, or more to taste

3½ to 4 pounds bone-in chicken pieces (8 to 10 legs, thighs, and/or halved breasts)

1½ cups chicken broth

Preheat the oven to 450 degrees F, with a rack in the middle. Generously oil a large baking sheet with olive oil. Place the remaining ⅓ cup oil, garlic, oregano, lime juice, salt, and pepper in a food processor or molcajete and process or mash to a coarse paste.

Rub the garlic paste all over chicken pieces and place them skin side down on the baking sheet. Roast for 15 minutes. Reduce the temperature to 375 degrees F, turn the chicken pieces skin side up, and pour the chicken broth onto the baking sheet. Roast for 45 to 50 minutes longer, or until the chicken is cooked through and the juices, if any, run clear when pierced with a knife.

Transfer the chicken to a platter. Scrape up the sauce remaining in the pan, spoon it over the chicken, and serve.

Cook's Note

► You can marinate the chicken for up to 2 days, covered, in the refrigerator.

ORANGE AND ANAHEIM CHICKEN / **POLLO A LA NARANJA Y CHILE VERDE**

Serves 4 or 5

I have never seen as many orange blossoms as I did the first time I visited Sonora. In every town, the streets were lined with trees in full bloom, their branches so heavy with blossoms that they almost touched the ground. Oranges are also very much a part of the local cuisine. In this Sonoran favorite, orange juice is paired with another one of the region's signature ingredients, Anaheim chiles. The chicken is browned, then simmered in a sauce made with Anaheims, orange juice, onions, and garlic. The pale green sauce is just a little spicy, just a little sweet, and just a little sticky. I like to serve this with rice.

3½ to 4 pounds bone-in chicken pieces (8 to 10 legs, thighs, and/or halved breasts)

1 teaspoon kosher salt, or more to taste

½ teaspoon freshly ground black pepper

3 tablespoons vegetable oil

¾ cup chopped white onion

2 fresh Anaheim chiles, seeded and chopped

3 garlic cloves, sliced

½ teaspoon ground canela or cinnamon

½ teaspoon dried oregano

3 cups freshly squeezed orange juice (from about 8 medium oranges)

Season the chicken with the salt and pepper; set aside.

Heat 2 tablespoons of the oil in a Dutch oven or a large deep skillet with a lid over medium-high heat. Add the onion and chiles and cook for 4 to 5 minutes, stirring often, until they start to soften. Add the garlic, canela or cinnamon, and oregano and cook for another couple of minutes, until the mixture is fragrant and the vegetables are soft. Scrape into a blender. Add 2 cups of the orange juice and puree until smooth.

Add the remaining 1 tablespoon oil to the pot and heat over medium-high heat. When the oil is hot, brown the chicken pieces in batches, skin side down first, until nicely colored, 4 to 5 minutes on each side. Remove to a bowl or plate as each batch is done.

When all of the chicken pieces have been browned, reduce the heat to medium-low and add the orange juice–chile puree to the pot, stirring. Add the remaining 1 cup orange juice and stir well. Bring to a simmer, stirring and scraping up all of the browned bits from the bottom of the pot. Return the browned chicken pieces to the pot, cover partially, and simmer for 40 minutes, or until the chicken is cooked through and the sauce has thickened and coats the back of a wooden spoon.

Taste and adjust the seasonings and serve.

CHORIZO CHICKEN TINGA / TINGA DE POLLO CON CHORIZO Y PAPA

Serves 6

The best-known versions of chicken tinga—shredded chicken cooked in a chipotle-tomato sauce—are from the state of Puebla, but the dish is popular throughout central Mexico. This take on it, though, is very specific to the region's capital, Puebla City. I love the combination of sweet tomatoes and tart tomatillos, and the chorizo contributes small bites of bold flavor. There are diced potatoes and plenty of very thinly sliced onions, garlic, and the traditional seasoning trio of thyme, marjoram, and oregano.

Chicken tinga works well as a topper or filler for tacos, tostadas, sopes, quesadillas, and tortas. But you can also serve it with rice and/or beans and warm corn tortillas.

2 pounds ripe tomatoes, quartered, or 2 (15-ounce) cans tomatoes

¼ pound tomatillos (about 2), husked, rinsed, and quartered

1 cup chicken broth

1 to 2 chipotle chiles in adobo, finely chopped, plus 2 tablespoons of the sauce, or more to taste

¼ cup vegetable oil

1 pound Mexican chorizo, casings removed and coarsely chopped

2 cups slivered white onions

2 garlic cloves, finely chopped

2 bay leaves

1 teaspoon dried oregano

½ teaspoon dried marjoram

½ teaspoon dried thyme

1 teaspoon kosher salt, or more to taste

½ teaspoon freshly ground black pepper

1 pound red or Yukon gold potatoes, peeled and cut into ¼-inch dice

6 cups finely shredded cooked chicken (page 251) or rotisserie chicken

Place the tomatoes, tomatillos, broth, chipotles, and adobo sauce in a blender or food processor and puree until smooth (do this in batches if necessary). Set aside.

Heat 2 tablespoons of the oil in a Dutch oven or large deep skillet with a lid over medium heat. Add the chorizo and cook, using a couple of wooden spoons or spatulas to break it into smaller pieces, until it has browned and crisped, 8 to 9 minutes. Transfer to a plate or bowl with a slotted spoon, leaving the fat in the pot.

Add the remaining 2 tablespoons oil and the onions to the pot and cook, stirring occasionally, until the onions are wilted and translucent and beginning to brown around the edges, 4 to 5 minutes. Add the garlic and cook until fragrant and beginning to color lightly, less than a minute.

Stir in the chile-tomato puree, along with the bay leaves, oregano, marjoram, thyme, salt, and pepper, cover partially, and cook for 5 minutes. Stir in the potatoes, cover partially, and cook for 10 more minutes, or until the sauce deepens in color to an earthier red and the potatoes are soft.

Add the chicken and chorizo and cook, stirring occasionally, until the chicken has absorbed almost all of the sauce, 10 to 15 minutes. The mixture should be moist but not runny.

Serve hot.

CHICKEN POZOLE WITH PINTO BEANS / GALLINA PINTA

Serves 6 to 8

Two essential ingredients of Mexican cuisine, beans and maize (hominy), contribute to the complexity of this Sonoran stew, a unique pozole verde. The pintos are smooth and earthy, the hominy slightly sweet, chewy-starchy, and subtle. The chicken is cooked with onion, garlic, Anaheim chile, and cilantro, and more color and depth of flavor is added with a pureed seasoning sauce made of a batch of these same ingredients that are fire-roasted and stirred in during the final stages of cooking.

Even before I tried gallina pinta, I was lured in by its name, which translates as multicolored speckled hen, the speckles being the white hominy and the brown pintos. Originally gallina pinta was made with beef or pork, but over time, more and more cooks have been using chicken, so now the dish really matches its title.

It's possible to make pozole with canned hominy (and with canned beans as well), but it is worth taking the time to cook dried hominy yourself because of the resulting flavorful broth, which you then add to the stew. What's more, home-cooked hominy has a better flavor than canned, and the kernels are more irresistible to bite into, with a sturdier, more substantial texture.

FOR THE HOMINY (SEE NOTE)

½ pound dried hominy (about 1 heaping cup), soaked in water to cover for 8 to 24 hours

1 head garlic, papery outer layer removed and halved horizontally

¾ teaspoon kosher salt, or to taste

FOR THE CHICKEN

3½ to 4 pounds bone-in chicken pieces (8 to 10 legs, thighs, and/or halved breasts)

½ white onion

4 garlic cloves, peeled

1 fresh Anaheim chile, seeded and cut into quarters

10 sprigs fresh cilantro

2 teaspoons kosher salt, or to taste

FOR THE SEASONING SAUCE

1 fresh Anaheim chile

¼ white onion, cut in half

2 garlic cloves, not peeled

10 sprigs fresh cilantro

½ recipe Basic Simmered Beans (page 156), made with pinto beans, with at least 1 cup of their broth

FOR GARNISH

1 cup chopped white onion

1 cup coarsely chopped fresh cilantro leaves and upper stems

Crushed dried chiltepín chiles, finely chopped dried chiles de árbol, ground chile piquín, or red pepper flakes

2 limes, quartered

To cook the hominy: Drain the soaked hominy in a colander and rinse it. Place in a large pot, add water to cover by 4 to 5 inches and the halved garlic head, and bring to a boil. Reduce the heat to medium, skim off the foam, cover partially, and simmer for 2½ to 3 hours, until the hominy "blooms," or opens like a flower. Add the salt, stir, and set aside to cool.

continued

Meanwhile, cook the chicken: Place the chicken in a Dutch oven or other large pot, cover with water by at least 2 to 3 inches, and bring to a simmer over medium-high heat. Reduce the heat to medium-low, skim off the foam, and add the onion, garlic cloves, chile, cilantro, and salt. Cover partially and simmer for 1 hour, or until the chicken begins to fall from the bones. Remove from the heat, transfer the chicken pieces to a bowl, and let cool.

Strain the broth (discard the solids) and set aside 1 cup. Return the rest of the broth to the pot and set aside. Once it has cooled, remove the skin from the chicken and discard. Remove the meat from the bones, tear it into small pieces, and return it to the strained broth. Set aside.

While you're waiting for the chicken to cool, make the seasoning sauce: Preheat the broiler, with the rack 2 to 3 inches from the heat source. Put the Anaheim chile, onion, and garlic cloves on a baking sheet lined with foil and broil, turning the vegetables halfway through, until completely charred on the outside and soft on the inside, 5 to 7 minutes for the garlic and 10 to 12 minutes for the other vegetables. Remove the garlic when it is charred and softened, and when it has cooled, peel it. Alternatively, you can roast the vegetables on a preheated comal or skillet over medium heat, turning them every 4 to 5 minutes, until charred. Remove from the heat.

Place the chile in a plastic bag and seal the bag, or transfer it to a small bowl and cover it with plastic wrap; let the chile sweat for 5 to 10 minutes.

Remove the skin, stem, and seeds from the chile. Cut the chile into pieces and place it in a blender, along with the charred onion, garlic cloves, and cilantro sprigs. Add the reserved cup of chicken broth and puree until smooth. Pour into the pot with the chicken and broth.

Stir the pinto beans into the pot, along with 1 cup of their broth, or more to taste, depending on how brothy you want it. Remove and discard the halved head of garlic from the hominy and add the hominy to the pot, along with 1 cup of its liquid, or more to taste, if you want a brothier stew.

Put the pot over medium heat, bring to a simmer, and simmer, partially covered, for 15 to 20 minutes. You will know the pozole is ready when the seasoning sauce pools on the surface into tiny green puddles that are a darker green than the rest of the stew. Taste and adjust the salt.

Serve, and let everyone garnish their pozole with onion, cilantro, chiles, and a squeeze of fresh lime, as desired.

Cook's Note

▶ You can make the pozole using 2 (15-ounce) cans hominy, drained, and 2 (15.5-ounce) cans pinto beans, drained and rinsed (skip the first step of cooking the hominy). Add the hominy and beans to the pot after you add the seasoning sauce, along with 2 cups chicken or vegetable broth, or more to taste for a brothier stew.

Pozole almost always contains hominy—*maiz cacahuacintle*—giant corn kernels that, when cooked, have a substantial, toothsome, starchy texture and an almost sweet taste. The hominy is added to a stew made with one kind of meat or another, usually bone-in chicken and/or pork, vegetables, aromatics, and a seasoning sauce. The stew is served with lots of garnishes—typically chopped onion, chopped cilantro, lime wedges, and, sometimes, shredded lettuce and tortilla chips, which are an important part of the ritual.

There are three main kinds of pozole, determined in the first two cases by the color of the seasoning sauce. Red pozoles (pozole rojo) are flavored with dried red chiles such as anchos and guajillos and sometimes with tomatoes. Green pozoles (pozole verde) are seasoned with fresh green chiles, often combined with tomatillos, cilantro, and other green ingredients, including pumpkin seeds, lettuce, or radish leaves. White pozoles (pozole blanco) have no seasoning sauce and depend for their flavor on a strong meat broth combined with the sweet hominy broth.

Pozole's main ingredient, dried hominy, is best soaked for 8 to 24 hours before cooking. It takes 2½ to 3 hours of simmering before the kernels "bloom," opening at the wide end. If you don't have the time to soak it, it's okay, but it will take a bit longer, from 30 minutes to an hour more, for the kernels to open up. You can add aromatics like garlic to the water, but don't add salt until the end of cooking; adding it too soon will prevent the hominy from softening properly. As soon as the kernels are soft, take the hominy off the heat; if they cook for too long, they will break apart and become mushy.

CHICKEN IN PECAN AND ANCHO CHILE SAUCE /
POLLO CON SALSA DE NUEZ Y CHILE ANCHO

Serves 4 or 5

Pecan groves stretch for miles through Chihuahua, where this dish is beloved. The rich, creamy pecan sauce, made with few ingredients and yet fabulous results, is similar to a mole—thick, nutty, barely spicy, and slightly sweet—with ancho chiles, whose flavor hints of chocolate and raisins, and prunes, which accentuate the taste of the anchos. Like so many dishes from Mexico's northern states, this boasts complex flavors but comes together in a snap.

3 dried ancho chiles, stemmed and seeded

½ white onion

1 garlic clove, not peeled

4 cups chicken broth

1 cup pecans

6 to 8 pitted prunes (about ¼ cup tightly packed)

3½ to 4 pounds bone-in chicken pieces (8 to 10 legs, thighs, and/or halved breasts)

1 teaspoon kosher salt, or more to taste

½ teaspoon freshly ground black pepper

3 tablespoons vegetable oil

Heat a comal or small skillet over medium-low heat. Add the ancho chiles and toast until the skin changes color and the chiles are fragrant, about 30 seconds on each side. Remove from the pan.

Increase the heat to medium and add the onion and garlic clove. Toast, turning the onion and garlic frequently, until charred and softened, 5 to 7 minutes for the garlic, and 10 to 12 minutes for the onion. Remove the garlic when it's charred and softened, and when it's cool enough to handle, peel it.

Bring the chicken broth to a boil in a medium saucepan. Add the pecans, prunes, and toasted anchos, reduce the heat to medium, and simmer for 10 to 12 minutes, until the chiles and prunes have plumped and the pecans have softened. Transfer to a blender (working in batches if necessary), add the charred onion and garlic, and puree.

Season the chicken with the salt and pepper. Heat the oil in a Dutch oven or large skillet with a lid over medium-high heat. When the oil is hot, brown the chicken in batches, cooking it skin side down until nicely colored, 4 to 5 minutes, then turning it and browning on the other side for another 4 to 5 minutes. As each batch is done, remove to a bowl or plate.

Reduce the heat to low and, using the lid as a shield, pour in the pureed pecan sauce. It will bubble and splatter dramatically. Stir well, scraping up all the browned bits from the bottom of the pot, then return the chicken pieces to the pot. Cover, turn down the heat to medium-low, and simmer for about 40 minutes, stirring and scraping the bottom of the pot from time to time, until the chicken is cooked through and the sauce is thick.

Taste, adjust the seasonings, and serve.

ALMOND CHICKEN / **POLLO ALMENDRADO**

Serves 4 or 5

Almendrado refers to a saucy dish containing almonds. In some instances, the sauce is chunky, as it is here, and in other versions, it is pureed and creamy. It is actually a simple-to-make-mole hailing from Oaxaca, the state known for its many moles. I love the streamlined, deliciously crunchy nature of this one, with its toasted almonds, briny olives and capers, sweet raisins, and spicy pickled jalapeños. Serve it with any type of rice, to soak up the sauce.

½ **large white onion, quartered**

6 garlic cloves, not peeled

2 pounds tomatoes (see note)

12 black peppercorns

5 cloves, stems removed and discarded

1 (1-inch) canela stick or ½ **teaspoon ground cinnamon**

1 teaspoon dried oregano

3½ **to 4 pounds bone-in chicken pieces (8 to 10 legs, thighs, and/or halved breasts)**

1 teaspoon kosher salt, or more to taste

¼ **cup vegetable oil**

2 cups chicken broth

1 cup slivered almonds

½ **cup dark raisins**

½ **cup sliced pimiento-stuffed green olives**

¼ **cup chopped capers**

½ **cup pickled jalapeño strips or slices, or more to taste**

Preheat the broiler, with the rack 2 to 3 inches from the heat source. Put the onion, garlic, and tomatoes on a baking sheet lined with foil and broil, turning the vegetables halfway through, until they are charred and the tomatoes are mushy, 5 to 7 minutes for the garlic and 10 to 12 minutes for the other vegetables. Remove the garlic when it is charred and softened, and, when it is cool enough to handle, peel it. Alternatively, you can roast the vegetables on a hot comal or large skillet over medium heat, turning them every 4 to 5 minutes, until charred. Remove from the heat.

Meanwhile, heat a small skillet over medium-low heat. Add the peppercorns, cloves, and canela stick, if using, and toast for a couple of minutes, turning them so they toast evenly. Transfer to a bowl and set aside. Toast the oregano for 10 to 15 seconds; transfer to the bowl.

Combine the charred onion, garlic, and tomatoes and any juices in a blender. Add the peppercorns, cloves, canela or ground cinnamon, and oregano and puree until smooth.

Season the chicken with the salt. Heat the oil in a Dutch oven or large deep skillet with a lid over medium-high heat. When the oil is hot, add the chicken in batches, skin side down, and brown until nicely colored on the first side, 4 to 5 minutes, then turn and brown on the other side for another 4 to 5 minutes. As each batch is done, remove it to a bowl or plate.

continued

Pour the tomato sauce from the blender into the hot oil, shielding yourself with the lid, as it will splatter dramatically. Reduce the heat to medium. Add 1 cup of the chicken broth to the blender and blend for a few seconds, so you can get the remaining sauce out of the blender, then pour into the simmering sauce. Stir, cover, and cook for 10 minutes, stirring occasionally, until the sauce has thickened and darkened slightly.

Stir the remaining 1 cup chicken broth, almonds, raisins, olives, capers, and salt to taste into the pot. Add the browned chicken pieces, cover, reduce the heat to low, and cook for 25 minutes.

Add the pickled jalapeños, increase the heat to medium, and cook, uncovered, for 10 to 15 minutes, or until the chicken is cooked through, the sauce is thick, and all of the flavors have mingled. Taste and adjust the salt.

Cook's Note

► You can substitute 2 (15-ounce) cans fire-roasted tomatoes for the fresh tomatoes (skip the broiling step for the tomatoes). Add them to the blender with the roasted onion and garlic.

CANELA, THE TRUE CINNAMON

There are two kinds of cinnamon: Ceylon cinnamon, called *canela*, which also goes by the name true cinnamon, and cassia, which is the most common type in the U.S., where it's usually just called cinnamon. In Mexico, we use canela. The sticks are much softer, more papery, and less uniform than cassia cinnamon, and the flavor is softer, warmer, kinder, and sweeter too. It's easy to break the papery sticks of canela into shorter lengths or whir it into sauces in a blender. You can find canela in Mexican markets, online, and, increasingly, in well-stocked supermarkets. If you don't have it, you can substitute regular cinnamon, but use it in powdered form if you will be blending it, since the sticks are too hard to pulverize.

CHICKEN MOLE WITH MUSHROOMS / **ATÁPAKUA DE POLLO CON HONGOS**

Serves 4 or 5

Atápakua (the word means the meal) is a type of mole, popular in the state of Michoacán, in west-central Mexico. The dish comes from the indigenous Purépecha people, who have inhabited the region since pre-Hispanic times. Their cuisine is one of the least known of the subregional cuisines in Mexico, but it boasts spectacular and simple dishes. The base of this sauce is a mixture of roasted tomatillos, onion, garlic, and serrano chiles blended with simmered guajillos and lots of fresh mint and cilantro. The sauce is then thickened with masa, giving it a luxuriously silky feel. Accompany this with warm corn tortillas and, if desired, rice.

3 dried guajillo chiles, stemmed and seeded

½ white onion, cut into quarters

1 pound tomatillos, husked and rinsed

3 garlic cloves, not peeled

1 to 2 serrano chiles

½ cup chopped fresh mint leaves, plus more for garnish

½ cup chopped fresh cilantro leaves and upper stems, plus chopped leaves for garnish

2½ teaspoons kosher salt, or more to taste

¼ cup vegetable oil

3 to 3½ pounds bone-in chicken thighs (8 to 10; or use a combination of thighs, legs, and/or split breasts)

1 pound wild or cultivated mushrooms, or a combination, rinsed and cut into bite-size pieces

½ cup masa harina

½ cup water

2 cups chicken broth

Place the guajillos in a small saucepan, cover with at least 3 cups water, and bring to a boil. Reduce the heat to medium and simmer for 10 minutes, or until the chiles have softened. Remove from the heat, remove the chiles with tongs or a slotted spoon, and measure out 2½ cups of the cooking liquid; set the chiles and liquid aside.

Meanwhile, preheat the broiler, with the rack 2 to 3 inches from the heat source. Put the onion quarters, tomatillos, garlic cloves, and serranos on a baking sheet lined with foil and broil, turning the vegetables halfway through, until they are charred and the tomatillos are mushy, 5 to 7 minutes for the serranos and garlic and 10 to 12 minutes for the onions and tomatillos. Remove the serranos and garlic when they are charred and softened and, when it is cool enough to handle, peel the garlic. Alternatively, you can roast the vegetables on a comal or large skillet over medium heat, turning them every 4 to 5 minutes, until charred. Remove from the heat.

Transfer the tomatillos, along with any juices, the onion, garlic, and serranos to a blender. Add the guajillo chiles, along with 1 cup of the reserved cooking liquid, the mint, cilantro, and 1 teaspoon of the salt and blend until smooth. Set aside.

continued

Heat 3 tablespoons of the oil in a Dutch oven or large deep skillet with a lid over medium-high heat. Season the chicken with 1 teaspoon of the salt. Working in batches if necessary to avoid crowding the pot, add the chicken, skin side down, and brown for 4 to 5 minutes, until nicely colored, then turn and brown on the other side for another 3 to 4 minutes. Remove the chicken to a bowl as it is done.

Add the mushrooms to the hot oil and cook, stirring occasionally, until they begin to brown, 2 to 3 minutes. Add the remaining ½ teaspoon salt and cook for another 3 minutes, or until the mushrooms have browned and the juices they release have just about evaporated. Transfer to the bowl with the chicken.

Reduce the heat to medium and add the remaining 1 tablespoon oil. Pour in the guajillo sauce, shielding yourself from splatters with the lid. Stir, partially cover, and cook, stirring occasionally and being careful of the spatters, until the sauce thickens and darkens slightly, 7 to 8 minutes.

Meanwhile, combine the masa harina with the water in a small bowl and mix together until you have a soft dough. Add the remaining 1½ cups guajillo cooking liquid and stir until the masa is completely dissolved and there are no lumps.

Add the masa mixture to the guajillo sauce and stir or whisk until completely incorporated. Bring to a simmer and simmer for 1 minute, then stir in the chicken broth.

Add the chicken, mushrooms, and all the juices from the bowl. Stir well, reduce the heat to medium-low, cover, and simmer for 35 to 40 minutes, until the chicken is cooked through. Stir often and scrape the bottom of the pot to make sure the sauce and/or the chicken does not stick. Taste and adjust the seasonings.

Serve garnished with chopped fresh mint and cilantro.

Cook's Note

▶ You can substitute boneless, skinless chicken thighs; cook them for 25 to 30 minutes after browning them.

Mole is not just one dish; it's a whole category. Moles range in complexity from easy family meals like Chicken Mole with Mushrooms (page 240) and Almond Chicken (page 237) to slightly more complex Coloradito Mole with Chicken (page 245) to the ambitious Mole Poblano with Chicken (page 248), which is worthy of a celebration.

The word *mole* comes from the Nahuatl word *molli,* meaning mashed or ground. All moles have a sauce—in most cases, a thick one—made by mixing together a number of ingredients that vary from dish to dish. All contain at least one type of chile, fresh or dried. And every mole is characterized by a multidimensional layering of flavors, the result of each ingredient being transformed in one way or another—through toasting, roasting, simmering, frying, or even, in the case of the famous mole called *chilchilo* from Oaxaca, burning—to bring out their maximum taste while at the same time introducing additional nuances. Often, the pureed sauce is cooked in oil or lard, and a second intensification occurs. A third one happens when the sauce simmers after the other ingredients are added to it. That's the magic of mole.

The flavor profiles in Mexico's moles vary widely. Some have complex layers of one or a number of different dried chiles, toasted sweet spices like canela or cinnamon and cloves, aromatics, and broth. They can have hints of chocolate, which may come from a small amount of chocolate, but sometimes just from the hints of cocoa flavor in the dried chiles. Many moles include nuts, which act not just as a flavoring component but as a thickener as well. Others, like Oaxacan Green Mole with Pork and White Beans (page 308), have a more vegetal quality from herbs like hoja santa, epazote, cilantro, and parsley, along with fresh green chiles and tomatillos.

All moles benefit from being made ahead and reheated. The elements need time to get to know each other and mature together. This is another reason why moles are great for large gatherings: You can make them in advance, even freeze them if you wish, and they'll be even better when you heat them back up.

COLORADITO MOLE WITH CHICKEN / **MOLE COLORADITO CON POLLO**

Serves 6 to 8

In Oaxaca, women always cook together for fiestas, and there seems to be a fiesta every day! Mole coloradito, one of the famous seven moles from the state of Oaxaca (though, truth be told, there are many more than seven), is just such a party dish, and it's a very special one.

Like many other dark moles, the coloradito is a mix of rehydrated roasted dried chiles, nuts and seeds, tomatoes, aromatics, and spices, with a little bit of Mexican chocolate. But there is one unique ingredient that contributes to its sweetness and thick texture—ripe plantain.

The name *coloradito*—reddish—describes the color perfectly: somewhere between red, orange, and brown. (The term can also be used in Spanish when someone is blushing.) If you have leftover sauce, it makes a terrific excuse for mole enchiladas.

Although the sauce is complex, it's not difficult. It's deep and multidimensional, because all the toasting and simmering brings out different hidden bits of the personality of each ingredient before they are blended together and cooked again.

1 ripe plantain

6 dried ancho chiles, stemmed and seeded

5 dried guajillo chiles, stemmed and seeded

1 pound ripe tomatoes or 1 (15-ounce) can whole tomatoes

4 or 5 garlic cloves, not peeled

1 thick slice (about ½ inch) white onion

1 (1-inch) canela stick or ½ teaspoon ground cinnamon

3 cloves, stems removed and discarded

6 black peppercorns

¼ cup slivered almonds

¼ cup sesame seeds

1 teaspoon dried oregano

2 tablespoons dark raisins

1 tablespoon dark brown sugar or grated piloncillo

2 teaspoons kosher salt, or more to taste

3 cups chicken broth

¼ cup vegetable oil

3½ to 4 pounds bone-in chicken pieces (8 to 10 legs, thighs, and/or halved breasts)

1 (3-ounce) Mexican chocolate bar, broken or cut into pieces (see note)

1 pound chayote squash, peeled and sliced into 1-x-⅓-inch strips

1 pound green beans, trimmed and cut into 1-inch pieces

Preheat the oven to 400 degrees F. Put the plantain on a baking sheet lined with foil and make a couple of ½-inch slits in its skin. Bake for 40 to 45 minutes, until cooked through. Remove from the oven, and when the plantain is cool enough to handle, peel and slice; set aside.

Heat a comal or large skillet over medium-low heat. Add both chiles and toast for 30 to 45 seconds per side, until the color changes and they are fragrant and lightly toasted. Transfer to a saucepan.

continued

If using fresh tomatoes, add them to the saucepan. Cover the chiles (and tomatoes) with water and bring to a boil. Reduce the heat to medium and simmer for 12 to 15 minutes, until the chiles are softened and the tomatoes are mushy. Remove from the heat.

Transfer the tomatoes and chiles to a blender, along with 1 cup of the cooking liquid; add the canned tomatoes, if using. Puree until smooth and pour into a large bowl. Don't rinse the blender.

Heat the comal or skillet over medium heat. Roast the garlic cloves and onion slice until completely blackened and soft, 5 to 7 minutes for the garlic and 10 to 12 minutes for the onion, turning them from time to time. Remove the garlic when it is charred and softened, and when it's cool enough to handle, peel it. Transfer the garlic and onion to the blender.

If using the canela stick, toast it on the comal or skillet over medium-low heat, turning often, until fragrant, 1 to 2 minutes; transfer to the blender. Toast the cloves and peppercorns until fragrant, and transfer to the blender. Toast the almonds for 1 to 2 minutes, until lightly browned, and add to the blender. Toast the sesame seeds. Set aside 1 tablespoon of the seeds for garnish, and add the rest to the blender. Toast the oregano until fragrant, 5 to 10 seconds, and add to the blender.

Add the plantain, ground cinnamon, if using, raisins, brown sugar, 1 teaspoon of the salt, and 1 cup of the chicken broth to the blender. Puree the mixture until smooth. Pour into the bowl with the tomato puree. (Do not rinse the blender.)

Heat the oil in a Dutch oven or large deep skillet with a lid over medium-high heat. Season the chicken with the remaining 1 teaspoon salt. Working in batches to avoid crowding the pot, add the chicken, skin side down, and cook for 4 to 5 minutes, until nicely colored, then turn and brown on the other side for 3 to 4 minutes. Transfer to a large bowl.

Reduce the heat to medium-low. Carefully, using the lid as a shield, pour the pureed mole sauce into the oil. There will be splatters! Stir, cover partially, and cook for 6 to 7 minutes, stirring occasionally, until the sauce is very thick and the flavors have intensified. Add ½ cup of the chicken broth to the blender and whir briefly to rinse it out, then add the liquid to the pot. Add the remaining 1½ cups chicken broth and the chocolate. Stir and cook for a few minutes, until the chocolate has melted.

Return the chicken to the pot, stir well, cover partially, and simmer for 35 minutes, stirring from time to time to prevent the sauce from sticking.

Add the chayote and green beans, give everything a good stir, cover, and cook, stirring occasionally, until the vegetables are crisp-tender, about 10 minutes. Taste and adjust the seasonings.

Serve garnished with the reserved sesame seeds.

Cook's Notes

► If you can't find Mexican chocolate, you can make an approximation by substituting the same amount of bittersweet chocolate and adding a pinch of ground canela or cinnamon and a teaspoon of sugar.

► You can use zucchini and frozen green beans in place of the chayote or fresh beans. Cooking time will be about 5 minutes.

Variation

To make coloradito enchiladas with leftover chicken and sauce, reheat the sauce in a saucepan. Shred the chicken. Heat corn tortillas on a comal or skillet over medium-low heat for about a minute on each side. Top each one with some shredded chicken and roll up. Arrange on a platter or on plates and pour the sauce over. Garnish with crema and crumbled queso fresco and serve.

MEXICAN CHOCOLATE

Mexican chocolate is bittersweet chocolate, but it has a completely different flavor profile and texture from regular bittersweet. It's sweeter and grainier—almost gritty, but in a pleasant rustic sort of way. It's usually made from a mix of toasted cacao beans, ground almonds, sugar, and canela.

The chocolate is traditionally shaped into hexagons, weighing 2 to 3 ounces each, and scored into six sections, which can be cut or broken apart. They are individually wrapped and packed about six to a package. You can find the most popular Mexican brands, Chocolate Abuelita and Chocolate Ibarra, in supermarkets that sell Mexican ingredients as well as in Mexican shops. Recently many smaller, more artisanal manufacturers, such as El Mayordomo, from Oaxaca, a city known for the quality of its chocolate, have entered the market.

MOLE POBLANO WITH CHICKEN / **MOLE POBLANO CON POLLO**

Serves 10

Mole poblano, so called because it's from the state of Puebla, is the most iconic of the many moles that Mexican cuisine has to offer and definitely one of the most delicious. It's a deep, dark, nut-thickened sauce with an enchanting flavor. The last time I visited Puebla with my family, they all poked fun at me because I ate it at every meal of the day all week, sauced over eggs for breakfast, over poached chicken with a side of rice for lunch (the most traditional way, and how it's served here), and in mole enchiladas for dinner. I never tire of it!

Above all other moles, mole poblano personifies the extensive intermingling of foods resulting from the intermarriage of native Mexican and Spanish cuisines. The long and varied list of ingredients, including seeds from dried chiles, which add a deep dimension of flavor and heat, is the most obvious reason why this sauce is so complex and memorable; the dish's complexity also has a lot to do with the preliminary steps you take to bring out the flavors of each ingredient before they are pureed together. Each one is essential, and they all contribute to the smooth multilayering of flavors.

I know, the length of this recipe may strike you as intimidating, yet few things compare to a mole made from scratch, and I 've come across more and more people who are eager to learn how to do it. The most time-consuming task is prepping all the ingredients, but as long as you have everything in place before you start putting them into the pot, you will find the recipe manageable. Every minute is worth it!

I like to make a big batch of the mole, partly because it freezes well (see note). You can save some time by poaching the chicken a day ahead, and that will also provide you with the chicken stock you'll need for this recipe.

Serve with rice and warm corn tortillas.

MOLE POBLANO SLIDERS

Mole poblano shows up at parties everywhere, dressed in many different outfits. One of Mexican cooks' favorite uses for it is *hojaldras de mole*. Hojaldras are mini brioche-like buns, and hojaldras de mole are like chicken mole sliders. The little buns are filled with shredded chicken that is drenched in mole poblano and sprinkled with powdered sugar. The sliders are a favorite at kids' parties, school gatherings, and pretty much any get-together.

continued

FOR THE MOLE POBLANO

1 tomato (see note)

3 ounces tomatillos (2 or 3 small), husked and rinsed

¼ white onion, cut in half

3 garlic cloves, not peeled

½ cup lard, vegetable shortening, or vegetable oil

4 dried pasilla chiles, stemmed and seeded, seeds reserved

3 dried ancho chiles, stemmed and seeded, seeds reserved

3 dried mulato or ancho chiles, stemmed and seeded, seeds reserved

2 dried chipotle chiles, preferably moritas (page 133), stemmed and seeded, seeds reserved

2 tablespoons raw unblanched almonds

2 tablespoons raw peanuts

2 tablespoons dark raisins

1 tablespoon raw hulled pumpkin seeds

1 corn tortilla, cut into 8 wedges

4 (½-inch) slices bolillo or baguette (about 1 ounce)

2 tablespoons sesame seeds

3 cloves, stems removed and discarded

½ teaspoon aniseeds

½ teaspoon coriander seeds

¼ teaspoon black peppercorns

1 (1½-inch) canela stick (see note)

⅛ teaspoon allspice berries

About 6 cups chicken broth (see headnote)

3 ounces Mexican chocolate (page 247), cut or broken into pieces

1 tablespoon dark brown sugar or grated piloncillo

1 teaspoon kosher salt, or more to taste

FOR SERVING AND GARNISH

8 to 10 boneless, skinless chicken breasts, poached (see note)

¼ cup sesame seeds, toasted

To make the mole: Preheat the broiler, with the rack 2 to 3 inches from the heat source. Put the tomato, tomatillos, onion, and garlic on a baking sheet lined with foil and broil, turning halfway through, until the vegetables are charred and the tomato and tomatillos are mushy, 5 to 7 minutes for the garlic and 10 to 12 minutes for the other vegetables. Remove the garlic when charred and softened, and when it is cool enough to handle, peel it. Alternatively, you can roast the vegetables on a preheated comal or skillet over medium heat, turning them every 4 to 5 minutes, until charred. Remove from the heat.

Heat the lard, shortening, or oil in a large Dutch oven over medium-high heat. It should be hot enough so that the chiles begin to cook and bubble gently as soon as you add them. Working in batches as necessary so that you don't crowd the pot, sauté the chiles, stirring often, until they crisp and turn darker, 2 to 3 minutes; do not let them burn. Remove with a slotted spoon or tongs as they are done, allowing the oil to drip back into the pot, and place in a large bowl.

Add the almonds, peanuts, raisins, and pumpkin seeds to the hot fat and cook, stirring often, until nicely toasted but not burned, 2 to 3 minutes. The raisins will puff. Remove with a slotted spoon and add to the bowl with the chiles.

Fry the tortilla and bread pieces in the hot fat until crisp and browned. Remove with a slotted spoon and add to the bowl.

Add the sesame seeds, reserved chile seeds, cloves, aniseeds, coriander seeds, peppercorns, canela stick, and allspice to the oil. Cook, stirring frequently and taking care not to burn the spices, for 2 to 3 more minutes, until they are fragrant and beginning to darken. Stir in the roasted tomatoes, tomatillos, onion, and garlic and cook, stirring, for a couple of minutes to blend the flavors.

Return all the ingredients in the bowl to the Dutch oven and pour in 2½ cups of the chicken broth. Stir everything together, pressing the chiles down into the broth with the back of a spoon so they are moistened and break up, and bring to a simmer. Add the chocolate, brown sugar, and salt, stir well, and simmer for 15 minutes, pressing the ingredients down to submerge them if necessary and stirring and scraping the bottom of the pot often to prevent sticking. Add up to ½ cup more broth if necessary to cover all the ingredients. Turn off the heat, cover, and let sit for 30 minutes so that all the ingredients soften thoroughly. (This will make the mixture easier to puree.)

To finish the mole: Working in batches, puree the mixture in a blender or food processor until completely silky smooth. Measure out the mole (you should have 4½ to 5 cups) and place in a large saucepan. Add 2½ cups chicken broth to the mole and stir together. If desired, thin with a little more chicken broth. Bring to a simmer over medium-low heat and simmer, stirring and scraping the bottom of the saucepan, for 2 to 3 minutes. Taste and adjust the salt, turn off the heat, and cover to keep warm.

Place the poached chicken breasts in a large pot or a wide deep skillet, add enough broth to cover, and heat gently over medium-low heat. When the chicken is hot, remove it from the broth and arrange on a platter. Spoon the mole over the chicken, sprinkle with the sesame seeds, and serve.

Cook's Notes

► You can substitute a fire-roasted canned tomato for the fresh one; add to the blender with the roasted tomatillos, onion, and garlic.

► Canela will give you the best flavor, but you can substitute ¾ teaspoon ground cinnamon, adding it with the chocolate.

► You can store the pureed mole, covered, in the refrigerator for up to a month, or freeze it for up to a year.

► To poach the chicken breasts, combine 4 quarts water; 1 white onion, halved; 4 garlic cloves, crushed; 1 bay leaf; 1 tablespoon kosher salt; 6 black peppercorns; and a large carrot, sliced, in a Dutch oven or other large pot. Bring to a simmer over medium heat. Add the chicken breasts and bring back to a simmer, then cover partially and simmer for 30 minutes. Turn off the heat and let the chicken cool in the broth. Remove the chicken breasts from the broth. Strain the broth and reserve for the mole. You can poach the chicken breasts a day ahead and keep covered in the refrigerator.

PLAZA CHICKEN AND ENCHILADAS / ENCHILADAS PLACERAS CON POLLO

Serves 4

This messy, irresistible one-dish meal comes from Morelia, the capital of the state of Michoacán. The enchiladas in the name are made with corn tortillas that are slathered in adobo and griddled until a little crusty and uber-delicious. The adobo sauce is key. Rich, with a bit of sweetness and some acidic zing from the jalapeño pickling brine, it expresses itself in three ways: You coat the tortillas in it, you simmer the seared chicken in it, and you finish cooking the accompanying carrots and potatoes in it.

Be sure to cook the sauce long enough, until it's thick and you see tiny puddles of fat floating on the surface, an indication that all of the flavors have had time to deepen.

FOR THE ADOBO SAUCE

1 pound ripe tomatoes or 1 (15-ounce) can whole tomatoes

4 dried ancho chiles, stemmed and seeded

3 garlic cloves, peeled

½ cup coarsely chopped white onion

2 tablespoons dark brown sugar or grated piloncillo

1½ teaspoons kosher salt, or more to taste

1 teaspoon dried oregano

¼ teaspoon ground cumin

½ teaspoon freshly ground black pepper

2 tablespoons brine from pickled jalapeños or apple cider vinegar

2 cups chicken broth

2 tablespoons vegetable oil

FOR THE CHICKEN

4 chicken thighs plus 4 chicken legs (about 3 pounds)

¾ teaspoon kosher salt, plus more to taste

½ teaspoon freshly ground black pepper

2 tablespoons vegetable oil

½ cup finely chopped white onion

½ pound ripe tomatoes, finely chopped, or half a 15-ounce can crushed tomatoes

1 cup chicken broth

FOR THE POTATOES AND CARROTS

2 teaspoons kosher salt

1½ pounds potatoes, peeled and cut into ½-inch dice

1½ pounds carrots, peeled and cut into ½-inch dice

2 tablespoons vegetable oil

FOR THE GARNISHES

1 head romaine lettuce, thinly sliced

¼ cup thinly sliced white onion

1 tablespoon brine from pickled jalapeños

1 tablespoon apple cider vinegar

2 tablespoons vegetable oil

½ teaspoon kosher salt

Pinch of freshly ground black pepper

½ cup crumbled queso fresco, or more to taste

8 pickled jalapeños, whole or sliced, as you like, or to taste

FOR THE TORTILLAS

2 tablespoons vegetable oil

8 corn tortillas

To make the adobo sauce: Combine the fresh tomatoes, if using, anchos, and garlic in a medium saucepan, add water to cover, and bring to a boil. Reduce the heat to medium and simmer for 10 to 12 minutes, until the tomatoes and chiles have softened.

Using a slotted spoon, transfer the tomatoes, chiles, and garlic to a blender. Reserve the cooking water in the saucepan; you will use it to cook the potatoes and carrots later. Add the canned tomatoes to the blender, if using. Add the onion, brown sugar, salt, oregano, cumin, black pepper, pickling brine or vinegar, and chicken broth and puree until smooth.

Heat the oil in a large saucepan over medium heat. Pour in the adobo sauce, using the lid to shield yourself from spatters, cover partially, and cook at a medium simmer for 20 to 25 minutes, stirring occasionally, until the sauce has thickened and the flavors have intensified. You will know it's ready when you see little puddles of seasoned fat on top of the thickened sauce. Transfer to a bowl and set aside.

To make the chicken: Season the chicken with the salt and pepper. Heat the oil in a Dutch oven or large deep skillet with a lid. Working in batches if necessary to avoid crowding, add the chicken pieces, skin side down, and brown for 4 to 5 minutes, until nicely colored, then turn and brown on the second side for 4 to 5 minutes. Remove the chicken to a large plate as it is browned.

Return all the chicken to the pot, add the onion, stir, and cook for 3 to 4 minutes, until it softens. Add the tomatoes, sprinkle with salt, stir, and cook for 5 to 6 minutes, until they soften. Add ½ cup of the adobo sauce and the chicken broth and stir to combine, then spoon the mixture over the chicken. Cover and cook at a medium simmer for 35 to 40 minutes, turning the chicken halfway through, until it is cooked through. Set aside, covered to keep warm.

Meanwhile, cook the potatoes and carrots: Bring the reserved ancho cooking water to a boil. Add the salt and potatoes, reduce the heat to medium, and cook until the potatoes are tender, about 10 minutes. Using a slotted spoon, transfer them to a bowl. Add the carrots to the pan and cook until tender, 7 to 8 minutes. Remove with the slotted spoon to the bowl with the potatoes.

Heat the oil in a large skillet over high heat. Add the potatoes and carrots and brown for 3 to 4 minutes, stirring occasionally. Add ¼ cup of the adobo sauce and cook, stirring, for 2 to 3 more minutes. Transfer to a bowl, cover, and keep warm. Set the skillet aside.

To prepare the garnishes: In a large bowl, combine the lettuce, onion, pickling brine, vinegar, oil, salt, and pepper and toss well. (Have the seared carrots and potatoes, pickled jalapeños, and queso fresco at hand.)

continued

To cook the tortillas: Heat the oil over medium-low heat in the skillet you used for the carrots and potatoes. Have the bowl of the remaining adobo sauce close by. Working in batches, slide the corn tortillas through the adobo sauce, coating them on both sides, and place in the skillet, adding as many as will fit in one layer. Let them brown, turning once, for a couple of minutes per side. They may seem wet and fragile at first, but as they cook and brown, they will become more sturdy and manageable, and you will be able to turn them. Fold the tortillas over in the pan after they've browned on both sides, and place 2 folded tortillas on each dinner plate.

Arrange a chicken thigh and leg next to the tortillas on each plate, as well as a big spoonful of the potatoes and carrots. Garnish the tortillas with the dressed lettuce and onion, queso fresco, and pickled jalapeños.

Cook's Note

► Much of this meal can be made ahead. The adobo sauce can be refrigerated, covered, for several days, and the potatoes and carrots can be cooked up to 3 days ahead and refrigerated, covered. You can also cook the chicken in the adobo sauce up to a day ahead.

FROM HOME COOKING TO STREET FOOD AND BACK

Enchiladas placeras con pollo is a quintessential example of how Mexican street food is really an extension of the home kitchen. For convenience, vendors traditionally precooked all the elements of the dish—simmered the chicken, cooked the carrots and potatoes, made the adobo sauce—and prepared the garnishes and corn tortillas before coming to work. At their stands, the sauced chicken got a quick sear in fat, as did the potatoes and carrots, which were splashed with the same adobo sauce until browned. The corn tortillas were passed through the adobo sauce and through the hot fat, then folded in half and dressed with lettuce, onion, and jalapeños. The meal became so popular that it evolved from the street to a dish offered in the little mom-and-pop restaurants known as *fondas*, and eventually in more formal restaurants and even hotels. But the flavors remain street flavors. With this recipe, you can now bring it into your home.

CHIPOTLE TURKEY MEAT LOAF / **ALBONDIGÓN DE PAVO**

Serves 6

Don't let anyone tell you Mexicans don't love meat loaf and ketchup. Meat loaf goes by the name *albondigón* and ketchup by *catsup*. Turkey meat loaf was one of my favorite foods growing up in Mexico City, and I can't get enough of it. It was one of the first things my mom made for me when she came to stay with us after our first son, Alan, was born. When my second son, Sami, got here, my mom made it again, and it was just as comforting. By the time Juju came along and my mom came to visit, the meat loaf was a regular staple in our kitchen and I made it for her. I like to add smoky-hot sauce from chipotles in adobo sauce to the glaze along with ketchup, and I also put some into the meat loaf mixture. I always try to have enough for leftovers so we can have fantastic cold meat loaf sandwiches on toasted thick bread, with lettuce, tomato, pickled jalapeños, and sliced avocado the next day.

2 tablespoons vegetable oil

1½ cups finely chopped onion

¾ cup finely chopped celery

1 teaspoon kosher salt, or to taste

½ teaspoon freshly ground black pepper

2 pounds ground turkey breast

1 large egg, lightly beaten

1 tablespoon Worcestershire sauce

2 teaspoons Maggi or soy sauce

1 tablespoon tomato paste

½ cup bread crumbs

½ cup plus 1 tablespoon ketchup

3 to 4 tablespoons sauce from chipotles in adobo sauce

Heat the oil in a large skillet over medium heat. Add the onion, celery, salt, and pepper and cook until the vegetables are very soft, 10 to 12 minutes. Scrape into a bowl and set aside.

Preheat the oven to 350 degrees F, with a rack in the middle. Oil a 9-x-5-inch loaf pan.

In a large bowl, combine the ground turkey, egg, Worcestershire sauce, Maggi or soy sauce, tomato paste, bread crumbs, 1 tablespoon of the ketchup, and 1 tablespoon of the adobo sauce. Mix well, and stir in the cooked vegetables.

Fill the loaf pan with the turkey mixture, spreading it in an even layer. Combine the remaining ½ cup ketchup and the 2 to 3 table-spoons adobo sauce, to taste. Spread the chipotle ketchup over the meat loaf.

Place the loaf pan in a larger baking dish and add ½ inch of hot water to the baking dish. (This will prevent the top of the meat loaf from cracking.) Bake for 1 hour and 15 minutes, or until the meat loaf reaches an internal temperature of 165 degrees F.

Remove from the oven and let the meat loaf sit for at least 10 minutes, then cut into slices and serve.

FIESTA TURKEY WITH CHORIZO AND CASHEW STUFFING / **PAVO DE FIESTA CON CHORIZO Y NUEZ DE LA INDIA**

Serves 10

If you need a stunner for Thanksgiving dinner, here's your recipe, which is modeled on the traditions of coastal Veracruz. It results in a moist, juicy bird, with an irresistible adobo marinade and a to-die-for stuffing. The turkey is marinated for a day (or two) in a pineapple and orange adobo sauce. The adobo is poured over the turkey before it goes into the oven, so it caramelizes as it thickens and seasons the bird even more. The sweet and tart flavors in the adobo harmonize with those in the stuffing, which is made with a soft bread and a colorful mix of ingredients that include cashews, tomatoes, and chorizo.

You will need to start at least a day ahead so the bird can marinate.

FOR THE ADOBO MARINADE AND TURKEY

4 dried ancho chiles, stemmed and seeded

4 dried guajillo chiles, stemmed and seeded

8 garlic cloves, peeled

4 cups peeled, cored, and chopped fresh pineapple

1 cup coarsely chopped white onion

½ cup packed dark brown sugar or grated piloncillo

¼ cup white vinegar

1 teaspoon dried oregano

½ teaspoon ground canela or cinnamon

1 tablespoon kosher salt, or more to taste

½ teaspoon freshly ground black pepper

1 tablespoon vegetable oil

2 cups freshly squeezed orange juice (from 5 to 6 medium oranges)

1 cup chicken broth

1 (14- to 16-pound) turkey, rinsed and patted dry, giblets removed, neck reserved

FOR THE STUFFING

¼ cup olive oil

8 cups diced brioche or challah (½-inch dice)

¾ teaspoon kosher salt, plus more for the croutons

½ teaspoon freshly ground black pepper, plus more for the croutons

¼ cup vegetable oil

1 pound Mexican chorizo, casings removed and chopped

2 cups finely chopped white onions

1 cup finely chopped celery

3 garlic cloves, finely chopped

1 pound ripe tomatoes, finely chopped, or 1 (15-ounce) can crushed tomatoes

½ teaspoon aniseseeds

½ teaspoon dried thyme

½ teaspoon dried marjoram

½ teaspoon dried oregano

¼ teaspoon ground canela or cinnamon

2 cups chicken broth

1 cup pitted prunes, finely chopped

1 cup cashews, finely chopped

FOR ROASTING THE TURKEY AND THE GRAVY

1 pound ripe tomatoes, chopped, or 1 (15-ounce) can crushed tomatoes

4 celery stalks, chopped

3 medium carrots, peeled and chopped

2 medium white onions, chopped

2 cups chicken broth

To marinate the turkey: One to two days ahead, combine the ancho and guajillo chiles and garlic cloves in a medium saucepan, cover with water, and bring to a boil. Reduce the heat to medium and simmer for about 10 minutes, until the chiles and garlic are softened. Drain and transfer the chiles and garlic to a blender.

Add the pineapple, onion, brown sugar, vinegar, oregano, canela or cinnamon, salt, and pepper to the blender and puree until smooth.

Heat the oil in a medium saucepan over medium heat. Add the chile puree and orange juice, stir, bring to a simmer, and simmer, stirring occasionally, for 15 minutes, or until the mixture has thickened and darkened in color and the flavors have intensified. Add the chicken broth, stir, and set aside to cool to room temperature.

Slide the turkey and the neck into a large brining bag or plastic bag (you can use a kitchen garbage bag) and place in a large bowl, with the turkey breast side down. Open up the bag and pour in the marinade. Reach in and massage the marinade into and over the turkey, working it into the cavity and all the crevasses. Seal the bag (leave it in the bowl). Place the bowl in the refrigerator and marinate for at least 12 hours and up to 48 hours (the longer the better), turning the turkey in the bag a couple of times to redistribute the marinade.

To make the stuffing: Preheat the oven to 375 degrees F, with a rack in the middle. Brush a large baking sheet with 2 tablespoons of the olive oil. Put the bread in a large bowl, sprinkle with salt and pepper to taste, drizzle the remaining 2 tablespoons olive oil over the bread, and toss well with your hands.

Spread the bread evenly on the baking sheet and bake for 5 to 6 minutes. Remove the baking sheet from the oven, turn the pieces of bread over, and return to the oven for another 5 to 6 minutes, or until golden. Return the croutons to the bowl and set aside. Move the oven rack to the lowest position and increase the heat to 400 degrees F.

Heat 2 tablespoons of the vegetable oil in a large skillet over medium heat. Add the chorizo and cook, breaking it apart with a couple of wooden spoons or spatulas, until it has browned, 7 to 8 minutes. Using a slotted spoon, transfer the chorizo to the bowl with the croutons, leaving as much of the fat as you can in the skillet.

Add the remaining 2 tablespoons vegetable oil to the skillet. Add the onions and celery and cook for about 5 minutes, until softened and just beginning to brown. Clear a space in the center of the skillet, add the garlic, and cook until fragrant, less than a minute, then mix with the onion and celery. Add the tomatoes and cook until they begin to soften, about 2 minutes. Stir in the aniseeds, thyme, marjoram, oregano, canela or cinnamon, ¾ teaspoon salt, and ½ teaspoon pepper and cook, stirring occasionally, for a minute or two.

continued

Stir in the chicken broth and prunes and cook for another 2 to 3 minutes to heat through. Scrape the mixture into the bowl with the croutons, add the cashews, and stir until well combined. Let cool before stuffing the turkey.

To stuff and roast the turkey: Spread the tomatoes, celery, carrots, onions, and turkey neck in a large roasting pan and pour in the chicken broth. Remove the turkey from the bag. Stuff it with as much stuffing as will fit. Scrape any remaining stuffing into a bowl and set aside. Close the cavity by crossing the legs and tying them with butcher's twine. Set a roasting rack over the vegetables and place the turkey breast side up on the rack. Tuck the wing tips under the turkey. Pour all the marinade remaining in the bag over the turkey.

Transfer the turkey to the oven and roast for 30 minutes.

Reduce the heat to 350 degrees F, cover the turkey loosely with foil, and roast for about 3½ to 4 hours longer, basting halfway through, until the temperature in the thickest part of a thigh reaches 165 degrees F. Remove the turkey from the oven and move the oven rack to the middle. Transfer the turkey, on the roasting rack, to a baking sheet, cover loosely with foil, and let rest while you prepare the remaining stuffing and the gravy.

Strain the liquid in the roasting pan through a sieve set over a bowl, pressing on the solids with the back of a wooden spoon to get as much flavor as possible. Measure out 1 cup and pour that over the stuffing you set aside in the bowl. Mix well and spoon the stuffing into an oiled or buttered baking dish. Place in the oven and bake until it's heated through and the top is lightly browned, 20 to 25 minutes.

Meanwhile, pour the remaining strained cooking liquid into a saucepan, bring to a simmer over medium heat, and simmer, stirring occasionally, until it has reduced by half, 15 to 20 minutes,.

Carve the turkey and serve with the stuffing (from inside the turkey and the baking dish). Serve the adobo sauce on the side.

DIVINE, ALWAYS TRENDY, IT'S THE TURKEY

Turkey is a traditional celebration meal all over Mexico and has been since pre-Hispanic times. In some places, it's known as *guajolote*; in others, *totole*; and in others, it's called *pavo*. The Maya considered the wild turkey to be sacred, and it had a prominent place in their rituals. By the time the Spanish arrived, the bird had been fully domesticated, and it soon became one of the hottest exports to Spain. It was in such demand there too that it was reserved for special occasions and enjoyed by the higher echelons of society.

In Mexico, turkey remains the centerpiece for major holidays, a must for Christmas, and very popular for New Year's. It is also a favorite dish for once-in-a-lifetime rituals like quinceañeras and for weddings.

BEEF, VEAL, LAMB, AND GOAT

When I was a teenager and had just begun to drive, many of my most memorable weekends with friends revolved around barbacoa outings. Whoever had access to a car would pick everybody else up and we'd head out on the highway from Mexico City to San Juan del Rio in Querétaro, about an hour and a half away. It wasn't far off the exit to barbacoa paradise. We'd park by the side of the road at our favorite spot, a stand on the highway next to a field, where we reveled in the most luscious, tender-to-the-point-of falling-apart lamb. The people who made that barbacoa cooked it all night long in an underground pit and brought it to the same spot on the highway every weekend. They were only there on Saturdays and Sundays, and if you didn't get to the place before noon, everything would be gone. Whenever and wherever I taste barbacoa today, I am back there in an instant.

Meat dishes have a way of tying us to experiences like that, whether long-cooking adobo-bathed lamb or goat braises or simple cuts of beef seasoned with nothing other than salt and grilled ever so quickly over the hottest mesquite fire at a carne asada in Sonora. We have developed many flavorful techniques for cooking meat, from the pre-Hispanic method of slow-cooking in a pit (for which I've developed a thoroughly modern work-around) to searing it in a repurposed plowshare over an open fire.

Our culture takes a tongue-to-tail approach to meat. We have a reverence for the whole animal—when we sacrifice a cow, or lamb, or goat, we do not waste any of it. Our butchers are highly esteemed, and even in chain supermarkets, meat generally does not arrive on the shelves precut and prepackaged. Go to any big or small grocery store and you will find customers waiting while the butcher prepares exactly the cut they need for a particular dish, so that they can be transported right back to home.

DURANGO-STYLE BEEF AND VEGETABLE STEW / **CALDILLO DURANGUENSE**

Serves 6

When I asked my friend Alberto Fierro, the former director of the Mexican Cultural Institute in Washington, D.C., who is from Durango, to name the most important dish from his state, he immediately said *caldillo Duranguense*. It's the meal he misses the most. The brothy beef stew is usually made with a tomato- or tomatillo-based stock seasoned with onion, garlic, and richly flavored dried red chiles, very frequently anchos. Roasted poblanos, which are anchos in their fresh form, are often added toward the end of cooking; this is the only dish I've come across that uses both the fresh and dried versions of the chile. The flowery, spicy, and buoyant flavor of the poblanos is balanced by the overtones of chocolate and prunes in the anchos. In Durango, this stew is always eaten with a side of freshly made flour tortillas. After you try it, you will see why caldillo is what Duranguenses crave when they think of home.

1 pound tomatillos, husked and rinsed

5 dried ancho chiles, stemmed and seeded

½ cup coarsely chopped white onion

2 garlic cloves, peeled

¼ teaspoon ground cumin

1 teaspoon kosher salt, or more to taste, plus more for the tortillas

4 cups chicken broth

3 tablespoons vegetable oil

3 pounds boneless beef sirloin or beef chuck, cut into 1-inch pieces

4 poblano chiles, roasted, sweated, peeled, seeded, and cut into 1-x-¼-inch strips (page 176)

Warm flour tortillas for serving

Place the tomatillos and ancho chiles in a medium saucepan, cover with water, and bring to a boil. Reduce the heat to medium and simmer for 10 to 15 minutes, until the tomatillos are soft and mushy and the chiles are softened.

Using a slotted spoon, transfer the tomatillos and anchos to a blender. Add the onion, garlic, cumin, ½ teaspoon of the salt, and 1 cup of the chicken broth and puree until smooth.

Heat the oil in a Dutch oven or other heavy pot over high heat. Season the meat with the remaining ½ teaspoon salt. Carefully add the meat to the hot oil, without crowding; you may need to do this in batches. Cook, stirring occasionally, until the beef is nicely browned on all sides, 6 to 8 minutes.

Add the tomatillo puree and the remaining 3 cups chicken broth to the meat and stir together. Bring to a boil, reduce the heat to medium-low, cover, and cook for 50 minutes, or until the meat is tender and the broth has thickened.

Remove the lid, add the poblano chiles, and cook, uncovered, for another 5 minutes. Taste and adjust the salt.

Serve the stew in bowls, with hot flour tortillas. Pass salt for sprinkling on the tortillas.

WEDDING STEW / **ASADO DE BODA**

Serves 6

When I took my first bite of this beef stew in the city of Zacatecas, the capital of the state of the same name, I immediately understood why asados are often served at weddings (*bodas*) as the centerpiece of the menu. Although they are much less involved than Oaxacan moles, their flavor is similarly complex, with a deep, fruity mix of chiles and a bit of chocolate in the sauce base. The sweetness of the orange juice and zing from the vinegar here cut through the richness of the chiles and chocolate, with orange peel bringing a delicious hint of bitterness to the party.

3 dried guajillo chiles, stemmed and seeded

3 dried ancho chiles, stemmed and seeded

3 garlic cloves, peeled

1 (1-inch) canela stick or ½ teaspoon ground cinnamon

4 cloves, stems removed and discarded

½ teaspoon cumin seeds

½ teaspoon dried oregano

1 teaspoon dark brown sugar or grated piloncillo

2 cups chicken broth

2 teaspoons apple cider vinegar

3 tablespoons vegetable oil

2 pounds beef chuck, cut into 1-inch pieces

1 teaspoon kosher salt, or more to taste

1 cup finely chopped white onion

½ cup freshly squeezed orange juice

Rind of 1 orange, cut or torn into large pieces

1 ounce Mexican chocolate, chopped or grated

Warm corn tortillas and cooked white rice for serving

Heat a comal or skillet over medium-low heat. Add the guajillos and anchos and toast, turning them a few times, until they become fragrant, begin to smoke a little, and their skin darkens, a minute or two.

Transfer the chiles to a medium saucepan, add the garlic cloves, cover with water, and bring to a boil. Reduce the heat to medium and simmer for 10 to 15 minutes, until the chiles are soft. Set aside in the liquid.

Meanwhile, toast the canela stick, if using, and cloves on the comal or skillet over medium-low heat for 1 minute, or until fragrant. Remove from the heat. Toast the cumin seeds and oregano, stirring often, just until fragrant, less than a minute; be careful not to let them burn. Remove from the heat.

When the canela is cool enough to handle, break it into small pieces.

Transfer the chiles and garlic, along with 1 cup of their cooking liquid, to a blender. Add the canela or ground cinnamon, cloves, cumin, oregano, brown sugar, chicken broth, and vinegar and puree until smooth.

continued

Heat the oil in a Dutch oven or large deep skillet with a lid over medium-high heat. Add the beef, working in batches so as not to overcrowd the pot, sprinkle with salt (use a total of ½ teaspoon of the salt for the meat), and brown on all sides, 7 to 8 minutes. Add the onion, stir, and cook for another 7 to 8 minutes, until softened; the beef will continue to brown. Stir in the orange juice and cook, scraping the bottom of the pot and stirring often, until most of the juice has evaporated.

Stir in the chile puree, orange rind, chocolate, and the remaining ½ teaspoon salt, mix well, and bring to a simmer. Cover, turn the heat down to medium-low, and simmer for 1½ hours, or until the meat is so tender that it is easily broken apart with a fork. If the sauce has not thickened slightly, cook uncovered for another 5 minutes or so, until it has. Taste and adjust the salt. Remove the orange rind.

I like to serve this with tortillas and rice.

Cook's Note

► You can substitute an ounce of bittersweet chocolate, along with a pinch each of canela or cinnamon and sugar, for the Mexican chocolate.

BEEF BRISKET IN COLORADO CHILE SAUCE / CARNE CON CHILE

Serves 8 to 10

Carne con chile is one of the emblematic dishes of both the Sonora and Arizona regions, which makes sense since they are contiguous and, in fact, were a single entity before the Mexican-American War. They have more in common gastronomically than they do with many other states in their respective countries. The stew is always made with the long, red dried colorado chiles that predominate in the area. Some versions of this recipe include a splash of vinegar, but I prefer the stew without it. And some recipes call for more than one chile. I can't resist adding the incredibly flavorful chiltepín chile and chile de árbol along with the colorados, both for the flavor and for some smoky heat. Carne con chile is different from the stews (*guisos*) in other parts of the country, which are thickened with masa or toasted corn tortillas. Typical of the wheat-growing northern part of Mexico, especially Sonora, this one uses a roux, a cooked mixture of flour and fat.

The stew can be eaten in so many ways: with rice or beans, in burritos (see page 271), or in chimichangas. Native American communities in Arizona eat their carne con chile over fry bread, and their relatives south of the border eat theirs in large flour tortillas. Because there are so many ways to repurpose carne con chile and it's so easy to make, it's worth cooking up a big batch.

FOR THE MEAT

6 pounds beef brisket, trimmed of some of the fat and cut into 2-inch chunks

½ white onion

5 garlic cloves, peeled

2 bay leaves

1 tablespoon kosher salt

½ teaspoon black peppercorns

FOR THE STEW

10 to 12 dried colorado chiles, stemmed and seeded

½ pound ripe tomatoes or half a 15-ounce can whole tomatoes

2 garlic cloves, peeled

¼ cup coarsely chopped white onion

5 to 6 dried chiltepín chiles, stemmed

2 dried chiles de árbol, stemmed

1 teaspoon dried oregano

½ teaspoon kosher salt, or more to taste

2 tablespoons lard or vegetable oil

2 tablespoons all-purpose flour

To cook the meat: Place the meat in a large pot and cover with at least 3 quarts water. Add the onion half, garlic cloves, bay leaves, salt, and peppercorns and bring to a boil. Skim off any foam that has risen to the top, reduce the heat to medium-low, cover, and cook until the meat is tender enough to pull apart easily with your fingers, 1¼ to 1½ hours.

continued

Using a slotted spoon, transfer the meat to a bowl. Strain the broth into another bowl; discard the solids. Measure out 4 cups broth and freeze the rest for another use.

Once the meat is cool enough to handle, shred into bite-size pieces, removing any excess fat. Set aside.

To make the stew: Place the colorado chiles, fresh tomatoes, if using, and garlic cloves in a medium saucepan. Cover with water and bring to a boil, then reduce the heat to medium and simmer for 10 to 12 minutes, until the chiles have softened and the tomatoes are mushy.

Transfer the chiles, tomatoes, garlic, and ½ cup of the cooking liquid to a blender. Add the canned tomatoes, if using, onion, chiltepín chiles, chiles de árbol, oregano, and salt and puree until smooth.

Heat the lard or oil in a Dutch oven or large deep skillet with a lid over medium-high heat. Add the flour and stir together well. Cook, stirring, for a minute or two, or until the roux is bubbling and browned. Add the chile puree and cook, stirring often and making sure the mixture doesn't stick and burn, for 5 to 6 minutes, until it has thickened and darkened slightly.

Stir in the reserved beef broth, add the shredded cooked meat, and bring to a simmer, stirring. Reduce the heat to medium, cover partially, and cook, stirring often and scraping the bottom of the pot, until the sauce has thickened and the meat is coated with the chile mixture and so tender it is falling apart, about 30 minutes. Taste and adjust the salt.

Ladle the stew into bowls and serve.

Cook's Notes

► You can also make this recipe with boneless pork butt instead of the beef, or a combination of beef and pork.

► If you can't find colorado chiles, you can substitute dried guajillos. It's ideal to have the chiltepínes, but you can simply omit them if you can't get them.

► The stew will keep for 5 days in the refrigerator and can be frozern for up to 3 months.

CARNE CON CHILE BURRITOS

Carne con chile burritos are my favorite way of serving carne con chile. To make them, heat flour tortillas for about a minute per side on a preheated comal or a large skillet until they are heated through and pliable. Top with a generous amount—about ½ cup—of carne con chile, and roll up into a burrito. Once the burritos are assembled, you can heat them for a minute or two on the comal or skillet if you want them a bit toasted, or just serve them right away. Either way, top with queso fresco, crema, sliced or diced avocado, and shredded lettuce.

ANCHO AND BEEF PATTIES / **PACHOLAS**

Makes 16 super-thin patties; serves 5 or 6

Pacholas, seasoned ground meat pressed into patties as thin as thick tortillas and seared on a hot griddle, are common in the central states—Guanajuato, Jalisco, Michoácan, Querétaro, and the state of Mexico. Though I call them patties, they are nothing like hamburgers. They more closely resemble what we call *bistec*, very thin, tender cutlets—beef, pork, or veal—that are simply seasoned and quickly cooked, a typical uncomplicated, satisfying weekday meal. Pacholas are usually made with beef or pork, but you get the best of both if you combine them. Then all you need to do is mix the meat with its super-flavorful seasoning paste, which typically includes mashed saltines, and let it sit for a while before pressing or rolling out very thin patties and flash-cooking them in hot oil. They're served with salsa and often with a simple salad (usually sliced cucumber, tomato, and lettuce drizzled with lime juice and oil and seasoned with salt and pepper) and a side of fries (like Mexican steak frites), white rice, or beans.

2 dried ancho chiles, stemmed and seeded

1 to 2 dried chiles de árbol, stemmed (optional)

½ cup crushed saltine crackers (10 to 12)

3 tablespoons milk

1 large egg

½ cup finely chopped fresh parsley

¼ cup finely chopped white onion

¼ teaspoon ground canela or cinnamon

3 cloves, stems removed and discarded

½ teaspoon dried oregano

½ teaspoon ground nutmeg

1 teaspoon kosher salt

1 pound ground beef, preferably sirloin

1 pound ground pork

About 2 tablespoons vegetable oil

Roasted Tomato and Jalapeño Salsita (page 130) or other salsa of your choice

Place the anchos and chiles de árbol in a small saucepan, cover with water, and bring to a boil. Reduce the heat to medium and simmer until the chiles are softened, 10 to 12 minutes.

Using a slotted spoon, transfer the chiles to a food processor. Add the saltines, milk, egg, parsley, onion, canela or cinnamon, cloves, oregano, nutmeg, and salt and process until finely ground.

Transfer the seasoning paste to a large bowl, add the ground beef and pork, and mix together with your hands. Let the mixture sit, uncovered, for about half an hour, so the flavors meld and the mixture settles and absorbs the seasoning paste.

Divide the meat mixture into 16 equal portions and gently roll into balls.

You'll be cooking the patties one by one as soon as you press or roll them out. Cut two 9-inch circles or squares from a thin plastic bag, such as a produce bag or ziplock bag.

continued

Heat 1 tablespoon of the vegetable oil in a large nonstick skillet over medium heat. If using a tortilla press, line it with one of the pieces of plastic. Place one of the balls of meat on top. Place the other piece of plastic on top of the meat ball, close the tortilla press, and press down, not too hard. Alternatively, you can roll out the plastic-covered balls of meat with a rolling pin. The patties should be between ⅛ and ¼ inch thick, as thin as you can get without tearing it. Remove the top sheet of plastic. Pick up the patty from the bottom, using the plastic, invert it onto your palm, remove the plastic and, with a sweeping motion, transfer the patty to the pan, as if you were laying down a tortilla.

Cook the patty on the first side until the meat juices rise to the top and the bottom has lightly browned, about 2 minutes. Turn and cook for another 2 to 3 minutes or so, until lightly browned and fully cooked but not dry. Transfer to a platter, cover loosely with foil, and keep warm in a low oven while you cook the remaining patties, adding more oil to the skillet as necessary.

Serve the pacholas hot, with the salsa.

Cook's Note

► You can prepare the meat mixture up to 24 hours ahead. Covered and refrigerate.

NOT YOUR AVERAGE BURGER-FLIPPER

The name *pachola* comes from the Nahuatl word for tortilla. (The patties also go by *bistec de metate* or *bistec de carne molida*.) In rural areas and small towns, the meat is mixed with the favorite local flavoring ingredients, then ground and rolled out on a metate, a large slab of volcanic rock, with a sort of rolling pin called a *metapil*, made of the same heavy, porous material. To make pacholas the traditional way, you have to use all your body weight, and it takes not just muscle, but also a certain dexterity. When you do it right, the movement of the metapil mixes the ingredients and grinds them at the same time. The real pros can roll the meat out, push it to the edge of the metate, and catch it as it forms a meat sheet. Every push of the metapil forms little waves in the sheet and creates a pattern on its surface.

Luckily, you don't need a metate and a metapil to make pacholas. A food processor works just fine, and you can start with already ground meat.

BEEF PICADILLO / **PICADILLO DE CARNE**

Makes about 4 cups

Picadillo, chopped or shredded meat with sweet, salty, spicy, and briny flavors, delivers everything you need for either a main dish served center stage, with rice and beans, or a versatile filling to be used in any number of Mexican antojos like tacos, quesadillas, empanadas, tostadas, enchiladas, chiles rellenos (page 333), and plantain molotes (page 93). The diced beef (or hamburger meat, if you prefer) is cooked with sautéed onion and garlic, and then tomatoes, almonds, olives, and raisins are added. Like many cooks, I include capers too.

2 tablespoons vegetable oil

1 cup finely chopped white onion

3 garlic cloves, finely chopped

1 pound boneless beef chuck, finely chopped, or lean ground beef

¾ teaspoon kosher salt

½ teaspoon freshly ground black pepper

¼ teaspoon ground canela or cinnamon

¼ teaspoon ground allspice

5 cloves, stems removed and discarded, crushed

1 pound ripe tomatoes, chopped, or 1 (15-ounce) can crushed tomatoes

¼ cup slivered almonds

¼ cup pimiento-stuffed green olives, diced

3 tablespoons capers, chopped

3 tablespoons dark raisins

Heat the oil in a large skillet over medium-high heat. Add the onion and cook until soft and translucent, 3 to 4 minutes. Add the garlic and cook for another minute, or until softened. Add the meat, salt, pepper, canela or cinnamon, allspice, and cloves and cook, stirring often, for 6 to 8 minutes, until the meat browns a little and its juices begin to evaporate.

Add the tomatoes and cook for 8 to 10 minutes, until they soften and cook down a bit. Stir in the almonds, olives, capers, and raisins, mix well, and cook for another 10 or 12 minutes, stirring often, until all the ingredients and flavors are nicely blended. The mixture should be moist but not wet.

Serve, or use as directed in your recipe as a filling or stuffing.

Cook's Notes

▶ You can substitute chopped or ground pork loin or tenderloin for the beef.

▶ The picadillo will keep, well covered, in the refrigerator for 3 to 4 days, or in the freezer for up to 3 months.

GRILLED OAXACAN AIR-DRIED BEEF / **TASAJO**

Serves 6

Salted air-dried meats are common all over Mexico. In Oaxaca, the name for air-dried salted beef is *tasajo*. Butchers slice the meat thin and pound it even thinner, then salt the strips and let them dry. The salt accentuates the flavor of the fat marbling in the meat and draws out just enough moisture so that the beef will sear instantly on the hot grill.

I feasted on tasajo tacos in the central market in Oaxaca, and I couldn't get those smoky, charred flavors out of my head. When I returned home from that magical city, I realized how easy it would be to make the air-dried beef at home. In the morning, I slice, pound, and salt the meat. Right before dinner, I take it out of the fridge and light up the grill, and in three minutes, dinner is on the table. My boys love it. We enjoy it in tacos and with rice. And we put it tortas, spreading refried beans on the bottom of a toasted Mexican roll or baguette, topping it with the tasajo, a tomato slice, and a generous scoop of Smoky Guacamole (page 151).

You'll need to start this recipe at least 3 hours ahead so the meat can cure a little.

2 pounds flank steak

1 tablespoon kosher salt

Oil for the grill

Warm corn tortillas for serving

Your choice of salsas, guacamole, and/or picked chiles (such as jalapeños or chipotles, page 144), with their accompanying vegetables, for serving

Place a cooling rack over a baking sheet lined with paper towels. Place the flank steak on a cutting board. Slice the meat across the grain about ¼ inch thick, or thinner if possible. One by one, place the slices between sheets of parchment or wax paper and, using a meat mallet or the bottom of a small heavy skillet, pound it very thin, about ⅛ inch thick. You should be able to see the paper underneath through the meat, but it should not break apart. Place the slices on the cooling rack as you go.

When all of the slices have been pounded, sprinkle 1½ teaspoons of the salt over the top of the slices. Turn the slices over and sprinkle with the remaining 1½ teaspoons salt. Leave on the rack to air-dry at room temperature for at least 3 hours, and up to 8 hours. (If you prefer, you can leave it at room temperature for just 2 hours and refrigerate it for the remaining time.) As it dries, the color of the meat will darken into a much deeper red, and the structure of the grain will be much more evident.

Prepare a medium-hot fire in a charcoal or gas grill, or heat a grill pan over medium-high heat. When it is hot, brush the grill or pan with vegetable oil. Cook the meat in batches for about 1 minute per side, until it is lightly charred and the edges are crispy. Remove from the heat and cover loosely with foil while you grill the remaining meat. Serve with tortillas and the accompaniments of your choice.

Cook's Note

▸ Once it's dried, the meat will keep, tightly wrapped, in the refrigerator up to for 5 days.

NORTHERN-STYLE SEARED MEAT PLATTER / **DISCADA NORTEÑA**

Serves 10 to 12

Discada norteña is traditionally cooked in a big pan over an open fire, but you can make it indoors, and it's the perfect meal for a big family gathering or celebration. This version features a mix of beef tenderloin and pork tenderloin, browned in rendered chorizo and bacon fat, then cut into smaller pieces and returned to the pan to finish cooking in the company of softened onion and poblanos, chorizo, and bacon. With all that going on, the meat needs little more to season it than cumin, a spice much loved in northern Mexico, and a generous splash of Worcestershire sauce.

The origins of the dish are in the fields of Chihuahua, where farmers began to use their worn-out plowshares, called *discos,* as large comales—rather like gigantic open-air woks—for cooking over wood fires in the fields. The tradition continues. The rounded side of the plowshare is used to toast giant tortillas and the other side for cooking a mix of whatever meats and fresh ingredients are available. The resulting dishes are known as *discadas.* Used discos can still be found, and contemporary discos, aka cowboy woks, made specifically for these outdoor cookouts can be ordered online. Or you can use a Dutch oven, large skillet, or paella pan.

1 pound Mexican chorizo, casings removed and chopped

½ pound (about 10 slices) bacon, coarsely chopped

1 (2-pound) beef tenderloin roast

2 pounds pork tenderloins

1 teaspoon kosher salt, or more to taste

Freshly ground black pepper

3 cups coarsely chopped white onions

3 poblano chiles, seeded and coarsely chopped

¼ teaspoon ground cumin

1 tablespoon Worcestershire sauce

2 teaspoons Maggi or soy sauce

Warmed corn and/or flour tortillas for serving

Lime wedges for serving (optional)

Heat a Dutch oven, large deep heavy skillet, or large paella pan over medium-high heat. Add the chorizo and bacon and cook, crumbling and breaking up the chorizo with two wooden spoons or spatulas as it cooks, until the meats render their fat and brown. With a slotted spoon, transfer the chorizo and bacon to a bowl and set aside, leaving the fat behind in the pot.

Season the beef and pork with the salt and pepper to taste.

Return the pot to medium-high heat. If it is large enough, add both the beef and pork tenderloins and brown on all sides, or do them one at a time. Don't crowd the pot, or the meat will steam rather than brown. Transfer the browned meat to a large cutting board and let rest for at least 5 minutes.

continued

Meanwhile, add the onions and poblanos to the pot and cook over medium heat until they are tender and the edges of the onions are beginning to brown, 7 to 10 minutes.

While the onions and poblanos are cooking, cut each piece of meat lengthwise in half and then slice crosswise into ½-inch-thick slices.

Add the meat to the pot, along with the chorizo and bacon. Sprinkle on the cumin, add the Worcestershire sauce and Maggi or soy sauce, stir well, and cook for a few more minutes, until the meat is cooked to medium or your desired degree of doneness.

Spoon everything onto a platter and bring to the table, along with hot tortillas so that people can taco their meat. If you want, pass fresh lime wedges for people to squeeze onto their meat or tacos.

Cook's Note

► Instead of the fresh poblanos, you can use rajas, roasted poblano strips (page 176); you can also add chopped bell peppers or jalapeños. If you like, add some chopped tomatoes and/or chipotles in adobo along with the onions.

JUST CALL IT W SAUCE

Mexicans call Worcestershire sauce *salsa Inglesa,* much easier for us to say than Worcestershire, and a lot easier to spell too! It is a very common condiment in pantries throughout the country. We use it extensively to season grilled meats, chicken, and seafood. We also add it to seafood ceviches and even alcoholic drinks like Micheladas.

When I moved to the U.S., I knew nobody would know what I meant if I called Worcestershire "English sauce," but I had a hard time pronouncing the name. I mentioned the problem in one of my TV episodes, and to this day I still get e-mails from viewers giving me tips:

"Think rooster from Wooster."

"Whatsishere."

"Force-ster plus sheer."

I got so many suggestions that I decided to stick with W sauce.

BEEF AND VEGETABLE SALAD /
SALPICÓN DE CARNE (PAGE 282)

BEEF AND VEGETABLE SALAD / **SALPICÓN DE CARNE**

Serves 4 to 6

Think of this as the Mexican version of a Niçoise salad, made with beef rather than tuna, that can be tucked into a taco. Salpicón de carne is a beautiful meal on a platter and a very convenient one too, so it's ideal for entertaining. All the components can be made ahead (see note), and you can dress the beef and vegetables with the vinaigrette and refrigerate them until ready to serve. They will get even tastier as they sit! Then all you need to do is dress the lettuce.

My favorite way to eat this is in a taco, with some avocado, shredded beef, chipotles, and jalapeños in a corn tortilla, chasing my bites with the vegetables on the side. My husband likes to enjoy his as a salad on the plate, alternating it with bites of warm corn tortillas. You can design your own experience with the salpicón. *The photo is on page 281.*

FOR THE MEAT

1 to 1½ pounds flank steak, cut into 2-inch chunks

1 white onion, peeled

5 garlic cloves, peeled

2 bay leaves

2 teaspoons kosher salt

FOR THE SALAD

1 large or 2 medium carrots (about ¼ pound), peeled, halved lengthwise, and sliced into half-moons

2 medium red potatoes (about ½ pound), peeled and cubed

¼ pound green beans, trimmed and cut into thirds on the diagonal

½ cup fresh or thawed frozen peas

3 large radishes, halved and thinly sliced into half-moons

2 tablespoons chopped fresh cilantro leaves and upper stems

FOR THE VINAIGRETTE

⅓ cup white vinegar

2 tablespoons fresh lime juice, or more to taste

½ teaspoon kosher salt, or more to taste

½ teaspoon freshly ground black pepper

½ teaspoon dark brown sugar or grated piloncillo

1 garlic clove, minced

⅓ cup olive oil

⅓ cup vegetable oil

⅔ cup slivered red onion

FOR SERVING

½ large head romaine, leaves separated, washed, and dried, large outer leaves torn into smaller pieces if desired

1 ripe avocado, halved, pitted, and sliced

Sliced pickled jalapeños

Sliced chipotles in adobo or Pickled Chipotles with Baby Potatoes, Onions, and Carrots (page 144)

Warm corn tortillas (optional but highly recommended)

To cook the meat: Combine the flank steak, onion, garlic cloves, and bay leaves in a large saucepan and cover generously with water. Bring to a boil and add the salt. Lower the heat to medium-low and skim off any foam that has risen to the top. Cover partially and simmer for 1½ to 2 hours, until the meat is so tender that it comes apart easily when poked with a fork.

With a slotted spoon, transfer the meat to a bowl. Set a fine strainer over another bowl and strain the broth into it. Wash out the pan and return the broth to it. When the meat is cool enough to handle, shred it and set aside in one of the bowls.

To make the salad: Bring the beef broth back to a boil. One vegetable at a time, cook the carrots, potatoes, and green beans, in this order, until tender: 3 to 4 minutes for the carrots and green beans, until crisp-tender; 4 to 8 minutes for the potatoes, until they are tender but not mushy. As each vegetable is done, remove with a slotted spoon and place in a large bowl. Cook the peas just until tender, about 1 minute. Transfer to the bowl with the rest of the cooked vegetables, add the radishes and cilantro, and set aside to cool.

To make the vinaigrette: Whisk together the vinegar, lime juice, salt, pepper, brown sugar, and garlic in a bowl. Whisk in both oils. Taste and adjust the salt, adding up to ½ teaspoon more, and lime juice. Add the red onion and let macerate for at least 15 minutes, then, using a slotted spoon, remove the onion from the vinaigrette and set aside for garnish.

To assemble: Whisk the vinaigrette well. Measure out ⅓ cup and toss with the reserved meat. Let sit for 10 minutes.

Meanwhile, measure out another ⅓ cup vinaigrette and toss with the cooked vegetables, radishes, and cilantro. Let sit for 10 minutes. When you're ready to serve, place the lettuce in a large bowl and toss with a few tablespoons of the vinaigrette. Line a large platter with the dressed lettuce. Give the salad vegetables a stir and arrange over the lettuce, pouring any remaining dressing in the bowl over them. Give the meat a stir and arrange over the vegetables, making sure that all of the dressing goes with it. Garnish with the macerated red onion, avocado, pickled jalapeños, and chipotles. Pour any remaining dressing over the top.

Serve cold or lukewarm, with warm tortillas, if desired.

Cook's Notes

► The meat, vegetables, and vinaigrette can be prepared up to 24 hours ahead. Toss the meat and vegetables with the dressing in separate bowls as directed, cover, and let marinate in the refrigerator. Toss the lettuce with vinaigrette and arrange the salad on the platter with the garnishes just before serving.

► Salpicón can also be made with shredded cooked chicken. There are lovely seafood takes too, made with cooked crabmeat, shrimp, or lobster.

VEAL CHOPS WITH PINE NUT MOLE / **MOLE DE NOVIA**

Serves 4 to 6

These big, thick veal chops make a special meal for a special night. The pale pine nut–thickened mole is so delicious you could eat it with a spoon. Pine nut moles, which go by the names *mole de novia* (bride's mole, for the white dress) and *mole de boda* (wedding mole), are considered delicacies, both because pine nuts are more costly than other nuts and because of their refined flavor. These moles are gently cooked, with an eye toward keeping the color light. No colorful ingredients are called for. Only the white parts of leeks and scallions are used in the sauce, with the green tops saved for a garnish, and the chiles are yellow banana chiles (though you can substitute jalapeños) or yellow habaneros.

I toast the pine nuts and sesame seeds just a bit, to keep the color and flavors subtle, and I simmer the leek, garlic, chiles, and apple slowly until they reduce to a lightly caramelized puree. The apple and a little honey give it a delicately sweet taste.

- 1¾ cups pine nuts
- 5 tablespoons sesame seeds
- 2 tablespoons olive oil
- 2 tablespoons toasted sesame oil
- 4 tablespoons (½ stick) unsalted butter
- 3 cups thinly sliced well-washed leeks, white parts only
- 2 cups thinly sliced scallions (keep the dark green parts separate to use for garnish)
- 2 to 3 fresh banana chiles, thinly sliced
- 1 tart green apple, peeled, cored, and diced
- 2 garlic cloves, thinly sliced

- ½ cup water
- 2 teaspoons kosher salt
- ½ teaspoon freshly ground white pepper
- Pinch of ground canela or cinnamon
- 4 cups chicken broth
- 1 tablespoon honey
- 2 bay leaves
- 1 whole star anise (optional)
- 2 slices soft egg-enriched bread, such as brioche or challah, lightly toasted and diced (about 1 cup)
- 4 to 6 bone-in veal chops, about 1 inch thick and 12 ounces each

Heat a medium skillet over medium-low heat. Add the pine nuts and toast for 3 to 4 minutes, stirring occasionally, just until they smell toasty and begin to change color; don't let them color or toast too much. Immediately transfer to a bowl; reserve 2 tablespoons of the nuts for garnish.

Lightly toast the sesame seeds in the same skillet for less than a minute, watching carefully so they don't brown or burn. Immediately transfer to a bowl; set aside 1 tablespoon of the seeds for garnish.

Heat 1 tablespoon each of the olive oil and sesame oil and 2 tablespoons of the butter in a Dutch oven or large deep skillet with a lid over medium-low heat. Once the butter has melted, add the leeks, scallions (except the dark green parts), chiles, apple, and garlic and cook, stirring occasionally, for 15 minutes, until softened.

continued

Add the water, 1 teaspoon of the salt, ¼ teaspoon of the white pepper, and the canela or cinnamon to the pot and continue cooking until all of the water has evaporated and the vegetables are soft, lightly caramelized, and beginning to fall apart, 10 to 12 minutes.

Pour the chicken broth over the vegetables and add the pine nuts and sesame seeds, honey, bay leaves, and star anise, if using. Stir, raise the heat to medium, and bring to a simmer. Cover partially and simmer for 10 minutes, until the vegetables are falling apart and there is no crunch left in the pine nuts.

Remove from the heat and remove the bay leaves and star anise, if you used it. Add the bread and let it soak in the sauce while it cools.

Transfer the mixture to a blender, working in batches if necessary, and puree until smooth. Pour into a saucepan and keep warm over very low heat while you cook the veal chops.

Season the veal chops with the remaining 1 teaspoon salt and ¼ teaspoon white pepper. Heat the remaining 1 tablespoon olive oil, 1 table-spoon sesame oil, and 2 tablespoons butter in a large skillet over medium heat. When the butter is just starting to color (don't let it smoke), add half of the chops, to avoid crowding the pan, and cook for 12 to 14 minutes per side, until an instant-read thermometer inserted in the center of a chop registers 135 to 145 degrees F for medium (I like them closer to 145 degrees F). Transfer to a platter and cover with foil to keep warm while you cook the second batch.

Arrange the chops on individual plates or on a platter, spoon the sauce over them (see note), and garnish with the scallion greens and reserved pine nuts and sesame seeds.

Cook's Note

► If you have sauce left over, you can spoon it over seared shrimp or veal scaloppini. It is also delicious over steamed vegetables like chayotes, zucchini, green beans, or beets.

PINE NUTS IN MEXICAN COOKING

You may be surprised to see a Mexican recipe based on pine nuts, but they are not uncommon in our cooking, especially in the central part of the country, where they grow. We love piñones (the beautiful word has one of my favorite letters, the ñ), and we use them in many traditional sweets, including ice creams and paletas (popsicles).

In Mexico, you find a pink variety of pine nuts as well as the more familiar pale white and beige varieties like the nuts we find in grocery stores in the U.S. The flavors are similar but the pink ones are softer and sweeter than the white and beige ones. If you come across them in Mexico, by all means try them in this recipe. Then you can call it pink mole—*mole rosa*. But whatever pine nuts you get at your grocery store will work fine.

WRAPPED SLOW-COOKED LAMB / **MIXIOTE DE CARNERO**

Serves 6

Mixiote de carnero is a wrapped package of falling-apart-tender lamb bathed in an adobo-like marinade and steamed with more aromatics for hours over a beer-spiked bath. Traditionally, pulque was used, but beer was gradually substituted, as it is easier to get.

The lamb cooks slowly, absorbing the flavors of the adobo and softening to an incredible luscious texture. When you unwrap your little bundle and empty it into your bowl, the meat tumbles out, falling apart into shreds and mingling with the broth. You can enjoy it with a spoon, or slip it into warm corn tortillas. Round out the feast with Basic Simmered Beans (page 156) and Seared Nopalito Salad with Radishes and Oregano (page 331).

Plan to marinate the lamb for at least 2 hours, or, preferably, for a day or two.

FOR THE LAMB AND MARINADE

3 to 4 pounds boneless lamb shoulder or leg, cut into about 2-inch pieces, or lamb stewing meat

5 teaspoons kosher salt

8 dried guajillo chiles, stemmed and seeded

3 dried pasilla chiles, stemmed and seeded

1 teaspoon ground cumin

1 teaspoon dried oregano

½ teaspoon dried marjoram

½ teaspoon dried thyme

½ teaspoon freshly ground black pepper

4 cloves, stems removed and discarded

4 garlic cloves, peeled

3 tablespoons unseasoned rice vinegar or white vinegar

FOR THE PARCHMENT PACKETS

12 bay leaves, lightly toasted

12 avocado leaves, lightly toasted (page 163; optional)

1 cup light beer

FOR SERVING

Lime wedges, chopped white onion, chopped serrano or jalapeños, and chopped fresh cilantro leaves

Warm corn tortillas (optional)

To marinate the lamb: Place the meat in a large bowl, sprinkle evenly with 4 teaspoons of the salt, and rub the salt in. Set aside while you prepare the marinade.

Heat a comal or large skillet over medium-low heat. Add the chiles, in batches if necessary, and lightly toast them, turning as they darken and begin to release their fragrance, 1 to 2 minutes.

Tranfer the chiles to a medium saucepan, cover with water, and bring to a boil. Reduce the heat to medium and simmer for 10 to 15 minutes, until the chiles have softened.

Transfer the chiles and 1 cup of their cooking liquid to a blender. Add the cumin, oregano, marjoram, thyme, black pepper, cloves, garlic, vinegar, and remaining 1 teaspoon salt and puree until smooth. Pour the marinade over the meat and rub it over the meat with your hands, making sure that all of the pieces are coated. Cover and refrigerate for at least 2 hours, and up to 48 hours, the longer the better.

continued

To make and steam the packets: Cut twelve 12-x-16-inch pieces of parchment paper. Heat a comal or large skillet over medium-low heat. Lightly toast the bay leaves and avocado leaves, if using, for about 30 seconds per side. Remove from the heat.

Divide the meat, with its marinade, into 6 equal portions. Place a sheet of parchment paper on your work surface and top with a portion of meat. Place a bay leaf and an avocado leaf, if using, on top of the meat. Gather up the four corners of the parchment paper and bring them together to completely enclose the meat, then twist and tie with kitchen twine. Place the packet on another piece of parchment paper and repeat, so the packets are double-wrapped. Assemble the remaining packets in the same way.

Pour the beer into a steamer or pot big enough to hold a large steamer basket. Add enough water to come almost to the bottom of the basket. To monitor the water so it doesn't evaporate during the long steaming time, place a coin in it; replenish the water when you no longer hear the coin jingling against the pan. Place the packets right side up in the steamer basket. Bring the water to a boil, cover the pot, reduce the heat to low, and steam for 2 hours. Keep your eye (and ear) on the simmering water.

Check one of the packets. The meat should be fork-tender. Turn off the heat and let the bundles sit for at least 30 minutes before serving.

Place the packets in wide soup bowls and let guests open their own. They can squeeze in a bit of lime, add some onion, chile, and cilantro, if desired, and eat it like a stew or put it into tacos.

Cook's Note

► You can steam the packets up to 4 hours ahead and leave them in the pot, covered. Reheat for about 20 minutes over medium-low heat before serving.

ANCIENT PLANT, NEW TRADITION

Mixiote gets its name from the Nahuatl word for the thin membrane on the surface of the large, thick, pointy leaves of the agave (maguey) plant, the source of our favorite Mexican spirits, tequila and mezcal, as well as agave syrup and the most ancient Mexican alcoholic beverage, pulque. When it is peeled from the leaves and dried, this membrane resembles very thin parchment paper. Like corn husks or banana leaves for tamales, agave membranes have been used for centuries as wrappers for cooking meat. Not only do they swaddle the meat and its marinade, but they also infuse it with their own flavor and fragrance. The larger membranes can be used to wrap large cuts of meat that are traditionally cooked in underground pits, or they can be cut into smaller pieces for individual bundles that are steamed.

Mixiote is so popular, especially in the central states of Hidalgo, Tlaxcala, and Mexico, that it threatens the survival of agave plants. Once the papery membrane is peeled off, the leaves are often too damaged to survive. Many states have passed laws prohibiting the use of agave for this dish, and people are starting to substitute other materials, though the dish is still called mixiote.

LAMB BARBACOA / **BARBACOA DE BORREGO**

Serves 10 to 12

Although barbacoa is traditionally made in a sealed underground pit, you can make a version at home that is just as good. This recipe, which I've tweaked over the years, is inspired by both my mother's barbacoa and one from El Caballo Bayo in Mexico City, where it was a specialty. I use a meaty leg or shoulder of lamb, bone-in, and a large roasting pan. I rub the meat all over with a thick marinade made with guajillo and ancho chiles, wrap it in banana leaves (or foil), and roast it over vegetables in the foil-sealed pan.

There is a lot of food to share here, making this is an especially welcome dish for a cold winter night or Super Bowl Sunday.

FOR THE MARINADE

8 dried guajillo chiles, stemmed and seeded

8 dried ancho chiles, stemmed and seeded

⅓ cup apple cider vinegar

1 ripe tomato, quartered, or 1 canned tomato

⅔ cup coarsely chopped white onion

4 garlic cloves, peeled

1 tablespoon dried oregano

½ teaspoon ground canela or cinnamon

½ teaspoon ground allspice

2½ teaspoons kosher salt, or more to taste

½ teaspoon freshly ground black pepper

5 cloves, stems removed and discarded

3 tablespoons vegetable oil

FOR THE MEAT

8 pounds bone-in lamb (such as a combination of leg, shoulder, and/or ribs)

1 pound banana leaves, rinsed (optional)

6 dried avocado leaves (page 163; optional)

FOR THE VEGETABLE BASE

2 white onions, coarsely chopped

1½ pounds carrots, peeled and coarsely chopped

1½ pounds red potatoes, peeled and cubed

1¼ cups garbanzo beans, soaked for at least 4 hours, or as long as overnight, in water to cover by 2 inches, then drained

3 cups water

1½ cups beer of your choice (preferably light)

3 bay leaves

1½ teaspoons kosher salt, or more to taste

FOR SERVING

4 limes, cut into wedges

Warm corn tortillas

Raw Salsa Verde (page 120) and/or Drunken Salsa (page 136), or other salsa(s) of your choice

To make the marinade: Heat a comal or large skillet over medium-low heat. Add the guajillos and anchos and lightly toast for 1 to 2 minutes, turning them as they darken and begin to release their fragrance.

Transfer the chiles to a medium saucepan, cover with water, and bring to a boil. Reduce the heat to medium and simmer for 10 to 15 minutes, until the chiles have softened.

continued

Transfer the chiles and 2 cups of their cooking liquid to a blender. Add the vinegar, tomato, onion, garlic, oregano, canela or cinnamon, allspice, salt, black pepper, and cloves and puree until smooth.

Heat the oil in a large saucepan over medium heat for 1 to 2 minutes, until hot. Add the chile puree and cover partially, as the sauce will splatter dramatically. Let the sauce simmer for 10 to 12 minutes, stirring often, until it deepens in color to a darker brown and the flavor intensifies. It should be thick, almost pasty. Remove from the heat.

To marinate the meat: Place the lamb in a large bowl or roasting pan and completely cover with the marinade, rubbing it all over the meat with your hands. Cover and refrigerate for at least 2 hours, and up to 24 hours, the longer the better.

To make the vegetable base: Preheat the oven to 350 degrees F. Arrange the onions, carrots, potatoes, and garbanzo beans in a large roasting pan. Add the water, beer, bay leaves, and salt and stir. Place a roasting rack on top of the vegetables.

To cook the meat: Unfold the banana leaves, if using, and layer a couple on top of the roasting rack, leaving a generous overhang for wrapping the meat. Place the meat on top of the leaves. Arrange the avocado leaves, if using, on top of the meat. Fold the banana leaves over and around the meat to make a neat package. (If the overhang is not large enough to enclose the meat, use additional leaves.) Alternatively, if you don't have banana leaves, wrap the meat in foil, poke about 15 small holes in the bottom of the package with a fork or knife, so the meat juices

can drip onto the vegetables, and set on the rack. Cover the whole roasting pan with heavy-duty foil, preferably from a 24-inch-wide roll (overlap two sheets if they are 12 inches wide), crimping it along the edges of the pan to create a seal. (Double the sheets if you don't have heavy-duty foil.)

Place the pan in the oven and cook for 4½ to 5 hours, until the meat is so tender it is falling off the bone.

Remove the pan from the oven and allow the meat to rest for 15 to 20 minutes in its package. Be careful when you remove the foil, as the steam will be very hot (I wear oven mitts).

To serve, unwrap the meat and remove and discard the avocado leaves, if you used them. Using your fingers or two forks, pull the meat off the bones and shred.

Arrange the vegetables on a large platter (discard the bay leaves). Top with the shredded meat and drizzle some of the flavorful broth on top. Set out the cut limes so people can squeeze fresh lime juice onto their meat if desired, warm corn tortillas so they can make tacos with the barbacoa, and the salsa(s).

Cook's Notes

▶ You can make the marinade a day ahead, if you wish; cover and refrigerate.

▶ There will be a lot of broth. If you wish, serve small bowls of broth first, or serve on the side (my preference) with the barbacoa.

BRAISED GOAT OR LAMB WITH GUAJILLO CHILES / **BIRRIA**

Serves 8 to 10

Mexicans are almost religious about their birria. It's a signature dish of Jalisco, but the devotion has spread to surrounding states, and beyond to the U.S. If there is a roadside stand or restaurant specializing in birria, no Mexican can resist stopping there for the full experience.

The name *birria* derives from a Spanish word that means messy looking, perhaps because the meat cooks for so long it falls apart. The resulting rich broth, fragrant with chiles and aromatics, is served on the side or as a first course. The meat is shredded and enjoyed in tacos with all the fixings.

One of my favorite recipes for birria comes from Rosa Arroyo, a Mexican cook who also lives in Washington, D.C., and has cooked with me at the Mexican Cultural Institute for years. There are only a few ingredients; you don't need many when you are working with a flavorful meat like goat (though you can also make this, with wonderful results, with lamb). What you do need is patience, for it's the long cooking time that makes the meat so good. Make sure to get bone-in meat; it will have more flavor.

4 to 5 pounds bone-in goat or lamb shoulder, ribs, or leg, or a combination, cut into approximately 3-inch pieces (see note)

¼ cup white vinegar if using goat

2 tablespoons kosher salt (4 teaspoons if using lamb), or more to taste

4 or 5 large dried avocado leaves (page 163; see note)

3 ounces dried guajillo chiles (about 10), stemmed and seeded

FOR SERVING

Warm corn tortillas

2 cups finely chopped white onions

2 cups chopped fresh cilantro leaves

2 or 3 limes, quartered

If using goat, place the meat in a large bowl and cover with cold water. Add the vinegar and 2 teaspoons of the salt, stir, and let sit for 20 to 30 minutes. Drain and rinse well under cold water.

Place the goat or lamb in a Dutch oven or other large heavy pot and cover with at least 3 quarts water. Add the remaining 4 teaspoons salt, stir, and bring to a boil. Reduce the heat to low and skim off the foam from the surface. Cover and simmer for 2 hours.

Meanwhile, heat a comal or small skillet over medium-low heat. Toast the avocado leaves, turning them as they cook, until fragrant, about a minute. Remove from the heat. Toast the chiles, for about a minute per side, until they smell fragrant and begin to change color.

Place the chiles in a small saucepan, cover with water, and bring to a simmer over medium-high heat. Simmer for 10 to 15 minutes, until softened. Transfer to a blender, add 1 cup of the cooking liquid, and puree until smooth.

continued

After the meat has cooked for 2 hours, add the chile puree, stir, and then drop in the toasted avocado leaves. Cover again and simmer for another 2 hours, or until the meat is so tender it is falling off the bones. Taste the broth and adjust the salt.

When it comes to serving, you have many choices: You can transfer the meat to a platter, moisten with some broth, and serve the rest of the broth alongside in soup bowls for people to sip as they assemble and eat their meat tacos. Or you can serve the broth as a first course. Or serve the meat and broth together in soup bowls so people can take the meat from their bowls to make tacos if they want, or they can just eat everything together. They can garnish both the broth and the tacos they assemble with the onion, cilantro, and lime.

Cook's Notes

► You can have your butcher cut up the meat, or buy it precut (the pieces may be larger than 3 inches, and that's okay).

► Do try to get the avocado leaves for this. You can substitute bay leaves, but it won't be the same.

GET YOUR GOAT!

Goat isn't raised on a large scale in the United States, which is a good thing. It's grass fed, and unlike commercial beef and pork, it is raised without antibiotics. You can get it at farmers' markets and from small suppliers, including health food stores, or from other purveyors of sustainable and local meat.

Don't shy away from goat meat because you think it will be gamey. Most of the goat we get here in the U.S. is mild and tender, not even as strong as some lamb. But it has real flavor, a taste that speaks of the country.

Long, slow stewing is the best way to cook goat. The fewer ingredients you use for seasoning the broth and the longer you cook the meat, the more nuanced it will be.

PORK

The little city of Mocorito in Sinaloa is famous for two cultural exports. The first is the caramelized, chile-bathed pork preparation called *chilorio*.

Mocorito has more than twenty factories that produce chilorio, most of which are actually in private dwellings. Cooks process it in pouches and cans for distribution all over Sinaloa and beyond. Whenever my family and I return from Mexico, we tuck the packages into our suitcases, because chilorio is not only addictively delicious but also highly versatile, fortifying tacos, quesadillas, egg dishes—even lasagna.

Although I had tasted many regional adaptations of chilorio, I was hoping somebody could teach me how to make the original version. I was lucky to be pointed in the direction of Victoria Eugenia González, a charming, generous cook in Mocorito who has a small chilorio factory and restaurant called Mely in her home. Her chilorio is humbling in its simplicity. Vicky believes that when it's cooked properly—very slowly—first in its own fat, then in a guajillo puree with just a few well-chosen seasonings, its sweetness braced by a little vinegar, a mild green chile, and a bit of tomato, it has no need for the extra ingredients like orange juice that characterized the recipes I'd followed in the past.

As we cooked and chattered, I noticed that Vicky's dining room was filled with mementos, including many photos of the legendary Grammy Award–winning band Los Tigres del Norte. When I asked why, she explained that they are members of her large family. I was amazed to learn that one of the biggest-ever acts in Latin music started here in this tiny town, and that they were related to the cook who was teaching me its secrets.

Just as you can't imagine Mexican culture without the pulsating rhythms of its music, it's impossible to think about Mexican food without pork or one of its by-products—lard, chicharrón, chorizo, and bacon, among others. Pork finds its way into every aspect of Mexican cooking, present in one form or another in all manner of dishes, even desserts.

Pork is hospitable to all the wonderful seasonings and chiles in the Mexican repertoire. We slather pork butts with adobo and roast them. We add pork to bean dishes of all kinds. Almost no party can claim to be a party without pork. And on the Christmas table, you will usually find a stuffed pork roast or a big glazed ham fighting with the turkey for attention.

A few months after leaving Mocorito, I ran into Los Tigres del Norte at the Hispanic Heritage Awards at the Kennedy Center. They were stunned to find out I had spent time in their off-the-beaten-track home with their aunt. Of course, our conversation was all about their tía's fabulous chilorio.

SINALOA-STYLE SHREDDED PORK / **CHILORIO DE MOCORITO**

Serves 10 to 12

Chilorio, rich adobo-seasoned shredded pork, is synonymous with Sinaloa. The dish has become so popular across the country that national brands distribute it commercially; you can even find chilorio in gas stations. Homemade is better, of course, and chilorio is not at all difficult to prepare. And once you have the dish on hand, you have the makings for other spinoff dinners.

To make chilorio, you simmer pork shoulder or butt for nearly two hours, until the meat almost caramelizes, but there is very little babysitting involved. Then you add a guajillo chile adobo and cook the luscious meat even more, until it is falling-apart tender, the strands of pork coated with the adobo. This version, which has an intense chile flavor but isn't spicy, adds a final step, cooking the chilorio base with onion, Anaheim chiles, and tomatoes, which brings even more vibrancy to the dish.

Victoria Eugenia González, one of the most famous chilorio makers in the cradle of chilorio, the small Sinaloa town called Mocorito, taught me the secrets of making authentic chilorio.

FOR THE CHILORIO BASE

4 pounds boneless pork shoulder or pork butt, with the fat left on, cut into 1-inch pieces

1½ teaspoons kosher salt, or more to taste

5 cups water

¼ pound dried guajillo chiles (14 to 15), stemmed and seeded

8 garlic cloves, peeled

2 bay leaves

1 teaspoon dried oregano

1 teaspoon freshly ground black pepper

½ teaspoon coriander seeds

Pinch of ground cumin

⅓ cup white vinegar

FOR FINISHING THE CHILORIO

1 to 2 tablespoons vegetable oil

1 cup finely chopped white onion

½ pound fresh Anaheim chiles (2 large or 3 smaller), seeded and chopped

1 pound ripe tomatoes, chopped, or 1 (15-ounce) can crushed tomatoes

Kosher salt

Warm flour or corn tortillas for serving

To make the chilorio base: Heat a Dutch oven or large deep skillet with a lid over medium-high heat until hot. Add the pork pieces, sprinkle with 1 teaspoon of the salt, and cook for 15 minutes, stirring as the meat begins to brown. Reduce the heat to medium, pour in the water, and stir, scraping the bottom of the pot with a wooden spoon to release the browned bits.

Cover the pot and cook for 1½ hours, stirring and continuing to scrape the bottom from time to time. By the end of the cooking time, the broth will have cooked off and the meat will be frying and browning in its own fat.

continued

Meanwhile, place the guajillo chiles, garlic, and bay leaves in a medium saucepan, cover with water, and bring to a boil. Reduce the heat to medium and cook for 10 to 12 minutes, until the chiles are softened.

With a slotted spoon, transfer the guajillos, garlic, and bay leaves to a blender, and add 1 cup of the cooking liquid. Add the oregano, black pepper, coriander, remaining ½ teaspoon salt, cumin, and vinegar and puree until smooth.

Pour the chile puree over the meat, mix well, and use a couple of wooden spoons or spatulas to break apart the meat, which should come apart very easily. Stir well and cook over medium heat for another 10 to 15 minutes, stirring energetically and scraping the bottom of the pot from time to time. By the end of the cooking time, the meat should be so tender that it breaks into shreds. There will be just a thin film of sauce on the bottom of the pot. Taste and adjust the seasonings. Transfer the chilorio to a bowl. (If not using it right away, cover and refrigerate.)

To finish the chilorio: Add 1 tablespoon oil and some of the fat from the chilorio to the pot. If you have just made the chilorio, some of the fat will have risen to the top; if you refrigerated it, the fat will have hardened over the top. If there is not a lot of fat, use 2 tablespoons oil. Add the onion and Anaheim chiles and cook, stirring and scraping the bottom of the pot, until tender, 4 to 5 minutes. Add the tomatoes and salt to taste and cook, stirring from time to time, for about 10 minutes, until softened.

Add the chilorio to the pot, mix well, and cook for 10 more minutes, stirring often. Serve with flour or corn tortillas.

Cook's Note

► You can make the chilorio up to 5 days ahead and refrigerate it, tightly covered, or freeze it for up to 3 months.

TWO FAVORITE CHILORIO DISHES

Chilorio Migas
Tear 10 corn tortillas into pieces. Heat a tablespoon or so of some of the chilorio fat and shallow-fry the pieces of tortilla. Once they have started to brown, add 1 cup chilorio and heat through. Add 8 eggs, lightly beaten, and scramble them. Garnish with slices of avocado and white onion, and salsa of your choice.

Quesadillas with Shredded Pork
Top a flour tortilla with about ¼ cup shredded melting cheese, add about ⅓ cup chilorio, top the chilorio with another flour tortilla, and heat it on a comal or in a skillet over medium-low heat, turning it a few times, until the cheese melts and starts to ooze out and the tortillas crisp. Cut the quesadilla into 4 wedges and, if you want, top it with avocado slices.

BROWN SUGAR CARNITAS / **CARNITAS CARAMELIZADAS**

Serves 8 to 10

Crisp on the surface, succulent, and so tender that the meat shreds when gently pressed between your fingers, carnitas is one of Mexico's most treasured pork dishes. There are many ways to make carnitas, ranging from recipes that have nothing but pork, its fat, and salt to those that call for the addition of spices, herbs, and, sometimes, even Coca-Cola.

This version is utterly simple: just one heavy pot required, where the meat browns in its own fat. Then orange juice and milk are added, along with onion, garlic, bay leaf, salt, and brown sugar. The recipe takes a cue from the famous carnitas of Quiroga in Michoacán, known as the carnitas capital of the world, where carnitas makers add brown sugar at the end of cooking for a caramelized finish.

For the meat, I use pork butt, which has a generous amount of fat in which the meat can fry, and country ribs, which are not ribs at all but are cut from the shoulder end of the loin.

6 to 7 pounds boneless pork butt and boneless country-style ribs, fat left on, cut into 2- to 3-inch chunks (I use 4 to 5 pounds boneless pork butt and 2 to 3 pounds boneless ribs)

2 teaspoons kosher salt, or more to taste

½ cup water

½ cup freshly squeezed orange juice

½ cup milk

1 tablespoon dark brown sugar or grated piloncillo

½ white onion, quartered

2 garlic cloves, peeled

3 bay leaves

Warm corn tortillas

Pickled jalapeños

Guacamole of your choice

Raw Salsa Verde (page 120)

Heat a large Dutch oven or large deep skillet with a lid over medium-high heat. Add the pork, sprinkle with the salt, and cook, stirring and turning the pieces as they begin to render their fat, and scraping the bottom of the pot, for 12 to 15 minutes, until most of the chunks of meat are lightly browned on all sides. Meanwhile, combine the water, orange juice, milk, brown sugar, onion, and garlic in a blender and puree until smooth.

Reduce the heat to medium-low and pour in the pureed mixture. Add the bay leaves and cover the pot. Cook, removing the lid to stir and scrape the bottom of the pot every 30 minutes, until the meat is fork-tender and nicely browned, about 1½ hours. It should come apart easily if you pierce it with a fork. Taste and adjust the seasonings.

Using a slotted spoon, scoop out the carnitas, leaving the bay leaves and fat behind, and transfer to a bowl or platter. Shred the meat with a fork, if desired.

Serve with warm corn tortillas, pickled jalapeños, guacamole, and salsa verde.

Cook's Note

▶ If you can't find boneless country ribs, you can substitute bone-in ribs, or use all pork butt.

DROWNED CARNITAS TORTAS / **TORTAS AHOGADAS**

Makes 8 to 10 tortas

Torta ahogada translates as drowned crunchy sandwich, which is exactly what these irresistibly rich carnitas tortas are, drenched with not one sauce but two. The first is a thickened mild tomato broth, and the second is a much thicker, spicy tomato salsa with a vinegary zing. People can choose between one or the other, but usually they want both.

The sandwich hails from Guadalajara, the capital of the state of Jalisco. The tortas are made there with the local bread called *birotes*, a chewy, crusty, dense, salty baguette that does not fall apart when stuffed and sauced. If you can't find birotes, make the sandwiches with a sturdy baguette or ciabatta with a nice firm crust. Don't use a soft roll, or the sandwich can quickly collapse into a soggy mess. It will still be yummy, though!

FOR THE TOMATO BROTH

1½ pounds ripe tomatoes, coarsely chopped, or 1 (28-ounce) can crushed tomatoes

¼ cup chopped white onion

1 garlic clove, peeled

½ teaspoon dried marjoram

1 teaspoon dried oregano

2 cloves, stems removed and discarded

½ teaspoon kosher salt, or more to taste

¼ teaspoon freshly ground black pepper

1 tablespoon vegetable oil

3 cups chicken broth

FOR THE SPICY SALSA

7 to 8 dried chiles de árbol, stemmed, or to taste

1 pound ripe tomatoes or 1 (15-ounce) can whole tomatoes

2 garlic cloves, peeled

½ cup coarsely chopped white onion

3 tablespoons white vinegar, or more to taste

¼ teaspoon ground cumin

½ teaspoon kosher salt, or more to taste

1 tablespoon vegetable oil

8 to 10 (6- to 7-inch) lengths dense, crusty bread, such as sturdy baguettes

½ recipe Brown Sugar Carnitas (page 301), heated

To make the tomato broth: Place all the ingredients except the vegetable oil and chicken broth in a blender and puree until smooth.

Heat the oil in a saucepan over medium heat until very hot but not smoking. Pour in the tomato puree, cover partially, and cook for about 5 minutes, until the sauce reduces slightly and thickens. Add the chicken broth, bring to a simmer, and cook for a few more minutes. Taste, adjust the salt, and remove from the heat. Set aside, covered to keep warm.

Preheat the oven to 425 degrees F.

To make the salsa: Heat a comal or large skillet over medium-low heat. Add the chiles and toast, turning them occasionally, until their color changes, about 1 minute. Transfer to a plate and set aside.

continued

Place the fresh tomatoes, if using, garlic, and chiles in a saucepan, cover with water, and bring to a simmer over medium-high heat. Reduce the heat to medium and simmer for 10 minutes, or until the tomatoes are soft.

Transfer the tomatoes, garlic, and chiles to a blender. Add the canned tomatoes, if using, the onion, vinegar, cumin, and salt and puree until smooth. Taste for vinegar, salt, and heat and adjust accordingly.

Heat the oil in a medium saucepan over medium heat. Pour in the pureed sauce, shielding yourself from splatters with the lid, cover partially, and cook, stirring often, for 2 to 4 minutes, until the salsa thickens and darkens and the flavors deepen. Turn off the heat and cover to keep warm.

Place the bread on a baking sheet and toast in the oven for 3 to 5 minutes, just until the crust is crisp. Remove from the oven. Holding the bread with a towel if it is too hot to handle, turn each piece on its side and split it open, leaving it hinged on the other side.

To assemble the tortas: Open each bread and tuck in a generous amount of the carnitas. Place in a soup bowl or deep plate, with the opening facing up. Ladle a generous amount of tomato broth over the sandwiches, then spoon on as much spicy salsa as desired and serve. Make sure you have lots of paper napkins on hand!

CARNITAS CAPITAL

It is said that carnitas was invented in Michoacán. Although the entire state makes carnitas, as do the surrounding states in central Mexico, Quiroga is known as the true carnitas capital. Establishments in the city use the whole hog, and customers yell out to the taqueros what parts of the pig they want—the *maciza* (part of the butt or shoulder with no bone), *costilla* (ribs), *cuerito* (the skin that is turned into chicharrones), and even the ears (*orejitas*). Carnitas stands have warm corn tortillas ready and the traditional garnishes of pickled jalapeños, guacamole, and one kind of salsa verde or another for people to add as much as they want to their tacos.

YUCATECAN PORK AND BLACK BEANS / **FRIJOL CON PUERCO YUCATECO**

Serves 8 to 10

When it comes to food, the entire city of Mérida dances to the beat of a single drum—tradition—and tradition dictates that if it's Monday, you'll eat this hearty bean and pork stew. The dish is super-simple to prepare but so delicious: Simmer black beans with onion, epazote or cilantro, salt, and pork until the broth becomes inky and rich and the meat is falling-apart tender. Dress it up as much as you want to with the garnishes and the chunky Yucatecan salsa.

2 pounds black beans, rinsed and picked over

6 quarts water

4 pounds boneless pork shoulder or pork butt, or boneless country-style ribs, or a combination, cut into 2-inch chunks

1 white onion, cut crosswise in half

4 to 5 fresh epazote sprigs or 15 cilantro sprigs

1 tablespoon kosher salt, or more to taste

Warm corn tortillas

FOR GARNISH

8 to 10 radishes, cut into matchsticks

1 cup coarsely chopped fresh cilantro leaves and upper stems

1 ripe avocado, halved, pitted, and diced

4 limes, quartered

Yucatecan Tomato-Habanero Salsa (page 126)

Habanero chiles, cut into strips or finely chopped (optional)

Place the beans in a Dutch oven or other large pot and add the water. Bring to a boil, cover partially, reduce the heat to medium, and simmer for 45 minutes, or until the beans have begun to soften.

Add the pork chunks, halved onion, herb sprigs, and salt and stir well. Bring back to a simmer and cook, partially covered, for another 1½ hours, or until the pork is fork-tender, the beans are soft, and the broth is inky. Check from time to time to make sure everything is covered with broth and add up to 4 cups boiling water if necessary. Taste and adjust the salt.

Serve with warm tortillas, passing the garnishes for people to mix and mash in their bowls to taste.

Cook's Note

► Don't cut off the root end of the onion, so it won't fall apart and will be easy to scoop out after cooking. If you want to pull the herb sprigs out after cooking, tie them in a bundle with kitchen twine before adding them to the pot.

SLOW-COOKED PORK WITH CARAMELIZED TOMATOES / **LOMITOS DE VALLADOLID**

Serves 5 or 6

Lomitos de Valladolid is about three ingredients: pork, tomatoes, and onion. The key is the way you cook them. The meat is simmered, covered, with the tomatoes and onions for more than an hour, and then it is cooked uncovered until the tomatoes and onions are reduced to a caramelized paste that coats the meat in an oh-so-tasty way. Resist the urge to stop when the meat looks like it's ready, and keep going until there is no liquid remaining at all.

The dish, one of the best-kept secrets in the Yucatán Peninsula, is a specialty of the Yucatecan town of Valladolid, which is a hidden gem, a charming colonial town where all of the buildings are painted a deep golden yellow. I fell for lomitos when I ate it at the Mesón de Marqués Hotel, and understood at once why the locals are so proud of the recipe that they have given it their town's name.

Elsewhere in the Yucatán, the pork is served with warm corn tortillas and soupy beans on the side. Valladolid cooks are more particular: First they toast corn tortillas on a griddle until they become crunchy tostadas, then they top the tostadas with refried beans and add a cascade of the lomitos, with some slices of ripe avocado on the side.

3 tablespoons lard or vegetable oil

2 pounds boneless pork loin, cut into ½-inch pieces, any fat left on

1 teaspoon kosher salt, or more to taste

¼ teaspoon freshly ground black pepper

1 cup chopped white onion

2½ pounds ripe tomatoes, chopped, or 1 (28-ounce) can crushed tomatoes

10 to 12 tostadas for serving (page 54)

3 cups Basic Refried Beans (page 158), made with black beans, or Oaxacan Refried Black Beans (page 162), warmed, for serving

1 to 2 avocados, halved, pitted, and sliced, for serving

Heat the oil in a Dutch oven or a large deep skillet over medium-high heat. Add the pork, sprinkle with the salt and pepper, and cook, stirring occasionally, for a couple of minutes, until the surface of the meat is no longer pink. Add the onion, stir, and cook for a couple of minutes, until it begins to soften.

Stir in the tomatoes, cover, and reduce the heat to medium-low. Cook, stirring occasionally, until the meat is cooked through but not falling apart and the tomato mixture has broken down but is still a bit juicy, about 1 hour.

Taste for salt, and add more if desired. Stir and continue to cook, uncovered, until there are almost no juices remaining in the pot and the tomatoes and onions have caramelized and coated the pork pieces, which will have started to brown, 20 to 30 minutes longer.

Serve with tostadas, refried beans, and avocado. I like to spread refried beans on my tostada, top with a big spoonful of pork, and serve the avocado on the side, but you can also serve the refried beans and tostadas on the side.

OAXACAN GREEN MOLE WITH PORK AND WHITE BEANS / MOLE VERDE OAXAQUEÑO CON PUERCO Y FRIJOL BLANCO

Serves 8 to 10

An abundance of fresh herbs gives this mole an unforgettable herbal, floral aroma. When I was learning to make the dish, I was startled to see so much parsley, and I was also surprised that no cilantro is called for; but you can certainly play around with it and add some, especially if you can't find epazote. The mix of parsley, epazote, and hoja santa is divine. The epazote contributes an earthy flavor that is perfect with the almost sweet, root beer–like taste of the hoja santa (which is, in fact, sometimes referred to as root beer plant or leaf). The other green elements are a generous quantity of tomatillos, which are charred, along with a couple of serranos or jalapeños; together they add a lovely acidic hit and a touch of heat to the pork and beans.

Like all moles, this one is incredibly versatile and keeps on giving. It's good with enchiladas or chilaquiles. It's great with cooked vegetables, particularly potatoes and green beans, or spooned over rice. And you can also make it using vegetable broth or bean broth for a vegetarian option and serve it with just the beans.

FOR THE PORK AND BEANS

4 pounds boneless country-style pork ribs and/or pork butt, cut into 2-inch chunks

1 head garlic, papery outer layer removed and cut crosswise in half

1 white onion, cut crosswise in half

3 bay leaves

10 black peppercorns

1 tablespoon kosher salt, or more to taste

1 pound dried small white beans, such as navy beans

FOR THE GREEN MOLE

2 pounds tomatillos, husked and rinsed

1 to 2 serrano or jalapeño chiles, to taste

½ cup coarsely chopped white onion

3 garlic cloves, peeled

4 cloves, stems removed and discarded

1 teaspoon kosher salt, plus more to taste

¼ teaspoon freshly ground black pepper

2 tablespoons vegetable oil

1 cup coarsely chopped fresh epazote leaves and upper stems (or substitute cilantro)

1 cup coarsely chopped fresh parsley leaves and upper stems

3 to 4 fresh hoja santa leaves (page 311), torn into pieces, or 1 teaspoon crumbled dried hoja santa (optional)

FOR GARNISH

Chopped white onions

Thinly sliced radishes

Quartered limes

To cook the pork and beans: Combine the meat, garlic, onion, bay leaves, peppercorns, and salt in a large pot. Cover generously with water and bring to a rolling boil over high heat.

continued

Skim off any foam from the top, reduce the heat to low, cover, and cook for an hour, or until the meat is tender. Remove from the heat, transfer the meat chunks to a bowl, and set aside. Strain the broth through a fine strainer into a bowl and measure out 4 cups of it.

Meanwhile, rinse and pick over the beans, place in a large pot, add enough water to cover by 3 inches (about 10 cups), and bring to a boil. Reduce the heat to medium-low, cover partially, and simmer for 1 hour, or until the beans are just about tender.

Add salt to taste to the beans and continue to cook until tender, 15 to 30 minutes. Drain and set aside.

To make the green mole: Preheat the broiler, with the rack 2 to 3 inches from the heat source. Place the tomatillos and chiles on a baking sheet lined with foil and broil, turning them halfway through, until charred and soft, 7 to 8 minutes for the chiles and about 10 minutes for the tomatillos. Remove from the heat and allow to cool slightly. Alternatively, you can roast the vegetables on a preheated comal or skillet over medium heat, turning them every 4 or 5 minutes. Remove from the heat.

Transfer the roasted tomatillos and chiles, along with any juices, to a blender. Add the onion, garlic, cloves, salt, and pepper. Add 1 cup of the reserved pork broth and puree until smooth.

Heat the oil in a Dutch oven or large deep skillet with a lid over medium-high heat. Add the tomatillo puree (don't rinse the blender), using the lid as a shield, since it will splatter. Stir well, cover partially, and cook for about 10 minutes, stirring often so that the sauce doesn't stick to the bottom of the pot, until it has thickened considerably and deepened in color.

Meanwhile, add the epazote, parsley, hoja santa, if using, and the remaining 3 cups broth to the blender and puree.

Add the herb puree to the sauce and stir well. Bring to a simmer and stir in the pork and white beans. Cook at a medium simmer for 25 minutes, or until the meat is beginning to fall apart and the sauce has reduced and thickened. Stir and scrape the bottom of the pot often, as the sauce tends to stick. Taste and adjust the salt.

Serve, passing chopped onions, radishes, and limes at the table.

Cook's Notes

▸ If you can't find boneless country ribs, you can substitute bone-in ribs, or use all pork butt.

▸ You can also make this mole with bone-in chicken pieces.

HOJA SANTA, A HOLY DELICIOUS HERB

Hoja santa translates as sacred leaf—the Virgin Mary is said to have hung out the baby Jesus' washed diapers on a hoja santa plant to dry. The flavor of the leaves is difficult to pinpoint, yet unmistakable and unforgettable. Hoja santa sometimes goes by the name root beer plant or leaf, because there are hints of root beer and sassafras, and of mint, eucalyptus, tarragon, anise, black pepper, and allspice as well. Mexican cooks use hoja santa judiciously; too much can be overwhelming.

The plant grows throughout Mexico, but it is used in cooking mainly in the southern states, where you will find it both fresh and dried in all sorts of dishes from tamales to pozoles to moles. The thick, velvety, heart-shaped leaves make edible wrappers for meats, mushrooms, cheese, seafood, and tamales. Hoja santa also has a sweet side. The Aztecs used to add it to their chocolate drinks, and some Mexicans still do that today.

You can find hoja santa in some Mexican and Latin supermarkets or online. If you have the dried leaves, use about a third of the amount called for in the recipe. But if you can't get hoja santa, simply omit it from the recipe—there is no substitute.

ADOBO-ROASTED PORK BUTT / **PIERNA DE CERDO ADOBADA**

Serves 8

Mexicans love food that screams "celebration!" If you are serving pork butt, it is a sure sign you are feeding a crowd. The most common way of preparing it is to bathe it in an adobo sauce and roast it. All the elements I love in adobo are here—the classic pairing of anchos and guajillos; orange juice and apple cider vinegar, which add brightness; and a touch of brown sugar to balance the flavors and help caramelize the sauce.

This makes excellent leftovers. The meat and luscious sauce are a perfect filling for tortas or tacos or a topping for tostadas.

FOR THE MARINADE

½ **pound tomatoes (see note)**

1 **medium white onion, quartered**

6 **garlic cloves, not peeled**

2 **dried guajillo chiles, stemmed and seeded**

2 **dried ancho chiles, stemmed and seeded**

1 **cup freshly squeezed orange juice**

2 **tablespoons apple cider vinegar**

2 **tablespoons dark brown sugar or grated piloncillo**

½ **teaspoon dried marjoram**

½ **teaspoon dried thyme**

½ **teaspoon dried oregano**

1½ **teaspoons kosher salt**

½ **teaspoon freshly ground black pepper**

FOR THE MEAT

1 **(4- to 5-pound) bone-in pork butt**

3 **bay leaves**

Rind of ½ **orange**

To make the marinade: Preheat the broiler, with the rack 2 to 3 inches from the heat source. Put the tomatoes, onion, and garlic on a baking sheet lined with foil and broil, turning the vegetables halfway through, until they are charred and the tomatoes are mushy, 5 to 7 minutes for the garlic and 10 to 12 minutes for the tomatoes and onion. Remove the garlic when it is charred and softened, and, when it's cool enough to handle, peel it. Alternatively, you can roast the vegetables on a preheated comal or large skillet over medium heat, turning them every 4 to 5 minutes, until charred. Remove from the heat.

Transfer the charred tomatoes, onion, and garlic to a blender.

Heat a comal or large skillet over medium-low heat. Add the guajillo and ancho chiles and toast for about a minute, turning a few times, until lightly browned and fragrant.

Transfer the chiles to a medium saucepan, cover with water, and bring to a boil. Reduce the heat to medium and simmer until the chiles are softened, about 10 minutes.

Transfer the chiles, along with 1 cup of their cooking liquid, to the blender. Add the orange juice, vinegar, brown sugar, marjoram, thyme, oregano, salt, and pepper and puree until smooth.

continued

To roast the meat: Preheat the oven to 325 degrees F. With a small paring knife, pierce the pork butt all over so it will absorb the marinade. Place it in a large roasting pan or a Dutch oven and cover with the marinade, turning to coat. Add the bay leaves and orange rind. Cover with aluminum foil or a tight-fitting lid.

Roast the pork for 3 hours, or until fork-tender. Carefully remove the foil or lid, baste the meat all over with the sauce, and return to the oven. Increase the heat to 375 degrees F and roast, uncovered, for another 20 to 30 minutes, until the pork is crusted and browned on top. Transfer the meat to a cutting board and allow it to rest while you cook down the adobo sauce.

If you used a roasting pan, transfer the sauce to a saucepan. Place the pan or Dutch oven over medium-high heat and cook the sauce until thickened to a gravy consistency, 15 to 20 minutes. Fish out the bay leaves and the orange peel.

Slice the meat, or coarsely chop it, place on a platter, dress with the sauce, and serve.

Cook's Notes

► You can use half a 15-ounce can of fire-roasted tomatoes instead of the fresh tomatoes (omit the broiling step for them). Add to the blender with the onion and garlic.

► You can marinate the pork, refrigerated, for up to 48 hours.

GRILLED OAXACAN ADOBO PORK / **CECINA DE OAXACA**

Serves 6

These thinly pounded pork cutlets, marinated in a guajillo-chile adobo sauce, then grilled or seared, make an almost-instant dinner with refried beans, tortillas, any salsa I have in the fridge, and guacamole. I slip them into tortillas or rolls, with avocado and a slather of refried beans, for tacos or tortas. I often flash-fry a slice and serve over leftover rice with some avocado for a quick lunch, or scramble the seared pork with eggs and a roasted salsa for breakfast.

In most of Mexico, *cecina* means air-dried beef. But in Oaxaca, *cecina* is the word for thinly pounded pork that is marinated for several hours or even days in a chile marinade or adobo. I learned how to make this dish in the city of Oaxaca, jotting down notes from vendors at the Pasillo de Humo in the Mercado 20 de Noviembre, the place to go for dried, cured, and marinated meats.

12 dried guajillo chiles, stemmed and seeded

4 garlic cloves, peeled

2 tablespoons apple cider vinegar

2 teaspoons dried oregano

½ teaspoon dried marjoram

½ teaspoon dried thyme

1½ teaspoons kosher salt

½ teaspoon freshly ground black pepper

2 pounds thin-sliced pork loin cutlets

Vegetable oil for cooking the meat

FOR SERVING

Warm corn tortillas

Oaxacan Refried Black Beans (page 162)

Pickled chiles of your choice

Salsa of your choice

Guacamole

Heat a comal or large skillet over medium-low heat. Add the chiles in batches and toast, turning, for about 1 minute, until they change color and begin to release their fragrance.

Transfer the chiles to a saucepan, cover with hot water, and bring to a boil, then reduce the heat to medium and cook for about 10 minutes, until the chiles are softened. Remove from the heat.

Transfer the chiles and 1 cup of their cooking liquid to a blender. Add the garlic, vinegar, oregano, marjoram, thyme, salt, and pepper and puree until smooth. Scrape into a bowl and set aside to cool.

One at a time, place each slice of meat between sheets of parchment or wax paper on a cutting board and, using a meat mallet or the bottom of a small heavy skillet, pound until very thin, about ⅛ inch thick. You should be able to see the paper under the meat, but it should not break apart. Transfer to a platter.

continued

When all of the slices have been pounded, generously brush each one on both sides with the chile marinade, coating the meat completely, and place on a baking sheet. Pour any remaining marinade on top.

Prepare a medium-hot fire in a charcoal or gas grill, or heat a grill pan over medium-high heat. Brush the grill or pan with vegetable oil. Grill or sear the meat for about 1 to 2 minutes per side, until cooked through and a little bit charred on the surface.

Serve with tortillas, refried beans, pickled chiles, salsa, and guacamole.

Cook's Note

▸ You can refrigerate the marinated pork, covered, for up to 3 days, or freeze it for up to 3 months. The longer it sits, the more flavor it will have.

WHERE A SMOKY CORRIDOR LEADS TO HEAVEN

On a visit to Oaxaca, a local historian named Miguel Marquez took me to lunch at the aptly named *Pasillo de Humo*, or Smoke Corridor, in the Mercado de 20 de Noviembre, one of the city's main markets. As you walk through the narrow passage, all the vendors cry out that theirs is the best grilled pork or beef in all of Oaxaca. Locals stay loyal to one stand or another for generations. The owners pass their stands down from one generation to the next too.

The moment you begin to linger at a stand, the vendor will begin to describe all of the different meats he has on offer. To order, you choose your meats and decide whether you want grilled spring onions and nopalitos (cactus paddles) to go along with them. You are then directed to a spot in the informal dining room at the end of the corridor, where long tables are covered with brightly colored plastic tablecloths. A few minutes after you sit down, your sodas and aguas frescas show up, and then the grilled meats. Local tradition requests that if you want some of the huge, soft, freshly made corn tortillas called *blandas* (the name means soft), you need to clap three times. The tortillas are brought to your table in a snap by someone from the stand where you bought your meat, and once you start preparing your tacos, a big tray of condiments appears to dress them up: guacamole, nopalito salad, pickled vegetables, and various salsas with different levels of heat. It's an interactive, delicious, and very satisfying quick lunch.

YUCATECAN GRILLED CITRUS PORK / **POC CHUC**

Serves 4 to 6

The literal translation of this dish, grilled meat, doesn't begin to describe the citrusy, pungent flavor of these thin slices of pork marinated in a Yucatecan mix of bitter orange juice and lots of garlic, then quickly grilled over hot coals. I learned to make poc chuc in Izamal, a town in the heart of the state of Yucatán that is famous for its deep golden yellow buildings, and for its Yucatecan restaurant, Kinich. It was there that Jina, who has been cooking at Kinich for over two decades and is a poc chuc expert, gave me my step-by-step lesson.

4 cups bitter orange juice or Bitter Orange Juice Substitute (page 206)

10 garlic cloves, peeled

2 tablespoons kosher salt

2 tablespoons freshly ground black pepper

2 pounds boneless pork butt, sliced very thin (see note)

FOR SERVING

Yucatecan Tomato-Habanero Salsa (page 126)

Yucatecan Pickled Red Onions (page 147)

1 bitter orange or 1 to 2 limes, cut into wedges

Basic Refried Beans (page 158), made with black beans

Warm corn tortillas

Combine the bitter orange juice, garlic, salt, and pepper in a blender and puree until smooth.

Place the pork in a large baking dish and pour the marinade over it. Cover the dish and refrigerate for at least 2 hours, and up to overnight.

Prepare a medium-hot fire in a charcoal or gas grill. Drain the pork and grill, turning once, until cooked through and a bit charred, 2 to 3 minutes per side.

Serve with the tomato-habanero salsa, pickled onions, citrus wedges, black beans, and warm tortillas.

Cook's Note

▶ The pork should be sliced very thin, about ¼ inch. If you prefer, you can slice it a little thicker than that and pound it to ¼ inch thick.

PORK LOIN IN PEANUT SAUCE / **ENCACAHUATADO DE CERDO**

Serves 6

For this dish, a boneless pork loin roast is seasoned and browned, then simmered in a saucy blend of dried chipotle and guajillo chiles, tomatoes, spices, and peanuts. The heat and smoke of the chiles, the toasty peanuts, the sweet spices, and the acidic cider vinegar make for a memorable sauce.

FOR THE SAUCE

1 pound ripe tomatoes or 1 (15-ounce) can whole tomatoes

2 dried guajillo chiles, stemmed and seeded

3 dried chipotle chiles, preferably moritas (page 133), stemmed

3 garlic cloves, peeled

⅓ cup coarsely chopped white onion

1½ cups unsalted roasted peanuts

1 (2-inch) canela stick or 1 teaspoon ground cinnamon

10 allspice berries

10 black peppercorns

5 cloves, stems removed and discarded

1 teaspoon kosher salt, or more to taste

1 teaspoon dark brown sugar or grated piloncillo

1 tablespoon apple cider vinegar

2 cups chicken broth

FOR THE PORK

1 (2- to 3-pound) center-cut boneless pork loin roast

½ teaspoon kosher salt, or more to taste

¼ teaspoon freshly ground black pepper, or more to taste

½ teaspoon ground canela or cinnamon

2 tablespoons vegetable oil

Cooked rice and/or warm corn tortillas for serving

To make the sauce: Combine the fresh tomatoes, if using, guajillos, chipotles, and garlic in a medium saucepan, cover with water, and bring to a boil. Reduce the heat to medium and simmer for 10 to 12 minutes, until the tomatoes are mushy and the chiles have softened. Remove from the heat.

Remove the chipotle chiles with a slotted spoon and, once they are cool enough to handle, open them and remove the seeds. Transfer the chiles, tomatoes, and garlic to a blender. If using canned tomatoes, add them to the blender, then add the onion and peanuts.

Heat a comal or large skillet over medium-low heat. Toast the canela stick, if using, for about a minute. Add the allspice berries, peppercorns, and cloves and toast, shaking the pan, until everything smells fragrant, about 1 minute. Transfer to the blender.

If using ground cinnamon, add it to the blender. Add the salt, brown sugar, vinegar, and enough chicken broth to moisten the ingredients, and puree until smooth, at least 1 minute. Add more chicken broth as necessary to blend the ingredients, but be careful not to overfill the blender.

To make the pork: Season the pork with the salt, pepper, and canela or cinnamon.

continued

Heat the oil in a Dutch oven or a large deep skillet with a lid over medium-high heat. Add the pork and brown on all sides, about 3 minutes per side. Carefully add the peanut sauce and any remaining chicken broth, shielding yourself with the lid, as it will splatter. Stir well, cover, and reduce the heat to medium-low. Cook, stirring often to make sure that the sauce doesn't stick and scorch on the bottom of the pot, until the pork reaches an internal temperature of 145 degrees F, 35 to 45 minutes.

Transfer the pork loin to a cutting board. Taste the sauce and adjust the salt.

Slice the meat, then return it to the pot and reheat gently. Serve with rice and/or corn tortillas, passing the remaining sauce in a bowl.

Cook's Note

► If the roasted peanuts you use are salted, be sure to reduce the salt in the recipe accordingly.

PORK CHOPS IN CHILE-SEED SAUCE / **VENORIO CON CHULETAS DE CERDO**

Serves 4

Hailing from the state of Durango, the spectacular velvety sauce called *venorio* is made with the seeds and veins of dried chiles, not the chiles themselves. The seeds are cooked in oil, along with cumin seeds. The frying intensifies the seeds' nutty, woodsy overtones, and they're then blended with roasted garlic and tomato. Surprisingly, the masa-thickened sauce is not particularly spicy, although it is deeply aromatic. It's served over thick, meaty pork chops, which I sear on top of the stove, then finish in the oven.

Once you've tasted the dish, you'll want to hold onto the seeds and veins from ancho and guajillo chiles whenever you seed them for other dishes. Make sure they are completely dry and then put them in a jar and store with your spices.

4 bone-in pork chops, about 1 inch thick and 12 ounces each

1½ teaspoons kosher salt

½ teaspoon freshly ground black pepper

5 garlic cloves, not peeled

1 large tomato

¼ cup olive oil

Seeds and veins from 3 ounces (7 or 8) dried guajillo chiles (about 3 tablespoons seeds)

Seeds and veins from 3 ounces (5 or 6) dried ancho chiles (about 3 tablespoons seeds)

1 teaspoon cumin seeds

4 cups chicken broth or water

1¼ cups masa harina, blended with ¼ cup water, or 3 corn tortillas, toasted and crumbled

8 to 10 scallions, white and light green parts only, thinly sliced

½ cup coarsely chopped fresh cilantro leaves

Season the pork chops with 1 teaspoon of the salt and the pepper.

Preheat the broiler, with the rack 2 to 3 inches from the heat source. Put the garlic cloves and tomato on a baking sheet lined with foil and broil, turning them halfway through, until they are charred and the tomato is mushy, 5 to 7 minutes for the garlic and 10 to 12 minutes for the tomato. Remove the garlic when it is charred and softened, and when it is cool enough to handle, peel it. Alternatively, you can toast the vegetables on a preheated comal or skillet over medium heat, turning them every 4 to 5 minutes. Remove from the heat.

Transfer the tomato and garlic cloves to a blender.

Preheat the oven to 400 degrees F. Heat 2 tablespoons of the oil in a Dutch oven or large deep skillet over medium heat. Add the chile seeds and veins and cook, stirring constantly, until lightly browned and coated in oil, 2 to 3 minutes; take care not to burn them. Stir in the cumin seeds and toast for about 1 minute.

Using a large spoon, transfer the seeds and veins to the blender, leaving the oil behind in the pot. Add 1 cup of the chicken broth or water and the remaining ½ teaspoon salt to the blender and puree until smooth; set aside.

continued

Reheat the Dutch oven or skillet over medium-high heat. Add the remaining 2 tablespoons oil, and when it is hot, add as many pork chops as will fit without crowding the pot and cook for about 3 minutes on the first side, until nicely browned. Turn and sear the second side for just 1 minute. Transfer to a baking sheet or roasting pan. Repeat with the rest of the chops.

Transfer to the oven and bake until their internal temperature reaches 145 degrees F, 10 to 12 minutes, depending on the thickness of the chops.

Meanwhile, reheat the fat remaining in the Dutch oven or skillet over medium heat. Pour in the chile seed puree (don't bother cleaning the blender) and cook, stirring and scraping all the browned bits from the bottom, until the sauce thickens and darkens and the flavors intensify, 4 to 5 minutes.

While the sauce reduces, break up the masa harina mixture with your hands, if using. Add it or the toasted tortillas to the blender, along with the remaining 3 cups chicken broth or water, and puree until smooth.

Pour the broth mixture into the sauce and stir together, scraping the bottom of the pot. Bring to a medium simmer and cook, stirring occasionally, for 12 to 15 minutes, until the sauce thickens slightly. It is ready when you see tiny puddles of fat on the surface. Taste and adjust the seasonings.

Arrange the chops on a platter and top with the sauce. Garnish with the scallions and cilantro and serve.

AMAZING ANCHOS

Ancho chiles are fleshy compared to other dried chiles, and their heat is mild, with a deep, bittersweet fruity flavor that has hints of chocolate and prunes. It's no wonder that these are probably the most widely used chile in Mexico.

Anchos are poblano chiles that have been allowed to ripen to a deep red and then dried, which concentrates their exuberant fruitiness. They are wide and chubby at the stem end and are more pliable than most other dried chiles, with dark, shiny reddish-brown, wrinkly skin.

The chiles are available in most supermarkets and all Mexican markets, but the packaging can be confusing, because they are sometimes labeled pasilla anchos. Pasillas are a different type of dried chile (see page 127), longer, darker, and more slender. If the package is labeled pasilla ancho, it is probably an ancho—look for that reddish-brown color and generous shape to be sure.

SALADS AND VEGETABLES

Vegetables and salads may not be the first thing you think of when you think of Mexican food. But get lost with me as I walk down the endless rows of produce in any Mexican market, or come along as kind and generous cooks from all over the country invite me into their kitchens for a meal, and you will see that there are many stories to tell about our vegetable dishes.

When I moved to the U.S., I searched in vain for my favorite vegetables. My problem was compounded by the fact that I didn't know the English words for the vegetables I missed the most. How was I to explain to the person in the produce department what I was looking for when I was searching for nopalitos? I could only imagine what they'd think if I said "cactus paddles." How could I describe the chayote I was craving? "It looks a little bit like a pear, but it's a squash, crunchy like a cucumber, and lighter green than a zucchini," I'd say. I would be met with blank stares and polite apologies. I could find plenty of zucchini, but where were their sweeter and more flavorful cousins, the chubby round light green calabacitas with feathery white markings, that I loved so much?

We have come a long way in the U.S. since then. I can get nopalitos in the supermarket, and chayote is now sold in most large grocery stores. I cook it with a thick, rich-tasting, but simple-to-make tomato sauce spiked with chiles de árbol, then sprinkle crumbled salty Cotija cheese on top. I always make a large batch, knowing that I will want to eat it for lunch the next day, because the dish keeps well and reheats even better. Most of our vegetable dishes are like that. You can make them ahead and reheat them before serving, if you like, and they make great leftovers.

In this chapter, you'll find both classics I grew up with, like Chard and Potatoes with Chorizo (page 341), and local treasures I've learned about as I've traveled the country, including stunners like Campeche's Mayan chulibul, green beans cooked in a flavorful sauce of pureed fresh corn, dressed with a chunky tomato salsa, and crowned with ground pepitas. Every one of these no-fuss, forgiving recipes is a beauty.

AVOCADO, WATERCRESS, AND PECAN SALAD /
ENSALADA DE AGUACATE CON BERROS Y NUEZ

Serves 4 to 6

Watercress dressed with oil and vinegar, often with lime juice and herbs added, is a favorite in Mexican kitchens. The simple salad is sometimes tucked into tacos for a touch of freshness or used as a garnish for tostadas. When served as part of a meal, it may have a few more ingredients, as in this one. I've added some sweetness and heat to the dressing, and I love the textures that the crunchy pecans and creamy avocado bring to the salad.

1 garlic clove, not peeled

2 dried chiles de árbol or chiles piquín, stemmed

3 tablespoons olive oil

2 tablespoons vegetable oil

2 tablespoons apple cider vinegar

2 tablespoons freshly squeezed lime juice

1 teaspoon honey

1 teaspoon kosher salt, or more to taste

¼ teaspoon freshly ground black pepper

½ pound watercress (2 big bunches), lower stems removed

5 to 6 scallions, white and light green parts only, thinly sliced

½ cup pecans, coarsely chopped

1 ripe avocado, halved, pitted, and cut into large chunks

Heat a comal or skillet over medium-low heat. Add the garlic clove and chiles and toast, turning often, until the chiles darken in color, 1 to 2 minutes, and the garlic is soft and charred, 5 to 6 minutes; remove the chiles as soon as they are done. When the garlic is cool enough, peel it. Mince the garlic and chiles.

In a large salad bowl, whisk the oils, vinegar, lime juice, honey, salt, and pepper together. Add the chiles and garlic and mix well with the whisk. Taste and adjust the salt.

Add the watercress, scallions, and pecans to the bowl and toss well. Arrange the avocado pieces on top, sprinkle with a little salt, and serve.

SEARED NOPALITO SALAD WITH RADISHES AND OREGANO / **ENSALADA DE NOPALITOS ASADOS CON RÁBANOS Y OREGANO**

Serves 4 or 5

Mexicans love nopales so much that we almost always refer to them in the diminutive, as *nopalitos*. I serve these seared nopalitos as a side with complex meat dishes like Wrapped Slow-Cooked Lamb (page 287), Braised Goat or Lamb with Guajillo Chiles (page 293), and Brown Sugar Carnitas (page 301). But I also wouldn't hesitate to use nopalitos as a taco filling or tostada topping, with just about any salsa.

I cook the nopalito strips in a bit of oil until they are barely browned and all of their juices have been released and then evaporated. It's a similar process to cooking and browning mushrooms, although the liquid from nopales is a bit viscous. Then I season them with a generous amount of dried oregano, take them off the heat, and toss them with just enough lime juice to brighten them up, a little chopped white onion, some sharp radishes, and, for an added kick, a minced jalapeño or serrano.

2 tablespoons olive oil

1 pound nopales (cactus paddles), cleaned (page 332) and cut into 1½-x-½-inch strips

1 teaspoon kosher salt

1 teaspoon dried oregano

½ pound radishes, halved lengthwise and thinly sliced

1 jalapeño or serrano chile, finely chopped

⅓ cup finely chopped white onion

½ cup coarsely chopped fresh cilantro leaves and upper stems

1 tablespoon freshly squeezed lime juice

Avocado slices for garnish (optional)

Heat the oil in a large skillet over medium heat. Add the nopales and ½ teaspoon of the salt and cook, stirring occasionally, until the nopales release their juice and it has almost evaporated, 8 to 10 minutes. Stir in the oregano and cook for a minute or two, until fragrant. Remove from the heat.

Combine the radishes, chile, onion, cilantro, lime juice, and the remaining ½ teaspoon salt in a serving bowl. Add the nopales and toss together, top with slices of avocado, if desired, and serve.

Some grocery stores and farmers' markets in the U.S. sell nopales already cleaned and cut up, but the demand for this fantastic, super-healthy vegetable isn't yet great enough for it to be commonly available that way. Don't let that deter you from cooking them. Once you've prepared a couple of paddles, you'll see that it isn't very difficult.

Buying Nopales

Look for paddles that are bright green and tender but not limp. They shouldn't be wrinkled or have dark spots. The smaller the paddle, the more tender it will be, though large ones are delicious too, especially for grilling.

Cleaning Nopales

Nopales are covered with little thorns, and they are very persnickety, so be careful. Wherever there is a bump, there will be a thorn in the middle of it. You may want to wear plastic gloves. Hold the nopales at the base and rinse under cold water. Lay each paddle on a cutting board and, using a vegetable peeler or a sharp paring knife, peel away the bumps, trying not to peel off all of the shiny dark green skin between the bumps.

Rinse the nopales again. Lay each paddle flat on the cutting board and trim off ¼ inch of it all the way around the edges, then cut away about ½ inch of the thick base. Once prepped, nopales will keep for 3 to 4 days in a covered container in the refrigerator.

Cooking Nopales

Roasting nopales on a comal, griddle, or grill, or searing them in a pan in a little oil, are my preferred methods of cooking. Lay the paddles, whole or cut up, directly on the pan or grill, maybe with a little bit of oil if using a pan, and cook until the surface is nicely seared or charred and the viscous juices emerge. At this point, you can add other ingredients, seasonings, and/ or spices, such as chopped onion, garlic, tomatoes, or corn kernels; fresh or dried chiles; and epazote, cilantro, or oregano in whatever combination you wish. The flavors will be absorbed by the nopales as they continue to cook and the sticky juices evaporate. You can also add these seasonings and ingredients to the cooked nopales after transferring them to a bowl. Another delicious way to dress cooked nopales is to toss them with a pico de gallo—onion, tomato, fresh chile, and cilantro.

You can also boil the paddles, but you'll need to rinse and drain them several times to rid them of the goo.

CHILES RELLENOS WITH CHEESE / **CHILES RELLENOS DE QUESO**

Makes 8 to 10 chiles rellenos; serves 8 to 10 as an appetizer, 4 to 6 as a main course

These chiles rellenos are stuffed to the gills with melty cheese, then swathed in a luxurious blanket of beaten egg whites folded together with the yolks, and fried until golden brown. You can tell they come from Mexico's northern states because they are made with the chile of choice there, the Anaheim (also called New Mexico or California chile). These chiles rellenos actually have a double dose of this chile, because the salsa that tops them is made with chiles colorados, the dried form of the Anaheim.

Serve them as a main dish, with rice and/or tortillas or beans, or as an appetizer or as a side with grilled meats.

> **8 to 10 fresh Anaheim chiles (about 3 pounds), roasted, sweated, and peeled (page 176; see note)**
>
> **3 cups grated melting cheese, such as Oaxaca, asadero, Monterey Jack, or mozzarella (12 ounces)**
>
> **½ cup all-purpose flour**
>
> **4 large eggs, separated**
>
> **Vegetable oil for deep-frying**
>
> **Colorado Chile Red Salsa (page 128)**
>
> **Shredded cabbage for garnish (optional)**
>
> **Crumbled Cotija cheese or queso fresco for garnish (optional)**

Make a slit down one side of each roasted chile and carefully remove the cluster of seeds and veins.

Stuff each chile with about ⅓ cup cheese, or as much as will fit and still allow you to close it. Close it and secure the opening with a toothpick.

Place the flour on a plate. Lightly roll the stuffed chiles in the flour and transfer to a baking sheet or platter. (The dusting of flour will help the batter stick to the chiles.)

With an electric mixer, beat the egg whites in a large bowl on medium speed until they hold stiff peaks. Lightly beat the egg yolks in a small bowl. Gently fold the egg yolks into the egg whites with a flexible spatula, just until they are incorporated.

Place a cooling rack on a baking sheet lined with paper towels. Fill a Dutch oven or large deep skillet with 1 inch of oil and heat over medium-high heat until it reaches 360 degrees F. You can test the oil by dipping a piece of tortilla or bread into it; the oil should immediately bubble happily all around the edges. Adjust the heat to keep the oil at around 360 degrees F.

Working in batches to avoid crowding the pot, dip each chile into the egg batter, making sure that it is entirely covered, and gently place in the hot oil, seam side up. Spoon some of the hot oil on top to seal the chile. Fry for about 2 minutes per side, until golden brown, turning the chiles over gently with rubber-tipped tongs, a slotted spoon, or two spoons. Drain on the rack.

continued

Transfer the chiles to plates or a platter, ladle on the salsa, sprinkle with shredded cabbage and grated cheese, if using, and serve.

Cook's Notes

► Anaheims have a brighter, more citrusy flavor than poblanos, but you can use poblanos for this dish.

► The chiles are best eaten as soon as they are ready, but you can make them ahead if necessary. Place them in a baking dish and, when ready to eat, reheat them in a 300 degree F oven for 10 minutes.

Variation

You can stuff these with the picadillo on page 275 instead of the cheese. You will need 3 to 4 cups.

OAXACA CHEESE, THE MOZZARELLA OF MEXICO

Oaxaca cheese is a cow's-milk cheese similar to mozzarella that is hand-stretched into long ribbons and rolled up like a ball of yarn. It's a creamy cheese that is also slightly, and deliciously, rubbery. It melts beautifully, with a mild, rich flavor that is a tad saltier than mozzarella. Fresh Oaxaca cheese is great for eating on its own, but it can also join many different dishes from soups to desserts.

If you can't find Oaxaca, substitute low-moisture mozzarella, asadero, or Monterey Jack.

GREEN BEANS IN CORN SAUCE WITH PUMPKIN SEEDS / **CHULIBUL**

Serves 4

This Mayan vegetable dish is a dream, and it comes together quickly. Green beans are cooked in a creamy fresh corn and epazote puree, topped with a chunky, spicy cooked tomato salsa, and garnished with pumpkin seeds. It comes from Campeche, in the Yucatán Peninsula. There, chulibul is often prepared more like a soup, with the green beans boiled and the rest of the ingredients stirred in. But searing the beans quickly in oil before finishing the cooking in the pureed corn preserves their crisp texture and bright flavor. Serve chulibul as the centerpiece of a vegetarian meal or as a side.

½ cup raw hulled pumpkin seeds (see note)

1¼ teaspoons kosher salt

1 cup fresh corn kernels (from 1 large ear)

1 cup water

3 to 4 fresh sprigs epazote or cilantro

3 tablespoons vegetable oil

1 pound green beans, trimmed

½ cup finely chopped white onion

1 fresh habanero, serrano, or jalapeño chile, finely chopped

1 garlic clove, finely chopped

1 pound ripe tomatoes, chopped, or 1 (15-ounce) can crushed tomatoes

Heat a small skillet over medium-low heat. Add the pumpkin seeds and toast until they are lightly colored and starting to jump or pop, 4 to 5 minutes. Transfer to a bowl and let cool.

Transfer the pumpkin seeds to a food processor, add ¼ teaspoon of the salt, and pulse until finely ground. Set aside.

Combine the fresh corn, water, and epazote or cilantro in a blender and puree until smooth.

Heat 2 tablespoons of the oil in a large skillet over medium-high to high heat. Add the green beans, sprinkle with ½ teaspoon of the salt, and cook for 3 to 4 minutes, stirring occasionally, until they begin to turn brighter green. Pour the pureed corn over the green beans, reduce the heat to medium, and cook for 8 to 10 minutes, stirring often so that the sauce doesn't stick to the pan, until the beans are tender and the puree has reduced to a creamy, thick sauce.

Meanwhile, heat the remaining 1 tablespoon oil in a medium saucepan or skillet over medium-high heat. Add the onion and chile and cook until softened and starting to color, 3 to 4 minutes. Add the garlic and cook until translucent, less than a minute. Add the tomatoes and the remaining ½ teaspoon salt and cook, stirring occasionally, until the tomatoes are softened and pasty, 5 to 8 minutes.

Scrape the beans with the corn sauce onto a platter. Top with the tomato salsa, garnish with the ground pumpkin seeds, and serve.

Cook's Note

▶ You can substitute roasted salted pumpkin seeds for the raw ones, but don't toast and salt them, just grind them.

CHAYOTES WITH CHILE AND CHEESE / **CHAYOTES CON CHILE DE ÁRBOL Y QUESO**

Serves 4 to 6

Those pale green pear-shaped vegetables that you sometimes see in the produce section of your supermarket are chayotes. They have a flavor similar to that of summer squash, to which they're related. With their juicy crunch, chayotes are wonderful raw, either grated, sliced, or diced, in salads, or you can cut them into sticks, sprinkle with lime juice and chile powder, and enjoy as a snack. I also love this cooked chayote dish from central Mexico, in which the vegetable's mild taste provides the ideal backdrop for a rustic, spicy sauce made with tomatoes and chiles de árbol.

- **1 pound tomatoes (see note)**
- **¼ large white onion**
- **1 garlic clove, not peeled**
- **¼ cup water**
- **2 dried chiles de árbol, stemmed, or more to taste**
- **1½ teaspoons kosher salt, or more to taste**
- **¼ teaspoon freshly ground black pepper**
- **2 tablespoons vegetable oil**
- **4 large chayotes (2½ to 3 pounds), peeled, quartered lengthwise, and sliced crosswise about ¼ inch thick (see note)**
- **½ cup crumbled Cotija cheese or queso fresco, or to taste**

Preheat the broiler, with the rack 2 to 3 inches from the heat source. Put the tomatoes, onion, and garlic on a baking sheet lined with foil and broil, turning the vegetables halfway through, until they are charred and the tomatoes are mushy, 5 to 7 minutes for the garlic and 10 to

12 minutes for the tomatoes and onion. Remove the garlic when it is charred and soft, and when it's cool enough to handle, peel it. Alternatively, you can roast the vegetables on a preheated comal or skillet over medium heat, turning them every 4 to 5 minutes, until charred. Remove from the heat.

Transfer the charred vegetables to a blender. Add the water, chiles, salt, and pepper and puree until smooth.

Heat the oil in a Dutch oven or a large deep skillet with a lid over medium-high heat. Add the pureed sauce, shielding yourself from splatters with the lid, and cook for a couple of minutes, stirring often, until it has thickened and darkened slightly. Add the chayote and toss with the sauce. Reduce the heat to medium, cover partially, and cook for about 7 minutes. Remove the lid and cook, stirring, for another minute, or until the sauce has thickened but the chayote is al dente and still crunchy. Taste for salt and add more if desired.

Transfer to a serving bowl, garnish with the cheese, and serve.

Cook's Notes

► You can substitute 1 (15-ounce) can fire-roasted tomatoes for the fresh tomatoes (skip the broiling step for the tomatoes). Add them to the blender with the roasted onion and garlic.

► Chayotes have a large, soft seed in the middle, which I love eating on its own with a sprinkling of salt. You can also just leave the seeds in the chayote, as in this recipe.

CHARD AND POTATOES WITH CHORIZO / **ACELGAS CON CHORIZO Y PAPAS**

Serves 4 to 6 as a side, 4 as a main course

Swiss chard and potatoes is one of Mexico's most popular combos. We refer to dishes like these as *de cajón,* in the drawer, meaning whenever you pull it out, it delivers. I add chorizo for a dish that can stand on its own as a main for those looking for meat, and it also makes a fabulous side, which is how I usually serve it. Sometimes I make a double batch so that I can fill tacos or enchiladas with the leftovers the next day. Feel free to make this vegetarian by omitting the chorizo.

Kosher salt

2 pounds Swiss chard, stemmed

2 tablespoons olive oil

½ pound Mexican chorizo, casings removed and coarsely chopped

¾ cup finely chopped white onion

2 pounds red potatoes, peeled and cut into ½-inch dice

¼ teaspoon ground cumin

¼ teaspoon ground allspice

¼ teaspoon freshly ground black pepper

1 pound ripe tomatoes, chopped, or 1 (15-ounce) can crushed tomatoes

Bring a large pot of salted water to a boil. Add the chard and cook just until tender, 2 to 4 minutes. Drain in a colander and press out the excess water with a wooden spoon. Coarsely chop and set aside.

Heat the oil in a large skillet over medium heat. Once it is hot, add the chorizo and cook, breaking it up with two wooden spoons or spatulas, until it begins to render its fat and brown, about 4 minutes. Stir in the onion and cook for about 3 minutes, until it begins to soften.

Add the potatoes and sprinkle with 1 teaspoon salt, the cumin, allspice, and black pepper. Stir together and cook for 10 to 12 minutes, until the potatoes are soft and just beginning to brown. Add the tomatoes and cook, stirring occasionally, until they soften, a few minutes. Add the chard, stir, cover, and cook for 10 minutes, until the chard is very tender; there will still be a small amount of liquid in the pan, but it should not be soupy.

Remove from the heat and serve.

CRACKED CORN IN TOMATO CHEESE SAUCE / CHACALES

Serves 4 to 6

This soothing, nourishing dish is made with chacales, cracked dried hominy, which is similar to grits, but much coarser and more toothsome. You can get chacales—it also goes by *chuales* or *chicales*—online, at Mexican groceries, and, increasingly, in large international supermarkets. It's often sold under the name golden hominy corn or *maíz trillado*, meaning cracked corn. Traditionally eaten during Lent in the northern states of Mexico, chacales (the name of this dish as well as the ingredient) makes a satisfying side at any time of year.

½ **pound chacales (maíz trillado)**

1 **pound ripe tomatoes or 1 (15-ounce) can whole tomatoes**

2 **garlic cloves, peeled**

8 **cups water**

1 **teaspoon kosher salt**

1 **cup vegetable or chicken broth or water**

2 **tablespoons lard or vegetable oil**

¾ **cup chopped white onion**

2 **cups melting cheese, such as asadero, Oaxaca, Monterey Jack, or mozzarella (8 ounces)**

¼ **cup chopped fresh cilantro leaves or chives for garnish (optional)**

Place the chacales in a bowl and cover with hot water. Soak for at least 30 minutes.

Put half the fresh tomatoes, if using, the garlic, and water in a medium saucepan and bring to a boil. Reduce the heat to medium-high and simmer for 10 minutes, until the tomatoes are soft. Using a slotted spoon, transfer the tomatoes and garlic to a blender. (Leave the water in the saucepan for cooking the chacales.) Add the salt and broth or water to the blender, along with half the canned tomatoes, if using. Puree until smooth. Set aside.

Bring the saucepan of tomato water to a boil. Drain the chacales, add to the boiling water, reduce the heat to medium, and simmer for 30 minutes.

Meanwhile, finely chop the remaining tomatoes.

Heat the lard or oil in a Dutch oven or large saucepan over medium heat. Add the onion and cook, stirring occasionally, for 3 to 4 minutes, until softened and just beginning to color. Add the chopped tomatoes and cook for 2 to 3 minutes, until they begin to soften.

Place a colander over a bowl and drain the chacales, reserving the cooking liquid. Add the chacales to the onion and tomato mixture and cook, stirring, for a minute. Stir in the pureed tomato mixture, along with 2 cups of the chacales cooking liquid, and bring to a boil. Reduce the heat to medium and cook for 10 to 15 minutes, until the sauce is thick and creamy and the chacales is cooked through; it will still be chewy.

Add the cheese and stir until it has melted. Garnish with the cilantro or chives, if using, and serve.

POTATO CROWN / **ROSCA DE PAPA**

Serves 8 to 10

This elegant-looking baked potato ring comes from Sonora, in the north of Mexico, a region that loves its potatoes as much as it does its cheese, and dairy products in general. Cooks there whip potatoes together with cream, butter, and cheese and bake them in a ring-shaped pan (I use a Bundt pan), creating a spectacularly delicious puffed crown. It emerges from the oven looking browned and gorgeous, ready to be sliced like a cake.

4 tablespoons (½ stick) unsalted butter, at room temperature, plus more for the pan

2 tablespoons bread crumbs

Kosher salt

4 pounds red potatoes, peeled and cut into chunks

⅓ cup heavy cream

2 tablespoons all-purpose flour

1 teaspoon baking powder

¾ cup grated melting cheese, such as asadero, Oaxaca, Monterey Jack, or mozzarella

½ cup grated añejo, Cotija, or Parmigiano-Reggiano

3 large eggs, well beaten

Preheat the oven to 400 degrees F, with a rack in the middle. Butter a 10-inch Bundt pan and dust with the bread crumbs.

Bring a large saucepan of salted water to a boil. Add the potatoes, reduce the heat to medium, and simmer until the potatoes are tender, about 20 minutes. Drain and place in a large bowl.

Add the butter and cream to the potatoes and mash with a potato masher or a fork until smooth.

Stir the flour, baking powder, and 2 teaspoons salt together in a small bowl, then stir into the potato mixture. Stir in both cheeses. Stir in the eggs and mix until thoroughly incorporated.

Scrape the potatoes into the Bundt pan and smooth the top. Bake for 55 minutes, or until the potatoes are puffed and golden. Remove from the oven and allow to sit for a few minutes.

Invert a serving plate over the Bundt pan, invert it onto the plate, and remove the pan. Serve immediately.

Cook's Note

► If you have any leftovers, you can slice them, panfry them in a bit of butter, and serve them under eggs topped with salsa.

ISTMEÑA POTATO CASSEROLE / **CAZUELA DE PAPA ISTMEÑA**

Serves 6 to 8

This traditional potato cazuela, from the Isthmus of Tehuantepec in Oaxaca (*Istmeña* means from the Isthmus), is like a souffléd version of chunky mashed potatoes, embellished with colorful bits of diced carrots, peas, pickled jalapeños, and green olives. The potatoes are coarsely mashed and blended with cream and egg. The casserole tastes rich and a little spicy in a slightly briny, lingering way because of the pickled jalapeños. Yellow mustard, a perhaps surprising ingredient that is popular in this part of Mexico, contributes to the tanginess of the dish, which is very different from other Oaxacan specialties. I first tasted it in the city of Oaxaca at the restaurant La Teca, whose welcoming owner-chef, Señora Deyanira Aquino (known to everybody by her nickname, La Teca), an extraordinary cook from the Isthmus, has made it her life's mission to share the food from her region.

3 tablespoons unsalted butter, plus more for the baking dish or ramekins

Kosher salt

3 pounds Idaho or Yukon gold potatoes, peeled and cut into large dice

½ pound carrots, peeled and cut into ½-inch dice

1 cup fresh or thawed frozen peas

1 cup chopped white onion

1 tablespoon yellow mustard

⅔ cup crema, heavy cream, or crème fraîche

1 large egg, lightly beaten

Freshly ground black pepper to taste

⅓ cup chopped pimiento-stuffed green olives, or more to taste

⅓ cup chopped pickled jalapeños, or more to taste

Preheat the oven to 375 degrees F. Butter a 9-x-11-inch baking dish or six to eight 6-ounce ramekins.

Bring a large pot of salted water to a boil. Add the potatoes and cook until a fork or paring knife slides in easily, about 12 minutes. Remove with a slotted spoon and place in a large bowl.

Drop the diced carrots into the boiling water and cook for just 1 minute; remove and set aside in a smaller bowl. Drop in the peas and cook for 1 minute. Drain and place in the bowl with the carrots.

Melt the 3 tablespoon butter in a small skillet over medium heat. Add the onion and cook, stirring occasionally, until wilted, 3 to 5 minutes.

To the bowl with the potatoes, add the onions, mustard, cream, egg, 1 teaspoon salt, and the pepper and gently mix together, leaving the potatoes mostly chunky but letting some of them mash just a little bit, until everything is incorporated. Stir in the peas, carrots, olives, and pickled jalapeños. Scrape the potatoes into the prepared baking dish or individual ramekins.

Bake for 25 minutes, until the top has just begun to brown a little. Serve hot or warm.

MASHED SWEET POTATOES WITH CARAMELIZED PINEAPPLE / **DULCE DE CAMOTE CON PIÑA**

Serves 8

Dulce de camote, candied sweet potatoes mashed with fruit and topped with toasted nuts, is a cherished dish throughout Mexico, eaten for breakfast with coffee and for dessert. The fruit varies—it can be oranges, coconut, or pineapple—as do the nuts, which can be pecans, almonds, or pine nuts. Fresh pineapple is the traditional pairing in the states of Colima and Nayarit. Here it's pureed and cooked down with brown sugar or piloncillo until it turns into a kind of hot, fruity caramel syrup that is then blended into the mashed sweet potatoes, bringing with it a tropical and refreshing tang. The dish makes a terrific addition to the Thanksgiving table. It's ridiculously easy to make, and your guests will absolutely love it. See if they can guess that there is pineapple in it.

4 pounds sweet potatoes, scrubbed

1 medium to large pineapple, peeled, cored, and diced, with its juice

¾ cup packed dark brown sugar or grated piloncillo

½ teaspoon kosher salt

⅔ cup pine nuts or slivered almonds

Preheat the oven to 425 degrees F, with a rack in the middle. Cover a baking sheet with foil or parchment paper. Prick the sweet potatoes 5 or 6 times each with a fork or the tip of a paring knife and arrange on the baking sheet.

Bake the sweet potatoes for 50 minutes to an hour, depending on the size, until they are very soft, with juices beginning to ooze and caramelize on the baking sheet. Remove from the oven and let cool until you can handle them.

Carefully remove the skins from the sweet potatoes. Place the potatoes in a large bowl and mash with a potato masher or fork until very smooth.

Place the diced pineapple with all of its juice in a blender, and puree until smooth. Transfer to a large saucepan or Dutch oven, add the brown sugar, and bring to a simmer over medium heat. Attach a candy thermometer to the side of the pan and simmer until the mixture thickens, caramelizes, and reaches 210 degrees F, usually 12 to 15 minutes. Stir in the sweet potatoes and salt and mix together thoroughly with a sturdy whisk. Cook for another 5 to 6 minutes, stirring and folding until you have a rich puree.

Meanwhile, toast the pine nuts or almonds in a small skillet over medium-low heat for a couple of minutes, stirring or shaking the pan, until lightly toasted and fragrant. Immediately remove from the pan.

Scrape the sweet potatoes into a serving bowl, garnish with the toasted nuts, and serve.

ZUCCHINI AND CORN IN POBLANO SAUCE /
CALABACITAS DE TAPACHULA

Serves 6

Mexicans prepare the trio of corn, zucchini, and poblano in every possible way, from soups and stews to quick sides like this one from the city of Tapachula in Chiapas. Here a mixture of zucchini and corn is enveloped in a creamy poblano sauce. Think of it as a Mexican version of ratatouille, but with more texture and much quicker to make. Be careful not to overcook the zucchini, and keep the corn crunchy.

4 fresh poblano chiles, roasted, sweated, peeled, seeded, and coarsely chopped (page 176)

⅓ cup chopped white onion

1 garlic clove, peeled

⅓ cup vegetable or chicken broth or water

2 tablespoons vegetable oil

½ pound ripe tomatoes, finely chopped, or half a 15-ounce can crushed tomatoes

1 cup corn kernels (from 1 large ear)

1½ pounds zucchini (about 3 medium), trimmed and diced

1¼ teaspoons kosher salt

¼ teaspoon freshly ground black pepper

1 cup diced panela cheese (see note)

Combine the poblanos, onion, garlic, and broth or water in a blender or food processor and puree until smooth. Set aside.

Heat the oil in a large skillet over medium-high heat. Add the tomatoes and cook until they soften, about 3 minutes. Clear a space in the middle of the pan and add the corn. Cook for 2 to 3 minutes, until it begins to color. Add the zucchini, season with the salt and pepper, stir, and cook for 2 to 3 minutes, until the zucchini begins to soften.

Stir in the poblano puree, bring to a medium simmer, and cook for 8 to 10 minutes, until the poblano sauce has reduced and thickened and the zucchini is tender but not mushy. Scrape onto a platter, top with the cheese, and serve.

Cook's Note

► If you can't find panela cheese, you can substitute queso fresco, for a more crumbly option, or Oaxaca for a mild, melty option.

Variation

You can turn this dish into a soup. At the end of cooking, add 6 cups chicken or vegetable broth, bring to a simmer, and cook for 5 more minutes. Ladle into bowls, top with the cheese, and serve.

PANELA CHEESE

Panela is a white skim-milk cheese. It's firm enough for slicing and eating as a snack or in sandwiches, yet soft enough to grate or shred. Its flavor is mellow, with just a hint of salt and tanginess. In a hot dish, it becomes soft and creamy but resists melting. In that way it resembles the Indian cheese paneer. Its firmness makes it perfect for a quick sear. I love it, thrown on a comal or skillet for a couple of minutes per side and topped with red or green salsa, for breakfast.

ZUCCHINI, POBLANO, AND CHEESE TORTE / **TORTA DE CALABACITA**

Serves 6 to 8 as a side, 4 to 6 as a main course

In Mexico, *torta* is the word for sandwich, but a torta can also be a dish that is like a cross between a soufflé, a bread, and a pudding. This one made with zucchini and poblano is rich, both sweet and savory, and a tad spicy. It can be gluten free if you use rice flour, which will make it pleasantly grainy. Serve as a main with a side salad, or as a side with meat, chicken, or fish.

½ **pound (2 sticks) unsalted butter, at room temperature, plus more for the baking dish**

2 **pounds zucchini (4 to 5 medium), trimmed**

1 **cup rice flour or all-purpose flour**

1 **teaspoon baking powder**

1 **teaspoon baking soda**

1 **teaspoon kosher salt, or to taste**

2 **tablespoons granulated sugar**

3 **large eggs**

3 **fresh poblano chiles, roasted, sweated, peeled, seeded, and cut into small strips (page 176)**

2 **cups grated melting cheese, such as asadero, Oaxaca, Monterey Jack, or mozzarella (8 ounces)**

Confectioners' sugar for sprinkling (optional)

Crema, crème fraîche, or sour cream for topping (optional)

Preheat the oven to 375 degrees F, with a rack in the middle. Butter a 9-x-12-inch baking dish.

Grate the zucchini on the large holes of a grater. Place in a colander and press on the zucchini with your hands or the back of a spoon to release the excess moisture. Leave for a few minutes and press again. Repeat one more time and set aside.

Whisk the flour, baking powder, baking soda, and salt together in a small bowl.

In the bowl of a stand mixer fitted with the paddle attachment, or in a large bowl using a hand mixer, beat the butter at medium-high speed for a couple of minutes, until creamy. Add the granulated sugar and continue beating until well mixed. Reduce the speed to low. Beat in one of the eggs, then add about a third of the flour mixture and beat until thoroughly mixed. Repeat with the remaining eggs and flour mixture, mixing until incorporated.

Press on the zucchini one more time to extract more moisture. Add to the mixer and beat at medium-low speed for another minute, until well incorporated. Add the roasted poblano strips and cheese and mix just until incorporated. Scrape into the baking dish.

Bake for 40 minutes, or until the torta is puffed and golden brown on top and a toothpick inserted in the center comes out moist but not wet. Sprinkle with confectioners' sugar and/or top with cream and serve warm, lukewarm, or cold.

DESSERTS

SANDWICH COOKIES WITH CAJETA / **BIZCOTELA VESTIDA** 356

CHOCOLATE-DIPPED PALMIERS / **OREJAS CON CHOCOLATE** 359

CARAMEL-FILLED PASTRIES / **COYOTAS** 363

FLOURLESS CHOCOLATE ALMOND CAKE / **PASTEL DE ALMENDRA Y CHOCOLATE** 365

FOUR-MILK CAKE WITH PLUMS AND APRICOTS / **PASTEL DE CUATRO LECHES CON CIRUELAS Y CHABACANOS** 367

DATE AND PECAN CAKE / **PASTEL DE DÁTIL CON NUEZ** 369

CLASSIC CREAMY FLAN / **FLAN NAPOLITANO DE QUESO** 372

CAJETA MOUSSE / **MOUSSE DE CAJETA** 374

COCONUT RICE PUDDING / **ARROZ CON LECHE DE COCO** 377

BURNT MILK ICE CREAM / **HELADO DE LECHE QUEMADA** 378

DAY OF THE DEAD BREAD / **PAN DE MUERTO** 381

CHOCOLATE-AND-VANILLA THREE KINGS' BREAD / **ROSCA DE REYES DE CHOCOLATE Y VAINILLA** 384

CINNAMON-SUGAR FRIED DOUGH / **CHURROS** 388

MIXED NUT AND SEED BRITTLE / **PALANQUETA DE NUECES Y SEMILLAS** 390

CANDIED PUMPKIN IN BROWN SUGAR SYRUP / **CALABAZA EN TACHA** 392

If you were to run into me in the Mexico City airport in January, you would see that I'm clutching an outsize carry-on, a two-foot-long cardboard box. This package is more valuable than all the rest of my luggage, and I relinquish it only reluctantly at security. I place it gently on the conveyer belt and watch anxiously as it passes through the scanner, worried that someone's suitcase will topple over and smash it. Inside, clearly visible through the plastic window on top, is a buttery, orange-scented sweet bread decorated with a sugar crust topping. Called *rosca de reyes*, kings' bread, it's the way Three Kings' Day, aka Epiphany, is celebrated in Mexico, and the holiday wouldn't be the same without it.

I'm hardly the only Mexican sharing my seat with a pastry. In departure lounges everywhere throughout the country at any time of year, you'll see travelers, on their way to visit family or friends, juggling beribboned boxes of cakes, plastic containers of cookies, and crinkly cellophane bags of candy. It's in our nature to spoil our loved ones, especially when we haven't seen them in a while, and we consider it a must to bring something sweet as a housewarming gift, a thank-you, or a treat for a festival day. It's our way of saying *hola*.

In Mexico, *postres* is a much broader concept than its translation, desserts. Sweets are more than the finish to a meal. They're an integral part of almost every time of the day and every important occasion. A piece of tres leches cake with a glass of orange juice and a cup of coffee can be a light breakfast. On our way to work, we stop to pick up a bag of pan dulce from our favorite panadería to share with colleagues during the morning coffee break.

While most of our treats simply make our daily lives a little sweeter, a few have deep symbolic meaning and are associated with specific holidays. As the calendar approaches November 1, the pastry cases and shop windows of panaderías, grocers, and even department stores fill up with sugar-coated loaves of decorated pan de muerto, Day of the Dead Bread (page 381). This rich brioche connects us to the afterlife and our relatives who have passed on. We wait for it all year long.

In this chapter, you'll find many of Mexico's beloved classic home desserts. Like churros, a number have jumped the border to become American favorites as well. Some, like coyotas, sweet, flaky pastries filled with delicious caramelized brown sugar, retain their regional roots while winning a cultish following nationally. Flan and rice pudding began as imports from Spain but took on slightly altered identities in their new country, made with different milks and embellished with more intense flavors. Other sweets like nut brittle predate the arrival of Europeans. I think you will fall in love with all of them.

SANDWICH COOKIES WITH CAJETA / **BIZCOTELA VESTIDA**

Makes 30 to 35 sandwich cookies

This has become our favorite cookie at home. It was inspired by my travels in Sinaloa, where sugar cookies are a local specialty. They go by many names, depending on what town you are in, but the most common one is *bizcotela*. I learned to make this easy flower-shaped rendition from Marta Gonzáles in Mocorito. Marta pinched off balls of sweet, buttery cookie dough, flattened them, and snipped the edges of each round with a pair of small scissors to make petals. I coat my cookies with sparkling sugar and sandwich them with cajeta. If you prefer, you can skip the crystal-sugar coating and filling, or, like me, dress them up.

> **8 cups all-purpose flour**
>
> **2 tablespoons baking powder**
>
> **Pinch of kosher salt**
>
> **1 pound (4 sticks) unsalted butter, cut into chunks, at room temperature,**
>
> **1 cup granulated sugar**
>
> **1 teaspoon vanilla extract**
>
> **4 large eggs**
>
> **1 cup whole milk**
>
> **1½ cups sparkling sugar (see note)**
>
> **1 cup cajeta (see note)**

Preheat the oven to 350 degrees F, with racks in the upper and lower thirds. Line two baking sheets with parchment paper.

In a large bowl, whisk together the flour, baking powder, and salt.

In the bowl of a stand mixer fitted with the paddle attachment, or in a large bowl using a hand mixer, combine the butter and granulated sugar and beat on medium speed for a couple of minutes, until creamy and fluffy. Beat in the vanilla. Beat in the eggs one at a time, mixing well after each addition. On low speed, beat in the flour mixture alternating with the milk in several additions, ending with flour. Turn out the dough and gather it into a ball.

Pour the sparkling sugar onto a small plate.

Lightly flour your hands. Pinch off pieces of dough and roll into balls 1½ to 2 inches in diameter. One at a time, flatten each ball slightly with the palm of your hand and, using scissors, snip the edges at intervals to make 5 petals, taking care not to cut all the way into the center. Press the dough down gently in the center to make an indentation, turn over, and press gently into the sugar crystals to coat the entire surface. Place right side up on one of the baking sheets, leaving about 1 inch of space between the cookies.

Bake the cookies for 30 minutes, switching the baking sheets from top to bottom and front to back halfway through, or until they are just beginning to brown around the edges. Cool completely on a rack. Repeat with the remaining dough, cooling the baking sheets between batches.

Spoon a heaping teaspoon of cajeta onto the flat side of half of the cookies and top with the remaining cookies, right side up.

continued

Stored tightly covered, the cookies will stay crisp for at least a week.

Cook's Notes

▸ Decorative sugars go by different names, including sanding sugar, rock sugar crystals, and sparkling sugar.

▸ You can use dulce de leche or caramel if you can't get cajeta.

CAJETA, MEXICO'S DULCE DE LECHE

You may know cajeta, the sweet, thick, sticky caramel sauce we make by boiling down milk with sugar, as *dulce de leche,* which is what it is called in South America. Our name for it probably has its origins in the little round boxes that this beloved sweet used to be packaged in (*caja* is the Spanish word for box). The ribbon-festooned boxes were sold on the streets and markets and present at every birthday party when I was a child.

We are addicted to cajeta and prefer it to dulce de leche. It has a stronger, more assertive flavor, because it is traditionally made with goat's milk, and it's cooked for a longer time, in big copper pots, until it is darker than dulce de leche.

You can find commercially made cajeta in Mexican markets and in many larger supermarkets. Fill sandwich cookies with it, top ice cream with it, or spread it on sliced bananas or apples, crepes, or toast. Use it to flavor flan. Stir it into your oatmeal or yogurt. Or just eat it with a spoon!

CHOCOLATE-DIPPED PALMIERS / OREJAS CON CHOCOLATE

Makes about 40 cookies

Orejas (the word means ears) are our version of French palmiers: puff pastry coated generously on both sides with cinnamon sugar, rolled up, and sliced into cookies that look like hearts— or the ears they're named after. As the cookies bake, the sugar coating melts and caramelizes; we like them dark, crusty, and crunchy. Many panaderías take orejas to the extreme, dipping them in a rich chocolate coating after they've cooled. You can find orejas ranging in size from 1-inch minis to gigantic 9- to 10-inch cookies, and in addition to classic sugar-coated orejas and chocolate-dipped ones like these, you'll see them edged in colored sugar, or covered with sprinkles (an option here), or a combination. The cookies are not difficult to make if you use store-bought puff pastry, but I have included my easy homemade version here for when you want to up your game.

FOR THE PUFF PASTRY (SEE NOTE)

2⅔ cups all-purpose flour, plus more for rolling out the dough

¼ teaspoon kosher salt

¾ pound (3 sticks) very cold unsalted butter, cut into ½-inch cubes

¾ cup ice water

FOR THE COOKIES

1½ cups sugar

1 teaspoon ground canela or cinnamon

¼ teaspoon kosher salt

FOR THE CHOCOLATE COATING

½ cup heavy cream

¼ pound bittersweet or semisweet chocolate, finely chopped, or ¾ cup chocolate chips

Rainbow sprinkles (optional)

To make the puff pastry: Place the flour and salt in a food processor, add the butter, and pulse a few times, until it has broken down into bits about the size of peas. Gradually add the water, pulsing until you have a very crumbly mixture; it should not come together into a ball of dough.

Lightly flour your work surface and your hands, and scrape the mixture out of the food processor. Gently press it together into one piece with your hands; do not knead. Lightly flour a rolling pin and roll out the dough into a more or less equilateral triangle that is ¾ to 1 inch thick. The dough will still be ragged and the corners slightly rounded.

Fold the two bottom tips of the triangle over to meet in the middle, then fold the top down, without overlapping the folded flaps (the dough will look like an envelope). Turn the dough clockwise a quarter turn and roll out it into a rectangle about ⅓ inch thick. (Folding and rolling the dough several times will create the pastry's flaky layers.) Fold the two long sides over to meet in the center, without overlapping, then fold the dough in half from top to bottom.

continued

Turn the dough clockwise another quarter turn and roll out into another rough triangle. Repeat the folding and rolling process 2 more times, for a total of 3 "turns." Tightly wrap the puff pastry in plastic wrap and refrigerate for at least 45 minutes.

To make the cookies: Mix the sugar, canela or cinnamon, and salt in a bowl.

Spread 1 cup of the cinnamon sugar into a large rectangle on a large work surface. Place the puff pastry on the center of the cinnamon sugar. With a rolling pin, gently roll the pastry out into a large rectangle about 12 x 26 inches and ¼ inch thick. Sprinkle the top of the rectangle evenly with the remaining cinnamon sugar.

Without cutting all the way through the dough, score a line lengthwise down the middle of the puff pastry rectangle with the back of a knife or a ruler. Tightly roll up each long side of the dough to the center line, creating two long rolled spirals that meet in the middle. Gently press the two rolls together in the middle

Cut the rolled pastry crosswise in half and wrap each roll in plastic wrap. Refrigerate for at least 30 minutes (see note). Scrape the cinnamon sugar remaining on the work surface into a wide bowl or onto a plate and set aside.

When you are ready to bake the cookies, preheat the oven to 400 degrees F, with racks in the upper and lower thirds. Line two baking sheets with parchment paper.

Take one roll at a time from the refrigerator and slice crosswise into ½-inch-thick slices. Dip both sides of the slices in the remaining cinnamon sugar to coat, and place on the baking sheets, leaving 1 inch between the slices.

Bake for 10 to 12 minutes, then switch the baking sheets from top to bottom and front to back. Bake for 8 to 10 minutes more, until the cookies are golden brown. If they appear to be browning too fast or if the caramel is burning at all, turn the heat down to 375 degrees F after the first 10 minutes. Transfer the cookies to a cooling rack and cool completely. Repeat with the remaining puff pastry and cinnamon sugar.

To make the chocolate coating: Bring the cream to a simmer in a small saucepan. Place the chocolate in a medium bowl and pour the hot cream over it. Let sit for 5 minutes, then stir until smooth. If using sprinkles, place them on a small plate.

Place a piece of parchment under the cooling rack to catch drips. Dip the top of each cookie into the chocolate and then, if using sprinkles, lightly press the chocolate-dipped side into them, and return to the cooling rack. Let the chocolate set before serving or storing.

Cook's Notes

▸ You can substitute 1 pound store-bought frozen puff pastry, thawed, for the homemade pastry.

▸ The dough can be refrigerated for up to 2 days before rolling it out. The rolls of dough can be refrigerated for 2 days or frozen, wrapped airtight, for up to a month. Thaw in the refrigerator before slicing and baking.

CARAMEL-FILLED PASTRIES / **COYOTAS**

Makes 12 pastries

With their light, crispy crust and sweet brown sugar filling, these round pastries, called *coyotas,* are one of the most loved desserts in the state of Sonora. I had tried a few renditions of coyotas in Mexico City, but I hadn't had the real thing until I landed in the city of Hermosillo, the coyota cradle of Mexico, where on one street there are more than twenty small family-run bakeries specializing in them. Everybody sent us to Doña Coyo, where the pastries, baked at high heat in wood-burning brick ovens, are absolutely incredible. "We make them with love, and we ship them all the way to Japan," one of Doña Coyo's granddaughters told me when I showed up for the third time.

The traditional dough is quite simple—flour, water, a little piloncillo, one or another kind of fat (lard, vegetable shortening, or, sometimes, butter), and salt. Some bakers use a bit of yeast, which results in a very light, easy-to-handle dough, and I have followed their lead. To make the crust, balls of dough are rolled out with special mini rolling pins into perfect circles that resemble thin flour tortillas. The most traditional filling is grated piloncillo mixed with some flour, which melts into a deep dark caramel as the coyotas bake. You can substitute brown sugar if necessary, but do try these made with piloncillo if you can.

FOR THE STARTER

1 tablespoon grated piloncillo or dark brown sugar

1 (¼-ounce) envelope active dry yeast (2¼ teaspoons)

½ cup lukewarm water

½ cup all-purpose flour

FOR THE DOUGH

¼ cup water

3 cups all-purpose flour

½ teaspoon kosher salt

½ pound (2 sticks) unsalted butter, cut into ½-inch cubes, at room temperature (see note)

FOR THE FILLING

1¾ cups grated piloncillo or packed dark brown sugar

2 tablespoons all-purpose flour

To make the starter: Combine the piloncillo or brown sugar, yeast, and water in the bowl of a stand mixer and whisk to dissolve the yeast. Whisk in the flour to combine well. Cover and place in a warm, draft-free spot until foamy and bubbling, about 30 minutes.

To make the dough: Add the ¼ cup water, the flour, salt, and butter to the starter. Attach the bowl to the mixer stand and fit it with the dough hook. Mix on low speed to combine, then increase the speed to medium and mix for 5 to 6 minutes, until the dough gathers around the dough hook, slaps against the sides of the bowl, and is very smooth.

continued

Line two baking sheets with parchment paper. Remove the dough from the mixer bowl and shape it into a ball. Divide it into 3 equal pieces, then divide each piece into 8 equal pieces (24 in all). Roll each piece into a ball and place on the baking sheets, leaving about 1 inch of space between them. Cover with a clean kitchen towel and let rise in a warm, draft-free place for 1 to 2 hours, until soft and slightly puffed.

Preheat the oven to 375 degrees F, with racks in the upper and lower thirds.

To make the filling and assemble the coyotas:
Combine the piloncillo or brown sugar and flour in a bowl and mix well.

Using a rolling pin, roll out each ball on a lightly floured surface into a 5-inch round about ⅛ inch thick (set the baking sheets aside for the moment). If you want perfect rounds, you can trim the rolled-out rounds with a 4½- to 5-inch biscuit or cookie cutter.

Spoon 2 tablespoons of the filling onto the center of 12 of the dough rounds. Cover with the other 12 rounds and press the edges together to seal. Then crimp the edges with the tines of a fork.

Place 6 coyotas on each baking sheet and make a 1-inch slit in the center of each coyota with the tip of a small knife.

Bake for 20 to 22 minutes, switching the baking sheets from top to bottom and front to back halfway through, until the coyotas are golden brown and the filling is bubbling out of the slits on top. Cool on racks.

The coyotas can be stored in an airtight container for about a week.

Cook's Notes

▸ You can use half vegetable shortening and half butter, or even all shortening, for the dough.

▸ You can also mix up the dough by hand in a large bowl.

▸ If the piloncillo you have is very hard, you may find it easier to chisel bits off with a sharp knife instead of grating it.

FLOURLESS CHOCOLATE ALMOND CAKE / **PASTEL DE ALMENDRA Y CHOCOLATE**

Serves 8 to 10

This moist, dense, nutty chocolate cake was my favorite dessert at Da Ciro, a restaurant in the town of Valle de Bravo, about two hours from Mexico City, where my family used to go for weekends and vacations when I was growing up. Sometimes the chef made the cake with almonds, sometimes with pecans, and sometimes hazelnuts. No matter which nuts he used, we loved it. The chefs at Da Ciro always refused to part with the recipe, and they have long since dispersed to other restaurants. But my taste memory of this cake is so vivid that, after much testing, I was able to re-create it, with almonds, chocolate (there's more in my version than in the restaurant's), and sweetened condensed milk. It is ridiculously easy to make.

½ pound (2 sticks) unsalted butter, cut into pieces

6 ounces bittersweet chocolate, cut into small pieces

4 large eggs

1 (14-ounce) can plus ¼ cup sweetened condensed milk

1½ cups almond flour or finely ground blanched almonds

½ teaspoon baking soda

½ teaspoon baking powder

Pinch of kosher salt

¼ cup boiling water

Confectioners' sugar for dusting (optional)

Whipped cream for serving (optional)

Preheat the oven to 350 degrees F, with a rack in the middle. Lightly butter a 9-x-2-inch round cake pan or a springform pan and line the bottom with a round of parchment paper.

Put the butter and chocolate in a heatproof bowl, set the bowl over a saucepan of simmering water (the bottom of the bowl should not touch the water), and heat, stirring occasionally, until the butter and chocolate are completely melted. Remove from the heat.

Put the eggs and condensed milk in a blender or food processor and blend or process to mix. Add the melted butter and chocolate and blend well. Add the almond flour or almonds, baking soda, baking powder, and salt and blend again. Add the boiling water and blend until smooth.

Pour the batter into the cake pan, scraping every last bit out of the blender or processor with a silicone spatula. Bake for 40 to 45 minutes, or until the top of the cake is springy to the touch and a toothpick inserted in the center comes out moist but not wet. Remove from the oven and let cool to room temperature on a rack; the cake will deflate as it cools.

Once it has cooled, invert the cake onto a plate, if using a cake pan, then invert it onto a platter or cake plate. If using a springform pan, remove the sides. Dust with confectioners' sugar and/or serve with whipped cream, if desired.

FOUR-MILK CAKE WITH PLUMS AND APRICOTS /
PASTEL DE CUATRO LECHES CON CIRUELAS Y CHABACANOS

Serves 10

Just about every Latin-American country claims to be the birthplace of tres leches cake, and Mexico is no exception. Served chilled, so moist that it's practically wet, tres leches is a sort of Mexican tiramisu. With this recipe, I've made it cuatro leches. Three of the milks—whole, evaporated, and condensed—are used in the sauce that infuses the layers. The fourth is a cajeta or dulce de leche filling. You could count the whipped cream as a fifth milk, I suppose, but we have always considered it to be a topping, not part of the cake. Even with all the milks, this dessert is surprisingly light and refreshing, with fresh summer fruit between the layers. It is great when just made, but it's even better if it is allowed to sit for at least a couple of hours in the refrigerator, as it becomes wonderfully moist and saturated with the sauce, making it a perfect do-ahead choice.

Softened butter for the cake pans

2 cups all-purpose flour, plus extra for flouring the pans

1 teaspoon baking powder

1 teaspoon baking soda

⅛ teaspoon kosher salt

8 large eggs, separated

1¼ cups whole milk

½ cup vegetable oil

1 teaspoon vanilla extract

1 cup granulated sugar

1 (14-ounce) can sweetened condensed milk

1 (12-ounce) can evaporated milk

1½ cups cajeta or dulce de leche

6 plums, halved, pitted, and thinly sliced (about 2 cups) or other fruit (see note)

6 apricots, halved, pitted, and thinly sliced (about 2 cups) or other fruit

2 cups heavy cream

¼ cup confectioners' sugar

Preheat the oven to 350 degrees F, with a rack in the middle. Butter and lightly flour two 9-x-13-inch baking pans.

In a medium bowl, stir or whisk together the flour, baking powder, baking soda, and salt.

In a very large bowl, whisk the egg yolks until thickened. Whisk in ¼ cup of the milk, the oil, and vanilla and beat until well mixed.

In the bowl of a stand mixer fitted with the whisk attachment, or in a large bowl, using a hand mixer, beat the egg whites until they hold soft peaks. Gradually add the granulated sugar and continue beating until the whites hold stiff but not dry peaks. Using a silicone spatula, alternately fold the flour mixture and egg whites into the yolk mixture, then continue to fold gently until well incorporated.

continued

Carefully scrape the batter into the two pans, dividing it evenly. Bake for 22 to 24 minutes, until a toothpick inserted in the center of a cake comes out with moist but not wet crumbs. Remove the cakes from the oven and cool in the pans on racks.

Whisk together the remaining 1 cup milk, the condensed milk, and evaporated milk in a medium bowl.

Once the cakes have cooled, poke holes all over both of them with a toothpick or fork. Pour half the milk mixture evenly over one of the cakes and let stand for at least 10 minutes, until it is absorbed. Drizzle the cajeta or dulce de leche evenly over the milk-soaked cake and top with the sliced fruit. Run a knife around the edges of the second cake and unmold it onto a rack or an upside-down baking sheet, then invert it onto the first cake. Pour the rest of the milk mixture evenly over the top and let it soak in.

Cover the cake with plastic wrap and refrigerate for at least a couple of hours.

Just before you're ready to serve, whip the cream with the confectioners' sugar in a large bowl until it holds stiff peaks. Spread the whipped cream over the cake and serve from the baking pan. Store any leftover cake, covered, in the refrigerator for up to 5 days.

Cook's Note

► Other fruit can be substituted if you can't find ripe plums and apricots. Sliced peaches, mangoes, or pears; sliced strawberries; and other berries will all work. You can also use thawed frozen fruit, drained thoroughly.

DATE AND PECAN CAKE / **PASTEL DE DÁTIL CON NUEZ**

Serves 10

The Spanish brought dates to Mexico in the seventeenth century. In the beginning, they were mostly cultivated by missionaries in Baja California Sur, and then, as more missions were established, in Baja California Norte. This moist, sweet cake has a rich, dense, marzipan-like texture. It's perfect not only for dessert but also as a midmorning or afternoon treat with a cup of coffee or tea.

1½ cups coarsely chopped pitted Medjool dates (about 8 ounces)

¾ cup boiling water

8 tablespoons (1 stick) unsalted butter, melted, plus more for the pan

2 cups all-purpose flour, plus more for the pan

1 teaspoon baking soda

1 teaspoon baking powder

Pinch of kosher salt

2 large eggs

1 teaspoon vanilla extract

1 cup granulated sugar

1 cup coarsely chopped pecans

Confectioners' sugar for dusting

Place the dates in a small bowl and cover with the boiling water. Let sit for at least 15 minutes, until soft. Every once in a while, press the dates down into the water.

Meanwhile, preheat the oven to 350 degrees F, with a rack in the middle. Butter and lightly flour a 9-inch round cake pan and line the bottom with a round of parchment paper.

Whisk together the flour, baking soda, baking powder, and salt in a large bowl. Set aside.

Transfer the dates, with their soaking water, to a blender or food processor and pulse to a coarse puree. Add the eggs and vanilla and pulse to combine. Add the melted butter and granulated sugar and pulse until well mixed. Add the pecans and blend to a smooth puree.

Make a well in the center of the flour mixture and scrape in the date mixture. Fold it into the flour with a silicone spatula until you have a thick batter. Scrape into the cake pan and smooth the top with an offset (or the silicone) spatula.

Bake for 45 minutes, or until the cake is browned and slightly crusty, with some cracks on top. A toothpick inserted in the center of the cake should come out with moist but not wet crumbs. Cool completely in the pan on a rack.

continued

Run a knife around the edges of the cake pan, place a plate over the top, and turn the cake out onto the plate, then invert onto a serving platter (rounded side up). Dust with confectioners' sugar before serving.

CALIFORNIA CUISINE

Mexico has its own Californias, two of them, in fact (it ceded a third one to the United States after the Mexican-American War). Baja California Norte and Baja California Sur, the last Mexican territories to become states, occupy the peninsula south of the Mexico-California border, with the Pacific Ocean on one side and the Sea of Cortez on the other. A newish regional Mexican cuisine has evolved in Baja, which profits from a Mediterranean terroir and climate, with hot days and cold nights and dry, rocky soil that lends itself well to growing olives, grapes, tomatoes, and dates. The food also profits from vigorous immigration into the Baja Peninsula from other states of Mexico that has brought along with it bold culinary ideas, new recipes, and talent.

CLASSIC CREAMY FLAN / **FLAN NAPOLITANO DE QUESO**

Makes 10 individual flans

Mexicans love flan, and most of us love it with the caramel on the darker side, so it contrasts with the sweetness of the custard. This is the traditional no-fuss, perfectly creamy, glossy flan, dripping with amber caramel, the kind you get in traditional Mexican restaurants and that your aunt brings to potlucks. It's called Napolitano because it includes cream cheese and uses sweetened condensed milk and evaporated milk instead of whole milk. But nobody knows how it got that name, since there doesn't seem to be a connection with Italy or Naples. The recipe is very simple, with no persnickety techniques.

> 1¼ cups sugar
>
> 2 tablespoons water
>
> 1 (14-ounce) can sweetened condensed milk
>
> 1 (12-ounce) can evaporated milk
>
> 3 tablespoons cream cheese
>
> 4 large eggs
>
> 1 tablespoon vanilla extract

Preheat the oven to 325 degrees F, with a rack in the middle. Have 10 (6-ounce) ramekins and a roasting pan at hand.

Combine the sugar and water in a medium saucepan over medium heat. The sugar will begin to melt, and the mixture will bubble. Swirl the pan occasionally, but do not stir. Continue cooking, swirling the pan from time to time, until the syrup is a rich caramel color, 7 to 10 minutes.

Divide the caramel evenly among the ramekins, tilting them so that it evenly coats the bottoms. Set aside to cool while you make the custard mixture.

Combine the condensed milk, evaporated milk, cream cheese, eggs, and vanilla in a blender and blend until smooth. Slowly, so that not too many bubbles form on the surface, pour the mixture into the caramel-lined ramekins, dividing it evenly.

Place the ramekins in the roasting pan. Carefully pour enough hot water to come about one third up the sides of the ramekins, making sure that you don't splash any water into the ramekins. Lay a sheet of foil loosely over the pan and very carefully transfer to the oven. Bake for 50 to 60 minutes, until the flans have set but still jiggle slightly in the center when shaken. Gently remove the foil—watch out for hot steam.

Let the flans cool to room temperature in the water bath. Remove from the water bath, cover each ramekin tightly with plastic wrap, and transfer to the refrigerator. Chill for at least 2 hours.

To serve, run a wet dinner knife around the edges of each flan to loosen it from the ramekin. Invert the ramekin onto a plate and let the flan slide out. Serve cold.

Cook's Note

► The flans can be refrigerated in the ramekins, covered with plastic, for up to a week.

CAJETA MOUSSE / **MOUSSE DE CAJETA**

Serves 10

This mousse, made with milk, cream, and gelatin, as well as cajeta, is ridiculously easy and a perfect ending to any meal. It falls into a category of desserts that we call *gelatinas espumosas,* and it has an irresistible texture, like a cross between a classic mousse, a jelled dessert, and a creamy pudding. Light, cold, and soothing, it melts in your mouth when you take a bite. If you want to be extra indulgent, serve it with a dollop of whipped heavy cream on top.

You can make the mousse in a ring mold or individual ramekins.

> **2 (¼-ounce) envelopes unflavored gelatin**
>
> **½ cup water**
>
> **1½ cups whole milk**
>
> **1¼ cups cajeta (see note)**
>
> **1 cup heavy cream**
>
> **1 cup diced fresh strawberries or other whole berries for garnish (optional)**
>
> **Whipped cream for serving (optional)**

In a medium heatproof bowl, combine the gelatin and water. Let sit until the gelatin softens and swells, 1 to 2 minutes.

Set the bowl over a saucepan of simmering water (the bottom of the bowl should not touch the water) and heat, stirring occasionally, until the gelatin has completely dissolved, about 2 minutes. Keep warm over low heat.

Heat the milk and cajeta in a small saucepan over medium heat, stirring, until the cajeta has dissolved and is thoroughly combined, 1 to 2 minutes. Remove the bowl of gelatin from the heat and whisk in the milk mixture.

In the bowl of a stand mixer fitted with the whisk attachment, or in a medium bowl, using a hand mixer, beat the cream until it holds medium-soft peaks. (Don't overbeat; if the cream is too stiff, it will break up when you fold it into the milk and cajeta.)

Working in batches, fold about one-third of the whipped cream into the cajeta mixture to lighten it, then gently fold in the rest until thoroughly combined.

Fill a large bowl with ice water and set the bowl with the mousse mixture in it. Stir the mousse gently with a whisk as it cools, making sure that it is smooth, with no lumps of gelatin.

Pour the mousse into a 6- to 8-cup nonstick ring mold or into 10 (6-ounce) ramekins. Cover with plastic wrap and refrigerate until set, at least 8 hours if using a ring mold, or at least 4 hours if using ramekins.

When you are ready to serve, fill a large bowl with hot water and briefly dip the bottom of the mold(s) into the water, just for a few seconds. Run a sharp small knife between the mousse and the edges of the ring mold, invert a platter over the top, and flip over to unmold the mousse. If using individual molds, you can invert them onto small plates or serve the mousse in the ramekins.

If desired, fill the center of the large mousse with the berries, or spoon some berries over each individual mousse. Top with whipped cream, if you like.

Cook's Notes

► You can substitute dulce de leche or caramel for the cajeta.

► The mousse (without the optional garnishes) can be refrigerated for up to 5 days.

Mexicans are wild about jelled desserts, which we call *gelatinas*. They are so popular that some shops specialize in only gelatinas, and they are always available, ready to go, in supermarkets. Homemade gelatinas are also sold on the street.

Gelatinas range from very simple versions, with a single flavor, to those with multiple flavors, in different colors, shapes, and patterns. Some are intended for children, others are spiked with rum or tequila or made with rompope (Mexican eggnog laced with liquor). The most intricate and retro gelatinas feature multicolored mosaics of different-flavored jelled cubes and shapes inside.

There are two main types of gelatinas: water-based and milk-based. I love both, but if pressed, I would have to opt for the milk-based variety. They are creamier and taste more luxurious. The ones with the most irresistible texture are *gelatinas espumosas* (spongy or foamy), which include whipped cream and are sometimes called mousses.

COCONUT RICE PUDDING / **ARROZ CON LECHE DE COCO**

Serves 6 to 8

Mexico inherited arroz con leche from Spain, but it didn't take long for the dessert to become a favorite all over the country. It is such a big deal that it is immortalized in a favorite Mexican children's song. I tropicalize mine with sweet coconut cream, as they do in Acapulco. I also add a whole star anise, some orange rind, and vanilla. The pudding can be eaten hot, warm, or chilled, and people feel strongly about which way is best. Some prefer it on the drier side and very thick, others like it soupy. I love it soupy and chilled!

1 cup long-grain white rice or jasmine rice

2 cups water

4 cups whole milk

¾ cup sweetened coconut cream, such as Coco Lopez, thoroughly mixed before measuring (see note)

Rind of half an orange

1 (2-inch) canela or cinnamon stick

1 star anise

3 tablespoons sugar

½ teaspoon kosher salt

3 to 4 tablespoons dark raisins (optional)

1 teaspoon vanilla extract

TOPPINGS (OPTIONAL)

Ground canela or cinnamon

Diced mango or other fresh fruit

Whipped cream

Combine the rice and water in a medium heavy saucepan and bring to a boil. Reduce the heat to medium and simmer for 3 minutes, stirring and scraping the bottom of the pan so the rice doesn't stick to it. Add the milk, coconut cream, orange rind, canela or cinnamon stick, star anise, sugar, and salt, stirring well to combine. Bring to a simmer, reduce the heat to low, and cook at a low simmer, stirring occasionally, until the rice is soft, about 20 minutes. The pudding will still be soupy. Stir in the raisins, if using.

Remove from the heat and stir in the vanilla until well combined. With a slotted spoon or tongs, fish out the canela or cinnamon stick, orange rind, and star anise. The rice will absorb more liquid as it cools, but the pudding will remain soupy.

Serve hot, warm, or chilled. If desired, sprinkle with canela or cinnamon and/or top with fresh fruit and/or whipped cream.

Cook's Notes

► Coconut cream tends to separate in the can, so be sure it's mixed well before you measure the cream. Shaking the can is not always sufficient: if it doesn't look well mixed, pour all of the cream out into a bowl, whisk well, and then measure.

► Without the optional toppings, the pudding can be refrigerated, covered, for up to 5 days.

BURNT MILK ICE CREAM / **HELADO DE LECHE QUEMADA**

Makes a generous 1 quart

Outside the main church in Teotitlán del Valle, a weaving village in the Oaxaca Valley, there are many ice cream stands. The different stands feature different flavors, but they all offer this one, and that's what the people of this beautiful village always recommend. The first time I tasted it, I was startled by its intense smoky, bitter taste. And then I couldn't stop eating it. *Leche quemada* means burnt milk. This ice cream balances the bitter-burnt with the sweet-creamy. You'll need a candy thermometer for the custard. I serve this with animal crackers.

- 1½ cups whole milk
- 1 (2-inch) canela or cinnamon stick
- ¾ cup plus 2 tablespoons sugar
- 2 teaspoons vanilla extract
- 2 large eggs
- 1½ cups heavy cream
- Animal crackers for serving (optional)

Combine the milk and canela or cinnamon stick in a small saucepan and heat over medium heat just until the milk barely begins to simmer and a skin forms on top, 6 to 7 minutes. Reduce the heat to low.

Meanwhile, put ¾ cup of the sugar in a medium saucepan and heat over medium heat. As the sugar begins to dissolve, swirl the saucepan occasionally, but do not stir. Continue cooking, swirling the pan a few times for even heating, until you have a richly colored caramel, 7 to 8 minutes.

As soon as the caramel is ready, remove the milk from the heat, remove the canela or cinnamon stick, and stir in the vanilla. Carefully pour the milk into the hot caramel in a very thin stream, whisking to incorporate it. The caramel will bubble up dramatically; just continue whisking until it is all well combined. If the caramel seizes or hardens on the bottom of the pan, return it to medium heat and whisk until any lumps are melted. Remove from the heat, attach a candy thermometer to the side of the pan, and cool the caramel to 185 degrees F; remove the candy thermometer.

Whisk the eggs until thick and foamy in a medium bowl. Whisk in the remaining 2 tablespoons sugar. When the caramel mixture has cooled to 185 degrees F, gradually whisk it into the beaten eggs in a very thin stream, being careful not to add it too quickly so the eggs don't cook.

Pour the mixture back into the saucepan and place over medium-low heat. Attach the candy thermometer again and, stirring constantly with a silicone spatula, being sure to get into the corners of the pan, heat until the mixture reaches 175 to 180 degrees F and coats the back of the spatula. Take care not to let the mixture come to a simmer, or the eggs will curdle. Remove from the heat and continue to stir for a minute to cool it slightly.

Place a sieve over a heatproof bowl and strain the custard into the bowl. Whisk in the cream.

continued

Fill a large bowl with ice and place the bowl of custard in it. Stir until the temperature of the custard drops to 65 degrees F, then cover and refrigerate for at least 1 hour, or for as long as overnight.

Pour the mixture into an ice cream maker and freeze following the manufacturer's directions. Serve the ice cream with animal crackers, if you like, or transfer to a freezer container and freeze until ready to serve. The ice cream can be frozen for up to 4 months.

DAY OF THE DEAD BREAD / **PAN DE MUERTO**

Makes 2 round breads

Pan de muerto is a signature treat for Día de Muertos, one of Mexico's most meaningful, colorful, and delicious holidays. Its brioche dough is enriched with butter and eggs and fragrant with orange flower water and orange zest; as is traditional in many places, I add anise seeds as well. Although the bread isn't difficult, it does take planning, as the dough requires four rises in all, including an overnight (or at least three-hour) rest in the refrigerator. Traditionally, pan de muerto is made as a very large bread, but I prefer to divide the dough into two loaves for easier handling. The bread is usually eaten plain, with hot chocolate or coffee.

FOR THE STARTER

½ cup whole milk, heated to lukewarm

1 tablespoon active dry yeast

1 teaspoon sugar

½ cup all-purpose flour

FOR THE DOUGH

2 tablespoons orange flower water, rose water, or water

2 teaspoons grated orange zest

1½ teaspoons anise seeds

4 large eggs, beaten

3½ cups all-purpose flour, plus more for dusting if needed

⅓ cup sugar

1 teaspoon kosher salt

½ pound (2 sticks) unsalted butter, cut into ½-inch cubes, at room temperature, plus more for the bowl

FOR THE TOPPING

6 tablespoons unsalted butter, melted

⅓ cup sugar

To make the starter: Whisk the milk, yeast, and sugar together in the bowl of a stand mixer. Whisk in the flour. Cover with a clean kitchen towel, set in a warm, draft-free place, and let stand until the mixture begins to bubble, 20 to 25 minutes.

To make the dough: Attach the bowl to the mixer stand and fit the mixer with the paddle attachment. Add the orange flower or rose water (or water), orange zest, anise seeds, eggs, flour, sugar, and salt and beat on low speed until combined. Scrape the bowl and beater and switch to the dough hook. Beat on medium speed for 10 to 12 minutes, until the dough pulls away from the sides of the bowl and starts to make a slapping sound.

On low speed, add the butter in 4 to 6 additions, incorporating each addition before adding the next one. From time to time, scrape down the bowl. When all the butter has been added, increase the speed to medium and beat for another 8 to 10 minutes, until the dough slaps against the bowl again. It will still be sticky, but don't be tempted to add more flour.

Butter a large bowl. Shape the dough into a ball and place in the bowl. Cover with plastic wrap or a kitchen towel and let rise in a warm, draft-free place until doubled, about 1½ hours.

continued

Gently deflate the dough with your fist, gather it into a ball, and turn it over, so the bottom is now on top. Cover with plastic wrap and refrigerate for at least 3 hours, or as long as overnight.

Remove the dough from the refrigerator and set, still covered, in a warm, draft-free spot for 30 minutes to an hour so it comes to room temperature and rises.

Line a baking sheet with parchment paper. Turn the dough out of the bowl. Cut off a quarter of the dough and divide it into 2 equal pieces; set aside. Divide the larger piece of dough into 2 equal pieces, shape each one into a ball, and place on the baking sheet.

To make the skull and crossbones, cut one of the smaller pieces of dough into 3 equal pieces. Shape one piece into a ball for the skull. For the bones, roll the other 2 pieces into ropes and pinch at intervals so they look like joints. Repeat with the other smaller piece of dough.

Flatten a dough ball into a 6-inch round. Place 2 of the bone strips on top of the dough, crossing them to make an X and pressing them lightly into the dough. Place the "skull" in the middle and press down lightly to secure it. Repeat with the other round of dough. If the dough seems sticky, dust it lightly with flour. Cover the breads lightly with kitchen towels and let rise in a warm, draft-free spot until doubled, 1 to 1½ hours.

Meanwhile, preheat the oven to 350 degrees F, with a rack in the middle. Bake the breads for 25 minutes, or until lightly browned on top. Cover the loaves loosely with foil. Bake for another 20 minutes, or until the breads are dark golden brown and sound hollow when tapped on the bottom. Cool on racks.

To make the topping: Brush the loaves with half of the melted butter. When they have cooled, brush with the remaining butter and immediately sprinkle with a generous amount of sugar, so that the sugar adheres before the butter cools and dries. Let the topping cool before slicing the bread.

Wrapped in foil or in a cake keeper, the bread will stay fresh for up to 5 days.

SWEETS FOR THE GRATEFUL DEAD

Even though both Day of the Dead and Halloween include graveyards and a lot of eating, they are quite different in nature. The Day of the Dead is a bittersweet festival in Mexico, when we remember those who have passed on, with gatherings and feasts that are simultaneously sad and joyous. The celebration lasts two days, November 1 and 2, when the departed have license to come back and visit the ones they've left behind. And if they're returning from another world, we'd better offer them a feast worth the trip! Altars decorated with bright orange marigolds are set up in cemeteries and homes, with candles lighting the way to ensure a safe journey. Favorite foods and drinks are left too, as well as other items like a preferred brand of cigarettes, playing cards, a favorite doll, or a special hat.

You might think all of this is a bit dark, but it's just another example of our devil-may-care approach to life.

CHOCOLATE-AND-VANILLA THREE KINGS' BREAD /
ROSCA DE REYES DE CHOCOLATE Y VAINILLA

Makes 1 large ring-shaped bread; serves 15

I once thought I could never come close to replicating any of the innumerable exquisite versions of the ring-shaped (*rosca* means wreath or crown) kings' (*reyes*) bread found in panaderías all over the country beginning the week of January 6, Three Kings' Day (Epiphany). The rich brioche is deeply tied to Catholic tradition in Mexico. The bakers hide anywhere from one to many plastic figurines representing the Baby Jesus inside. Whoever gets one has to organize a tamalada—a tamal-making party—on February 2, which is Día de la Candelaria, or Candlemas, the Feast of the Presentation of Jesus (and for us Mexicans, yet another reason to get together and make and eat tamales).

I wanted to create a bread for my family, featuring just the parts we love, because it is a well-known fact that every Mexican picks and chooses among the various toppings when eating the breads. So why not make a chocolate-and-vanilla marbled bread with a chocolate-and-vanilla sugar coating in place of the traditional dried-fruit decorations, which many of us just remove? Ask anyone in my house, and they'll tell you that our favorite part of the topping is that sugar coating! I add an exuberant splash of orange blossom (or rose) water to the dough, which is also traditional in many of our yeast breads—and, in my view, essential, but you can omit it, if you like. My rosca turned out to be just as wonderful as I had hoped.

Keep in mind that the dough needs three rises, including one in the fridge for at least three hours or overnight. If you want to hide little plastic Baby Jesus figures inside your rosca, you can find them online and in some Mexican grocery stores.

FOR THE STARTER

½ cup whole milk, heated to lukewarm

1 tablespoon active dry yeast

1 teaspoon granulated sugar

½ cup all-purpose flour

FOR THE DOUGH

1 tablespoon orange blossom water or rose water (optional)

1 teaspoon vanilla extract

1 teaspoon grated orange zest

4 large eggs

3½ cups all-purpose flour, plus more for dusting

½ cup granulated sugar

1 teaspoon kosher salt

½ pound (2 sticks) unsalted butter, cut into ½-inch cubes, at room temperature, plus more for the bowls

3 tablespoons unsweetened cocoa powder

FOR THE TOPPING

1 cup all-purpose flour

1 cup confectioners' sugar

10 tablespoons (1¼ sticks) unsalted butter or ½ cup plus 2 tablespoons vegetable shortening, at room temperature

continued

1 teaspoon vanilla extract

1 heaping tablespoon unsweetened cocoa powder

1 large egg, beaten with 1 tablespoon milk, for brushing

To make the starter: Whisk the milk, yeast, and granulated sugar together in the bowl of a stand mixer. Whisk in the flour. Cover with a clean kitchen towel, set in a warm, draft-free place, and let stand until the mixture begins to bubble, 20 to 25 minutes.

To make the dough: Attach the bowl to the mixer stand and fit it with the paddle attachment. Add the orange flower or rose water (if using), vanilla, orange zest, eggs, flour, granulated sugar, and salt to the starter and beat on low speed just until combined. Scrape the bowl and beater and switch to the dough hook. Beat on medium speed for 10 to 12 minutes, until the dough pulls away from the sides of the bowl and starts to make a slapping sound.

On low speed, add the butter in 4 to 6 additions, incorporating each addition before adding the next one. From time to time, scrape the bowl. When all of the butter has been added, increase the speed to medium and beat for another 8 to 10 minutes, until the dough slaps against the sides of the bowl again. It will still be sticky, but don't be tempted to add more flour.

Butter two medium bowls. Remove the dough from the mixer bowl, divide it in half, and return one half to the bowl. Shape the other piece into a ball and transfer to one of the buttered bowls.

Add the cocoa powder to the dough in the mixer bowl and mix on low speed until incorporated. Turn the dough out, shape it into a ball, and place in the other buttered bowl. Cover each bowl with plastic or a clean kitchen towel and let the dough rise in a warm, draft-free place until doubled, 1 to 1½ hours.

Gently deflate both portions of dough with your fist and shape into balls again. Cover and let rise in the refrigerator for at least 3 hours, or for as long as overnight.

Remove the dough from the refrigerator and set, still covered, in a warm, draft-free spot for about an hour so it comes to room temperature and rises.

Line a baking sheet with parchment paper. Remove the doughs from the bowls and shape each one into a ball. Press each ball down to flatten it slightly. Place the vanilla round on top of the chocolate round and stretch it so that it completely envelops the chocolate round, turning the dough over to stretch it over the bottom. Make a hole in the center of the dough by pushing your fist through it, then gently stretch the dough out to make a 9-x-13-inch oval.

Place the dough on the baking sheet. Insert a couple of plastic Baby Jesus figurines into the dough, if using. Cover with a clean kitchen towel and let rise for an hour or so, until the dough has puffed.

Meanwhile, preheat the oven to 350 degrees F, with a rack in the middle.

To make the topping: Combine the flour, confectioners' sugar, butter or shortening, and vanilla in a medium bowl and mix together into a smooth paste with your hands. Divide the paste in half. Add the cocoa powder to one half and knead and mix well until evenly incorporated. Divide each of the pastes into about 6 portions and shape into balls.

Gently brush the bread with the egg wash. Roll each paste ball into a log and then press to flatten it into a strip about 7 inches long, 1 inch wide, and ⅛ to ¼ inch thick. Arrange them on the bread, alternating chocolate and vanilla strips, at approximately 2-inch intervals.

Bake for about 45 minutes, or until the bread is golden brown and makes a hollow sound when tapped on the bottom. Cool on a rack before slicing.

Variation

For a traditional version, omit the cocoa and don't divide the dough. Make the topping as directed, but omit the cocoa; divide the paste into 12 portions and shape into strips. Decorate the bread with the topping and with dried and candied fruits of your choice, such as candied pineapple, figs, and cherries, and with candied lime and orange peel.

CINNAMON-SUGAR FRIED DOUGH / **CHURROS**

Makes about 16 churros

Churros, another of the many desserts we inherited from the Spanish, are a popular nighttime treat, served with Mexican hot chocolate. When I was growing up in Mexico City, churros were sold plain and simply dusted with sugar, but over the past couple of decades, cooks have been filling them with cajeta, chocolate, or different jams. I remain faithful to the classic—super-crisp on the outside, yielding on the inside, and generously coated with cinnamon sugar, ready to dip into hot chocolate or cajeta.

I tried many recipes without getting the results I wanted. But then Oaxacan chef Alam Mendéz, the son of my friend, chef Celia Florián, shared his technique with me, and finally, my churros were all that I wanted them to be. Alam's secret is sparkling water and eggs, both of which help create a pliant yet sturdy dough with a tender interior. I use the eggs and half sparkling, half flat water to get a crisp exterior.

2 cups plus 2 tablespoons all-purpose flour, plus more for dusting

1 tablespoon baking powder

1 cup water

1 cup sparkling water

1 teaspoon vanilla extract

3 tablespoons unsalted butter

Pinch of kosher salt

2 large eggs

⅔ cup sugar

2 teaspoons ground canela or cinnamon

Vegetable oil for deep frying

Combine the flour and baking powder in a bowl.

Combine the water, sparkling water, vanilla, butter, and salt in a medium saucepan and bring to a boil; once the butter has melted, turn off the heat. Add the flour mixture all at once, whisking vigorously to prevent lumps. Change to a wooden spoon or silicone spatula and stir vigorously, in one direction, until the mixture is uniform and smooth, with no lumps, about a minute.

Immediately scrape the mixture into the bowl of a stand mixer fitted with the paddle attachment. Beat on low speed until you no longer see any steam rising and the dough has cooled to lukewarm, about 2 minutes. (This helps make a uniform dough that is not too stiff and is cool enough to add the eggs without cooking them.)

One by one, beat in the eggs, making sure the first one is incorporated before adding the second one. Scrape down the bowl and beat until the dough is smooth. Scrape down the bowl again, then beat at high speed for another minute, or until the dough is soft, smooth, and malleable. It should resemble Play-Doh.

Scrape down the bowl and beater, remove the bowl from the mixer, cover with a clean kitchen towel or with plastic, and let the dough rest for at least 20 minutes. The rest will help the gluten in the flour relax so that the dough will be easier to work with and the churros won't crack.

Meanwhile, combine the sugar and canela or cinnamon in a bowl and spread on a large plate. Place a cooling rack on a baking sheet lined with paper towels. Line another baking sheet with parchment and very lightly dust it with flour.

In a Dutch oven or deep heavy skillet, heat about 2 inches of vegetable oil to 350 to 375 degrees F. You can test the oil with a teaspoon of dough; the oil is ready when it bubbles energetically around the dough.

Transfer all or some of the churro dough to a pastry bag fitted with a large (½- to ¾-inch) open star tip, or use a churro press, if you have one. Pipe the dough into 6- to 8-inch-long strips on the parchment-lined baking sheet. You can begin frying the churros as soon as you have piped out 5 or 6.

Working in batches, carefully place the shaped churros in the hot oil, taking care not to crowd the pot. They should float to the top almost immediately. Fry for 4 to 6 minutes, or until golden and crisp, turning as soon as one side is golden brown, about halfway through. The churros may resist being turned, but use tongs and be persistent to make sure they are evenly browned. Then use the tongs or a slotted spoon to remove them and let cool for a few seconds on the cooling rack. While they are still hot, toss them in the cinnamon sugar to coat. Serve hot or warm.

Cook's Note

► You can serve the churros with cajeta or dulce de leche, chocolate syrup, Nutella, jam, or honey, if you like.

MIXED NUT AND SEED BRITTLE / **PALANQUETA DE NUECES Y SEMILLAS**

Serves 10 to 12

Palanqueta, Mexico's nut brittle, is one of the most popular candies in the country. Home cooks sell the candies in markets, or street vendors buy them from the cooks. They are wonderful to break into small pieces and munch on, and they are an absolute delight as a topping for ice cream.

Although the most common variety of palanqueta is peanut brittle, you also find the brittle made with pumpkin seeds in southern Mexico, and with pecans in the north. In this recipe, I use all three—peanuts, pecans, and pumpkin seeds. But you can use whatever nut or combination you prefer.

Adding baking soda and butter to the hot syrup with the nuts makes the brittle easy to bite into. You will need a candy thermometer to make palanqueta.

- ⅔ **cup raw hulled pumpkin seeds**
- ⅔ **cup raw unsalted peanuts**
- ⅔ **cup pecan pieces**
- 1 **tablespoon unsalted butter, at room temperature**
- ½ **cup water**
- 1 **cup packed dark brown sugar**
- 1 **cup granulated sugar**
- 2 **tablespoons grated piloncillo or dark brown sugar**
- 2 **tablespoons corn syrup**
- ½ **teaspoon baking soda**
- **Kosher or flaky sea salt (optional)**
- **Vegetable oil**

Heat a medium skillet over medium-low heat. Add the pumpkin seeds and toast, shaking the pan or stirring, until they start popping and are just beginning to color, 3 to 4 minutes. Remove to a bowl to cool. Add the peanuts and pecans to the pan and toast, shaking the pan or stirring, for 4 to 5 minutes, until they just begin to darken. Transfer to the bowl with the pumpkin seeds.

Use ½ tablespoon of the butter to grease a baking sheet.

Combine the water, brown sugar, granulated sugar, piloncillo (or additional brown sugar), and corn syrup in a medium saucepan and heat over medium-low heat, stirring with a silicone spatula, until all the sugar dissolves. When the mixture begins to bubble dramatically, attach a candy thermometer to the side of the pan and heat until the mixture reaches 300 degrees F (the hard-crack stage).

Coat another silicone spatula with vegetable oil, remove the saucepan from the heat, and very quickly but carefully stir in the baking soda, the remaining ½ tablespoon butter, and the nuts and seeds. The mixture will continue to bubble for a few seconds but will then begin to harden very quickly. Stir well and immediately scrape the mixture onto the baking sheet, spreading it thin so that the nuts and seeds are in one layer. Sprinkle salt on top, if desired.

Let the brittle cool for 20 to 25 minutes, then break into pieces. Let cool completely, until hardened. The brittle will keep for a month in an airtight container (but I guarantee you will finish it long before that).

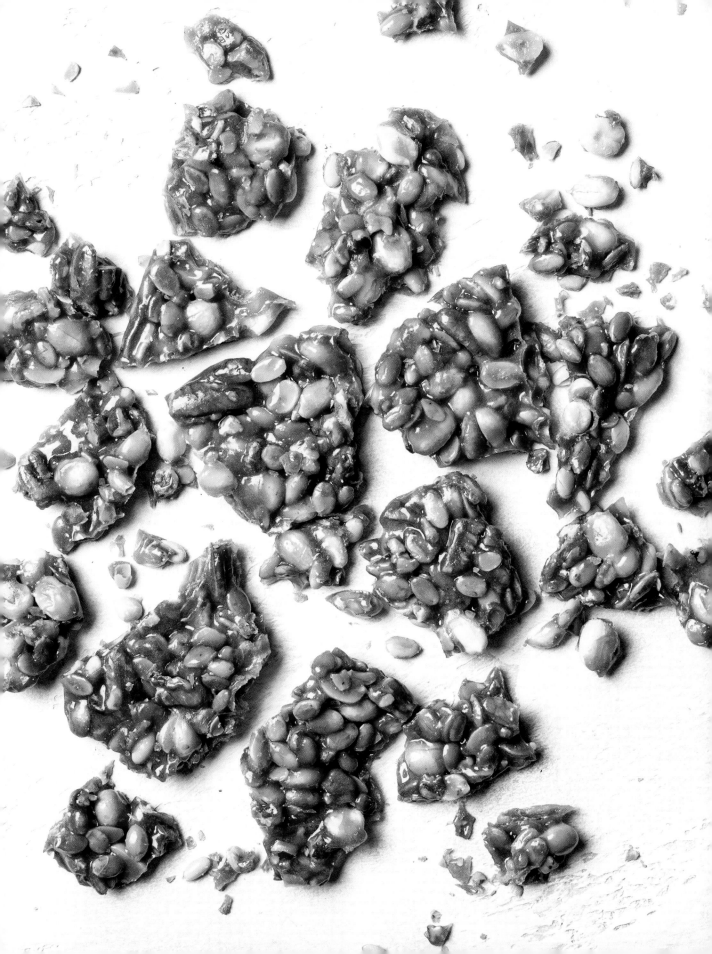

CANDIED PUMPKIN IN BROWN SUGAR SYRUP /
CALABAZA EN TACHA

Makes about 4 cups

Sweet pumpkin slices cooked in a piloncillo syrup with a stick of canela and orange juice and rind is traditional for Day of the Dead, but we also like to serve this sweet right through the Christmas holiday season, and you can find it year-round. In the U.S., it makes a great addition to the Thanksgiving dessert spread. The flavor will be more intense if you use piloncillo, but you can make this with dark brown sugar. I include the seeds and strings of the pumpkin, because as this cooks, the strings are transformed into something wonderful, and the sweet, crunchy candied seeds are to die for. The orange rind becomes candied too, and I always dive in for it.

My favorite way to eat the candied pumpkin is cold, with crema or crème fraiche, but it's wonderful with ricotta and it's irresistible on top of vanilla ice cream. I also enjoy it with my morning yogurt.

2 pounds piloncillo, broken or cut into chunks, or about 6 cups packed dark brown sugar

3 cups water

1 (3- to 4-inch) canela or cinnamon stick

Juice of 1 large orange (⅓ to ½ cup), plus the rind

1 small (5- to 6-pound) pumpkin

Place the piloncillo or brown sugar in a large heavy pot, add the water, canela or cinnamon stick, orange juice, and rind, and bring to a boil. Reduce the heat to medium-low and simmer, stirring occasionally, until all the sugar has dissolved, about 15 minutes.

Meanwhile, rinse and scrub the pumpkin and cut away the stem. Cut the pumpkin from top to bottom into 1- to 2-inch-wide slices and remove the seeds and strings if you wish (I recommend leaving them; see headnote). Using the tip of a paring knife, score the skin so that the pumpkin slices can absorb the syrup from both sides.

When the sugar has dissolved, remove the pot from the heat and arrange the pumpkin pieces in the syrup, skin side down. Return to the heat and bring back to a simmer, then cover and simmer over medium-low heat for 1 hour. From time to time, spoon some of the syrup over the top of the pumpkin slices if they are poking out. The pumpkin should be drenched in the simmering syrup.

Uncover and simmer for another hour, or until the pumpkin is a rich brown color and saturated with syrup. Turn off the heat and let cool; the pumpkin will continue to absorb the syrup and the syrup will thicken and darken.

Serve the candied pumpkin warm, at room temperature, or chilled. It will keep in a covered container in the refrigerator for a month.

INDEX

Note: Page numbers in *italics* indicate illustrations.

BAJA CALIFORNIA

Sea of Cortez (Gulf of California)

SONORA

CHIHUAHUA

BAJA CALIFORNIA SUR

SINALOA

DURANGO

ZAC

NAYARIT

NORTH

PACIFIC

JALISCO

OCEAN

COLIMA